UNITED STATES
of hysteria

UNITED STATES
of hysteria

Anne Dixey

Monday Books

© Anne Dixey 2008
First published in Great Britain in 2008 by Monday Books

A CIP catalogue record for this title is available
from the British Library

2008 ISBN: 978-1-906308-01-8

Printed and bound by Cox and Wyman
Typeset by Andrew Searle
Cover Design by Paul Hill at Kin Creative

www.mondaybooks.com
info@mondaybooks.com

For friends in America

Contents

Acknowledgements

Amalie, Josie and Roland were the perfect fellow adventurers. Also many thanks to all those at Monday Books, David Luxton, and friends and relatives in Britain for their faith and encouragement. Thank you to friends across the water for their unwavering kindness, generosity and support during my American journey – I couldn't have done it without you.

Foreword

This book begins in America but my life before that was in Britain. I lived and worked across the country as a newspaper reporter and news editor. My career began covering golden weddings and flower shows and ended, before the American adventure, producing national politics and social issues for BBC Radio 4.

I knew my country, with all its imperfections, pretty well. I felt completely at ease in the chaotic, urban Victoriana of my London, with its corner shops, street markets, double decker buses and frequent rain. My education was on the state and my babies on the NHS. My family were native Brits for as far back as anyone could remember.

When my partner got offered a job as Washington correspondent for *The Times*, I really didn't want to go – why uproot when life was good already?

I knew from visits as a tourist that Washington DC was a small city of government offices and museums with easy access to the mountains and the beach. We would get a bigger house and garden but would leave behind family, friends, familiarity and a job, childcare and a good school.

What made me crack was curiosity.

Nearly one in ten British nationals live part or all of the year abroad, according to the Institute for Public Policy Research, and the US is among the top ten destinations. When we joined the exodus, we were ready for an adventure – but not for what awaited us.

This is what happened to me, a mum living in a suburban community, and those around me. It is based on diary notes, interviews and extra research where necessary. Some names have been changed though everything took place.

Chapter 1:
Welcome to America

IT IS 3am in America. I am woken by two small girls (who think they're still in Britain and that it's 8am) bouncing round the hotel room and leaping from bed to bed, practising somersaults. This is no time for perfect parenting. I grab the TV controls and skim through 123 channels, rejecting real time fishing, Mexican soaps, Bible studies and a man selling a lethal looking range of hunting knives. At last, a reassuring American icon – Mickey Mouse circa 1928, before corporate merchandising and when life was black and white.

Today is going to be 'hot and humid in DC' says the radio, but inside the air conditioning machine blasts out an icy, howling gale. I curse the baffling controls, mutter about the waste of energy and pull every spare blanket out of the cupboards.

Finally it is 6.30am and the breakfast bar is open. 'And how are you today, Ma'am?' asks my beaming 'server'. I am just about to launch into a detailed reply when I realise she has already gone to the next table. It seems 'how are you' is a pleasantry not to be taken literally. The hotel is above a shopping mall, all chrome, escalators and musak. Dizzy and jetlagged, I lean over the atrium balcony for a glimpse of life below and spot Starbucks. Meanwhile the girls have found some garish-coloured guinea pig food which they claim is cereal and I have no energy to argue. Three bowls later and they can't stop running – down the escalators, up the stairs, six times round the fountain and twice round the food court. 'Stop! You will get told off,' I hiss, but the Asian and Latino catering workers just smile indulgently.

1

I step outside the artificially chilled mall and walk straight into a wall of heat. The Weather Channel says today will be in the 90s but will feel like 100 with the humidity. The bright sunlight and breakfast coffee (forgot my teabags) give me spots before the eyes. I find my sunglasses and focus, wondering how the sky is so blue and the streets so clean – no litter or dog poo. Not a drunk or a beggar in sight. *Don't they have any here?* None on the Metro either. The platform is shiny and bright with a ceiling like a giant waffle. There is a seat for everyone – the suited office girls, with painted faces and Monica Lewinsky hairdos, and homespun American tourists in shorts and baseball caps.

Twenty minutes later I am sitting, zombie-like, with all the other aliens in the social security office, waiting for a number so that I have the right to work, so that I can be legal. The man next to me looks familiar. I can't possibly know him, we haven't met anyone yet. Then it dawns on me he is a dead ringer for a hoodlum featured on last night's TV crime show *America's Most Wanted*. We smile weakly at each other. The room is filled with Latinos. They wear 'I love New York' baseball caps, cheap jeans and T-shirts claiming allegiance to American sports teams, as if dressing like a native will guarantee them their magic number. Security staff in navy blue shirts and trousers patrol between the plastic chairs looking for signs of defiance in faces lit by strip lights. We don't look them in the eye.

Disney cartoons are on the TV but you can only see the screen from certain chairs. All the children, including mine, are bored and tired, moaning in different languages, whimpering, threatening to throw up. The toilet reeks and soiled nappies litter the floor.

Five hours later, the woman at the front desk calls me up. A tough lady with unflinching eyes, she furiously turns down my application – 'I won't accept this, Ma'am!' (Never mind that my letter from a potential British employer has the exact wording recommended by the US embassy in London.) I start to plead my case as the children fight back tears but she is already looking past me, calling the next person.

We sit on the pavement outside in the searing heat. Amalie, aged four, says it's too hot and she is going to be sick. Josie, aged two, says it's too hot and she is hungry. We all cry.

Roland, whose job is the reason we are here, realises he is fast losing his argument that 'moving to America will be a great adventure'. And it is only day one. He goes back inside to ask politely, but firmly, to speak to the manager.

The rest of us dodge the speeding cabs to cross the road to a deli. There appear to be at least 57 different sandwich combinations to choose from. It's all too much and we settle for one 'just egg' and one 'just butter' on white bread which happens to be the same price as a deluxe, four fillings combo with two salads or 'sides'. The assistants are clearly horrified at our frugal tastes.

An hour later, we are relaxing in a tranquil cubicle at the back of the social security complex. It is a world away from the crying babies, the shouting and the Disney Channel. This man doesn't have a big enough desk to be the manager but I'm guessing he knows one. They might even have a cold beer and watch the basketball together. 'That is all fine, Ma'am,' beams my new friend as he passes my application. A plump African American man oozing warmth and charm, he shakes me by the hand, pats the children on the head and says, 'Have a nice day, Ma'am.' I think he means it.

Next stop the bank to open an account. We seem to have picked the fanciest one in America – on Pennsylvania Avenue across from the White House – with white pillars, mahogany desks and meticulously dressed clerks speaking in hushed tones. Our immaculately groomed female assistant sits us down on upholstered chairs to fill in the forms. The girls, relieved to be anywhere but the social security office, play happily under the chairs with coveted plastic footballers that came free with Tetley teabags. But this is taking longer than we thought. We may have bank records in Britain, but in America we have no more credit history than the average Mexican immigrant and they have no intention of trusting us with much cash. Another form to fill, and another, while the whispering and giggling under the chairs gets louder. The clerk kindly pretends not to notice. Suddenly the girls shoot out backwards, whipping up their sundresses and shouting at the top of their voices, 'We're showing our bottoms!' The Brits have only just arrived but they are already mooning at the locals.

After a hasty exit from the bank, we sit down exhausted in the cool comfort of the Metro. Three stops on and Amalie throws up everywhere. I start apologising, bracing myself for the handful of other passengers to glare and move away but they don't. Instead they ask how she is – 'Are you OK, honey?' – as I reach for wet wipes and tissues. The station worker who has to organise the clean-up is equally sympathetic when we break the news. Not sure we would have got such a generous response on the London Underground.

Living in a mall hotel, with all the chrome, musak and multi-coloured cereal, is a surreal existence – not good for your mental health. And we really need a washing machine for all the sicky stuff. We have put down the rent for an empty house in a DC suburb but there is no furniture for four weeks while the cargo ship with our worldly belongings chugs across the Atlantic. Our carefully packed box of air freight – kitchen utensils, bedding and toys – should arrive today. But bad news. The freight company has lost it. Staff swiftly change the subject and ask me how I am. Not great, I say, as they don't know whether my possessions are 3,000 miles away in Washington State (instead of Washington DC), or New York, or still in London. They suggest trying another office. This is on an answer phone with a message telling me to have a nice day. Try New York who can't help either but they really want me to have a nice day too. No one actually admits to losing it and they don't return our calls.

Decide that living in an empty house is better than staying in a mall. But the feeling of living in a dream continues when we arrive in Chevy Chase. The sun is too bright, the sky too blue and the trees too green. We seem to have moved in to a suburban film set. Every house is different in the neighbourhood – pale wood southern-style with verandas, all moonlight and magnolias, red brick colonials, angular modern affairs and low-rise chalets that the estate agents call 'ramblers' (we have one of these). Some even have faux White House entrances. Many have something other than lush front lawns in common: the American flag sends flashes of red, white and blue through the trees. All the houses are detached, even if there is only a sliver of land in between. Some gardens run straight to the street with nothing to stop dogs and kids on bikes passing through. It is pretty quiet here.

This is Chevy Chase, Montgomery County, Maryland, USA.

Chevy Chase is also the name of the Seventies comedian whose catchphrase on *Saturday Night Live* was, 'I'm Chevy Chase and you're not.' He was born Cornelius Crane Chase. Apparently, his granny nicknamed him Chevy after the place.

Our house is completely empty save for plastic basics bought the day before from Ikea, mattresses loaned from a kind British family connected through journalism and cardboard boxes for tables. A piece of paper sticks out from the rusty mail box beside the front door. It is from the local neighbourhood association and it says we are invited to a picnic tonight in the park. How kind.

It is dusk and the cicadas in the shadows are starting to hum. Runners pound by, sweating in the heat, on their way to the leafy trails which weave through the city. Dogs pant on their evening walk and children wander round the playground, itching from the mosquitoes. Earlier it was deserted here. Only mad dogs and newly arrived English families were out in the midday sun. Everyone else stayed indoors or went to the outdoor pool.

This evening, families are sitting under the trees on blankets between the playground and the baseball field, eating chicken and pretzels, drinking still lemonade. Almost everyone here started off somewhere else – mostly another part of America with a handful from South America or Europe – and came to Washington DC for work. One is a journalist like us, some work for the government or law firms, others for the World Bank. We have ended up in this suburb, seven miles from the White House, for much the same reasons – a house with a garden, a park, a public swimming pool, good local schools and a Metro stop.

Nobody seems to be drinking but we ask the question anyway – 'Where do you get alcohol around here?' (We called into a supermarket for food but it didn't sell any.)

'You can only get it in the liquor store,' we are told. 'And you will need photo ID.' I wonder if it is even polite to ask such a question in puritanical America. Will we now be known as 'the alcoholics just arrived from England'?

Darkness is falling and the chirruping cicadas are reaching a crescendo so we all pick up our blankets and rubbish before walking home. Back at the house I fumble to find unfamiliar light switches and the air conditioning dial.

The doorbell rings for the first time. It is an American neighbour we met an hour earlier in the park, bringing us frozen vodka and orange juice. We will probably never see him again – he is about to leave the area – but he does it anyway. 'Guessed you wouldn't make it to the liquor store tonight,' he smiles.

The night is long, the choice is either noisy, energy wasting air conditioning or the sweats and a blinding headache. At last morning comes and by nine o'clock it is already sweltering in the shade. The doorbell again. It is an elderly neighbour, Lena, bearing fresh raspberries. She has been here since the 1950s. 'The best fruit is from the farmers' market on Wisconsin Avenue,' she says. 'It is open on Wednesdays and Saturdays. Call if you need anything.'

We spot another neighbour across the street in her garden, in patched corduroys and a floral shirt, and go and say hello. 'The big ones are for the children,' she instructs firmly as she picks some apples from her tree and hands over two large rosy ones and two small maggoty specimens. 'Usually,' she adds, 'one calls on a new neighbour *before* they call on you.'

A retired librarian, Sally, lives in a red brick house built in the 1930s by the elephant keeper at the national zoo, with a veranda to sit out on steamy summer nights. It was 1969 when she bought it, the year Richard Nixon was inaugurated president and Neil Armstrong took man's first walk on the moon.

Has much changed? 'Yes! People pulled down nice, charming houses and put up monstrous ones in their place,' she says, crossly. 'Everything is bigger – the houses, the cars and the dogs. Oh, and the man who used to get drunk and fire his gun in the air has moved away.'

Chevy Chase apparently gets its name from a 14th century battle between the English and the Scots in Northumberland and refers to a field in the Cheviot Hills. The area here was named when the land was given to an 18th century settler.

There is a high concentration of English street names in the neighbourhood – Warwick, Essex, Dorset, Stratford and

6

Nottingham to name but a few. More evoke the English countryside – Sycamore, Meadow, Chestnut, Thornapple and Rosemary. And, in the style of English parishes, areas are split into 'incorporated municipalities', some dating back to the turn of the century. They call themselves towns or villages, elect officials and organise their own rubbish collection, road maintenance and landscaping. Some have their own police department, others an outdoor swimming pool and all a roadside sign to reaffirm their importance. My favourite is The Village of Drummond, named after a Civil War general. It is half a street with a mayor and no facilities whatsoever. A taxing district of 43 houses since 1916, original rules ban 'any horse, mule, swine, cow or other cattle' from wandering about Drummond. I wonder if residents living down the hill and out of the 'village' have ever been tempted to let a few loose.

My new home is in Chevy Chase West. This is not a municipality and services are run by the local council. But we do have a tree planting committee and volunteer 'block captains' in each street, who give out flyers and collect membership money for the neighbourhood association which organises community business and social events. Orderliness at all times is the watchword.

A few days later and it is time to have a go at driving the company lease car, a Honda CRV. It looks like a Mini compared with many SUVs around here but to me it feels like a Hummer. I hear there is a great supermarket called Wholefoods not far away. I work out I can get there doing only right hand turns apart from one junction controlled by traffic lights. This means I can concentrate on staying on the right side of the road. All is going well until I head down a road with gardeners' and builders' pick-up trucks parked along one side. They all have wing mirrors that stick a foot further out into the road. I haven't got the hang of the car width yet and ever so gently I clip one, and another, and another... That might have been shouting in the distance but I keep going.

I walk in the supermarket door and gasp at the sight before me. It is fruit and vegetable nirvana, produce as art, stacked in glistening pyramids. Perfect broccoli florets are arranged to show their best profile. And, for customers to taste, there is sweet pineapple on sticks, pink watermelon, zucchini bread and cheeses. It's a harvest festival without the church and the charity.

Another sun-filled morning (does it ever rain here?). Decide to walk to the Metro to go to the zoo. Need to work off all that free food at Wholefoods and don't have the nerve to get in the car again. Wonder why no one else is walking on such a perfect day as I push two children in the buggy along the leafy streets. Coming home early afternoon I see why. It is so hot I am panting and drenched in sweat in minutes. The children look like overripe tomatoes under their sunhats. Then we run out of water. It feels like the desert, just a matter of time before I hallucinate. I get slower and slower. Finally, we make it back to a cold bath, dabbing each others' mosquito bites with ice. Then we lie on the cool basement floor, still empty of any possessions, waiting for our skin colour to change from red to white. It takes hours.

By dusk, the heat has lost its intensity after a ferocious 15-minute storm and the cicadas are chirruping in the breeze. Night is drawing in and the streets are deserted save for some late dog walkers. Lights come on in the houses. A handful have half-closed shutters or blinds but most have their windows left open to passers by. There are no heavy drapes to shut off the night. Nosey neighbours don't lurk behind twitching net curtains here. Passers-by can just look right in until the lights go out. The first week I habitually close our blinds. Then Sally gives some friendly advice – 'You know, here if you do that, people think that you have something to hide.'

Today is Amalie's first day at nursery school, three weeks after arriving in America, and we wake up to an electric blue sky and brilliant sunshine. Another beautiful day in suburbia. I pack the children plus emergency map and directions in the car in plenty of time to get there. We pass leafy roads named after places from home and try not to clip the wing mirrors of gardeners' pick-ups. Waiting at the lights on Massachusetts Avenue, I marvel at the number of huge leafy trees and queues of people carriers around me, all with window stickers proclaiming allegiance for schools, colleges or sports teams. I turn off past a colonial white Baptist church to the nursery and join a queue of cars. The smiling young school assistants stand at the door, poised to whisk small pupils out of their car seats and into class. Safety regulations say you cannot park and walk them in except in special circumstances.

After pulling up round the corner to check the map again, I drive Josie towards a public library where a kids' *What's On* guide says there is 'Time for Twos' storytelling. The radio is tuned in to NPR (National Public Radio) – the closest station I can find to the BBC's Radio 4.

The presenter's voice shakes as he says it: *Reports are coming in that a passenger plane has crashed into the north tower of the World Trade Center in New York.*

My mobile rings. Roland is calling from Miami where he has been covering a local politics story, to say he is heading for the airport to try to get a plane to New York. 'I'll ring you when I get there,' he says and breaks off.

An emergency news flash comes on the radio – another plane has hit the south tower.

Once could be an accident... but *twice*? I resist the overwhelming urge to go straight home and switch on the TV. Be calm, be normal.

Minutes later we arrive at the library and find a parking space opposite. I'm careful to park pointing in the direction of the traffic. (I got a fine yesterday for parking in the right place but facing the wrong way – a violation.) Inside, the librarians and a few customers are huddled round a television. I glimpse shocking pictures of the smoking Twin Towers before walking upstairs to the children's section. A handful of other mothers and toddlers are there too. I ask the librarian when the storytelling starts. 'There is no storytelling here today, it's on at the Chevy Chase library in Maryland – this is Chevy Chase library in Washington DC.'

Decide not to drive on to the other one. Don't want to be too far from nursery school on the first morning, especially now. The women around me all try to act normally for the children but you can feel the tension. We settle down, kids on laps, with piles of books about furry animals and fairy tales. 'Time to move to Ohio, sweetie,' a pale-faced mother says to her young son, as he passes *Thomas the Tank Engine*.

Read the books without hearing the words until the last one, *Chicken Licken* – 'Oh Henny Penny, the sky is falling and I'm going to tell the king!' Suddenly I hear shouts and wails from below. We walk downstairs and see more people around the television. People are crying with their hands over their mouths in shock. A tearful pensioner comes over and touches my arm. 'They have hit the Pentagon, dear. And there is another hijacked plane circling Washington DC.' I freeze for a moment, just long enough to see the first picture of the Pentagon in flames. President Bush is in Florida. He has just said the country is under an 'apparent terrorist attack'. His voice sounds strange. I pick up a reluctant toddler and run past a grim-faced librarian to the door. The sound of sirens fills Connecticut Avenue as I call the nursery school on my mobile. I try repeatedly but can't get through, then ring home to test the line. No luck. The network must be down. This is an ordinary American street with a Safeway supermarket, a CVS pharmacy and a Starbucks. But it doesn't seem so ordinary anymore. Everything feels different to an hour ago. I drive off, telling myself to keep calm and stay on the right. The blank going-to-work faces of drivers have been replaced by worried, taut ones. You can feel the fear through their change in behaviour – incessantly honking horns, jumping red lights and cutting up other cars. I'm terrified of having an accident or losing my way – not now, please. I make it back home, en route to school, and run in to check the phone. The school has left a message saying they are shutting down. We must collect our children at once.

In the car again. From over the nearby Washington DC border, cars are driving bumper to bumper out of the city. I am the only one going in. The whirr of helicopters is overhead and the sound of sirens in the distance. Now Josie is crying for her sister and her Dad. Almost reunited with one, but the other? Maybe he is on a plane to New York – I just don't know. And how am I going to find out if the phone lines are down? Now the radio says the south tower of the World Trade Center has collapsed.

As I arrive at school, I hear overwhelming noise. It is the sound of military jets flying over the playground. Find my daughter sitting on a step with her Barbie lunchbox, demanding to know why the other new girl had been picked up before her. I say that the little girl was from New York where something bad had happened. 'What has happened?' she asks. I stare at the artwork on the wall. Someone is on the phone, fighting back the tears as she speaks to a relative who works near the Pentagon. Part of the building has now collapsed.

She shakes her head. 'You try to understand these people, but how can we now?'

Wild-eyed parents continue to rush in, trying to act normal for their children's sake. More military planes roar overhead as we leave.

The World Trade Center's north tower is collapsing. The radio says there are reports of another plane crashing in Pennsylvania. All flights have been stopped at US airports. Roland won't have made it in time. I concentrate on remembering the way home and staying on the right side of the road. We inch along. Queues of cars are heading out of the city towards the suburbs, towards Maryland. The other carriageway is deserted accept for emergency vehicles speeding past. Ashen drivers try their mobiles one more time. Dog walkers pass by, clutching radios to their ears. The White House has been evacuated, so have the State and Justice departments. It feels unreal. Has there been a mass exodus like this since the thirties when Orson Welles broadcast *War of the Worlds* on the radio? (Terrified listeners believed that Martians were invading New York.) This time it is no hoax. We are all driving home, assuming it is safer than downtown but how do we know? Is there more to come? The unthinkable has already happened.

After a 40-minute drive that should have taken ten minutes, we finally turn off Wisconsin Avenue into the quiet normality of leafy suburbia. Put the key in the door but it won't open. Please don't let us get locked out today. 'You need to give it a shove, Mummy,' my daughter reminds me. A big push later and we are inside. I turn on the TV and for the first time see the pictures of the planes crashing into the World Trade Center and the horrifying moment when the towers collapsed. I try and distract the children with dolls and jigsaws. The US Capitol has been evacuated. No sign of the President. Where is Dick Cheney? Are any members of Congress out there? New York Mayor Rudolph Giuliani is publicly leading his city through the crisis, urging people to stay at home during the evacuation of Lower Manhattan.

But who is in charge in Washington DC?

The girls say they are hungry. I let them eat chocolate chip cookies like there is no tomorrow because it feels like there really might not be a tomorrow. Realise I haven't eaten yet today but feel too sick to try. Drink black coffee instead. Imagine relatives in Britain having a cup of tea in front of the television. Try calling repeatedly but can't get through. The phone doesn't ring. Still can't connect to Roland's mobile. CNN says that the Centers for Disease Control and Prevention are preparing emergency response teams as a precaution. The local news reports that Washington hospital staff fear biological warfare and the US military is reportedly on nuclear alert. American Airlines say it has lost two planes – one hit the North Tower, the other the Pentagon. United Airlines confirms that one aircraft has crashed in Pennsylvania (was this the one thought to be over DC?) and later identifies another as the one that hit the South Tower.

We have now done three animal puzzles and dressed and undressed a selection of dolls. They demand children's TV – 'Why can't we watch Mickey Mouse?'

Try the all-American classic peanut butter and jelly sandwiches for lunch. One daughter only likes the peanut butter and the other only likes the jelly so have to start again. Add a glass of milk and some grapes as a token gesture to health. Sit back on the sofa to read Winnie the Pooh. They worry when Tigger gets stuck up a tree and clap when his friends rescue him.

'I'm so happy I could bounce all the way home!' he says.

Have turned the TV sound off and feel sure the children are not looking at the pictures. The script rolls across the screen – US borders with Canada and Mexico are on the highest state of alert. Mayor Giuliani appears live and completely calm. Try dialling a succession of numbers on the phone again but with no luck. It still doesn't ring. Have more chocolate chip cookies. The images of the Twin Towers crashing and the bloodied survivors keep coming back. It is still a beautiful day outside – we should be in the garden or the park – but feel like I should stay near the TV and the phone, just in case. Look out the window and the street is deserted. Not even a kid on a bike or a dog walker. No people carriers or pick-up trucks driving by. Everyone is waiting.

We are around seven miles from the likely targets downtown. Would a toxic cloud reach Chevy Chase? What are you supposed to do in a chemical attack anyway? Move on to Winnie the Pooh's *The Most Grand Adventure* when Christopher Robin had his first day at school.

'Will we always be together?' asks Pooh. 'Forever and ever!' smiles Christopher Robin.

Glance up at the TV to see President Bush speaking from an air base in Louisiana, 1,000 miles from DC. (Does he know something we don't?) 'Make no mistake, the United States will hunt down and punish those responsible for these cowardly acts,' he says. I barely hear the words, transfixed by his frightened face.

'Read, Mummy, read!'

Finish the book and try to rally our spirits with a game of animal dominoes. Too distracted to tell the difference between the hippo and the rhino, I lose without even trying. A state of emergency is declared in Washington. What does that mean, exactly? Now Bush is reported to be aboard Air Force One: whereabouts unknown. Democrat Senator Joe Biden from the foreign relations committee appears on the screen. At last, an elected politician who thinks it is safe to come out of the bunker. Warships are heading out to sea to protect the East Coast. The phone rings. I leap on it before it stops. It is my Mum from Britain, calmness itself and calling as if she was just ringing to ask about the weather. She promises to pass on to relatives and friends that we are fine. I try to ring out but still can't get a connection. No other calls get through. I wonder if it is our phone line. It took ages to get connected and the hapless workman with a mullet haircut who finally did the job put a call through to the police by accident. But no, the radio says all phone lines are overloaded.

The TV screen yet again shows the image of a plane hitting one of the Twin Towers. I hear my eldest daughter tell her sister matter-of-factly, 'Daddy is going to be killed. He went on an aeroplane.'

I tell them it wasn't his plane and he wouldn't have got on another one before the airports shut down. He was either waiting in Florida or driving back up the East coast. They listen politely but don't look convinced. Neither are they upset – when their toys die in games they come straight back to life.

If we are all going to die anyway, why not outside in the sunshine? Find shoes, pack some drinks and a snack. Do we need sun screen and mosquito repellent in September? Probably. Give it a gratuitous squirt and head off up the road.

We are all relieved to be outside. There is no one about as we walk up the residential side street to the park. But the playground is busy with schoolchildren and toddlers, all getting rid of some energy after the morning's confinement. Unusually for a weekday afternoon, there are no nannies in sight. The playground is full of dads on park duty in their regulation baseball caps, chino shorts and polo shirts. Their government, corporate or World Bank offices have shut down early. But today, no mobiles ring, no pagers bleep, we are all cut off from the outside world. The dads help their sons practise baseball strokes, watch their daughters' gymnastics and play hide-and-seek with the little ones. This is more than quality time. We are thankful to be alive and, just for a moment, forget the earlier events of the day.

Then a tearful airline worker rushes over to a child on a swing to give her a hug. She is still in uniform, a flight attendant or front desk staff. She looks white and shaken, a sudden reminder of what has happened.

We sit on the grass under the trees drinking apple juice and eating Goldfish (a recently-discovered cheesy, fish-shaped snack). The girls sidle up to new playmates, someone to swing with or hang upside down on the bars. The 'moms' watch their children from the shade. A new neighbour, Leah, introduces herself. Conversation keeps coming back to the inevitable.

'It is unbelievable.' We all nod in agreement.

'It is worse than the movies.' So true.

'You just couldn't have imagined it.'

Everyone knows someone close to the tragedy – a relative in New York, a friend at the Pentagon. We pause to drink in the sounds of the children playing and the breeze in the trees. Our new neighbours commiserate that this has happened three weeks after we arrived to live in their country. 'Welcome to America,' one says, grimly.

The sunny afternoon cools into a beautiful evening, some players venturing onto the tennis courts and baseball field, dog walkers in the distance in contemplative huddles. 'Call us if you need us,' Leah says, as we leave. I think she means it.

Back at home the sun is still streaming in the windows, bouncing off the white walls and the wooden floor. I turn on the radio to check the latest news but cannot hear for the clamour.

'What's for tea, Mummy? I'm hungry!'

'Well, I'm starving.'

'I stroked a dog.'

'I went upside down on the monkey bars...'

I manage an uninspiring macaroni cheese and carrots, and two cups of very strong tea for me.

Hundreds are dead and thousands injured in New York. The Pentagon is still burning. The president is reported to be flying back to Washington. Vice President Dick Cheney is in a 'secure facility' at the White House, Defense Secretary Donald Rumsfeld is at the Pentagon. The plane that crashed in Pennsylvania could have been heading for Camp David, the US Capitol or the White House, CNN says.

Run a bath but forget to check it in time and it is too full. They are already leaping in with water and foam everywhere. Finally have clean, dry children. They sit on the sofa in their pyjamas, a book at the ready – *101 Dalmatians*, again.

In the background, the TV, America's modern day campfire, flickers. I feel compelled to sit before it, to hear the horror stories, to have the company. President Bush arrives back at the White House to speak to the nation. Donald Rumsfeld gives a live press conference. Is the United States at war and if so who with?

'Read, Mummy, read!'

Perdita and Pongo help the Dalmatian puppies escape from Cruella De Vil's henchmen Horace and Jasper. Now they must get back home without being recaptured.

Josie falls asleep on the floor.

Back at the campfire, congressmen walk out onto the steps of the Capitol building. There is Senate Majority leader Tom Daschle, back from his 'secure location'.

As darkness falls on a shaken city, they launch into an impromptu song before the cameras – 'God bless America, land that I love, stand beside her and guide her thru the night with a light from above....'

I try not to cry.

'Can I have Marmite sandwiches in my lunchbox tomorrow?' asks Amalie. I say that will be fine (even though I expect school to be shut). She pauses for a moment before adding brightly, 'Are we all going to be killed, Mummy?'

'Oh no, we are all safe,' I reply as I tuck her up in bed. But I'm honestly not sure anymore.

I pad back into the kitchen and make tea and toast as a New York Police Department spokesman says at least 78 officers are missing. As many as half of the first 400 firefighters at the scene are thought to have been killed. I try the phone again. Still no luck. The street outside remains deserted. A few lights are on in the houses now. I think I catch the flickering of a TV. All is quiet apart from the distant sounds of sirens. The panic conveyed on the TV screens has gone. Now the focus is on the harrowing aftermath, the victims and the perpetrators. Amalie can't get to sleep and we read some more about Perdita and Pongo.

Later, President Bush addresses the nation. 'Good evening. Today, our fellow citizens, our way of life, our very freedom, came under attack in a series of deliberate and deadly terrorist acts....'

Then more talk of 'evil', 'terror' and 'freedom' before the inevitable, crowd-pleasing call to prayer and quote from the Bible. 'Even though I walk through the valley of the shadow of death, I fear no evil, for You are with me.' He adds, needlessly, 'None of us will ever forget this day.' I put away the toys and fold up the washing. The earlier frenetic pace of the day's news is now a trickle. Government offices will reopen tomorrow. Panic over...for now.

The phone rings. I can just make out Roland's voice at the end of a crackly line. With all planes grounded, he is driving through the night on a two-day journey from Miami to Washington. He sounds half crazed from caffeine and the stress of filing stories from southern roadside motel rooms. The line breaks up almost immediately but I am so relieved to hear him.

Too tired to stay up any longer, so I head for bed. Stop and watch the children as they lie motionless, in deep sleep amid cuddly toys. I lie awake, alone, listening to the sirens and fearing for the future.

Chapter 2:
I Love the USA

THE SIRENS and the helicopters seem incongruous in suburbia. Despite being surrounded by the sounds of a war zone, we can still buy a grande decaf skinny vanilla latte and have a gourmet Thai dinner delivered to the door.

Days after 9/11, the factories are pumping out patriotic merchandise to satisfy the need for Americans to show their national spirit. *God Bless America* car stickers are everywhere and the flags, mostly put away after the Fourth of July, fly outside peoples' houses again. I wonder if those who fly the Stars and Stripes all year round have bought bigger versions. They are all over the neighbourhood, from ostentatious ones on poles, on the walls at the front of houses, to little ones, the kind you wave at the parade, defiantly stuck in the ground.

Strosniders Hardware ('True Value') is flag central, with Cape Cod lighthouses for summer, harvest fruit and autumn leaves for 'fall', pumpkins for Halloween, snowmen, spring flowers and of course the Stars and Stripes. This is a shop for all seasons. When I first go to buy a broom the pavement outside is full of barbecues, lawnmowers, garden tools and mosquito repellent. There's a whole shelf of cool bags. Now giant rakes for the autumn leaves are coming in. Assistants in red waistcoats bustle about, helping customers find the right three-inch nail.

It is perfect weather: the humidity is gone and with it the mosquitoes. Guidebooks mention that Rock Creek Park,

Washington's green lung, is a nice place to go at this time of year. I read up: It was established in 1890 'for the benefit and enjoyment of the people of the United States'. This is one of the largest urban parks in the world, 1,755 acres of forest and trails passing within walking distance of the White House.

I've heard the name of the park somewhere before. I realise it is the place where police searched in connection with the disappearance of Chandra Levy, the Washington intern who had a relationship with politician Gary Condit. She was among the many joggers who use the park.

Today we are here for a park birthday celebration at its woodland nature centre. Inside it is full of stuffed wildlife in glass cases and park rangers poised to meet their people. They wear brown trousers, short-sleeved shirts and Mountie-style hats, like giant scouts. 'Hey kids, how *are* you? Wanna see something cool?' Evangelists for nature, they lead children off, like the Pied Piper, to look at a frog, a bird or animal tracks. This is called a nature hike.

The parents are dressed in beige khaki shorts and T-shirts which proclaim what race they ran, who they work for or what college they went to. They call their children 'sweetie' and 'bud' ('buddy' if being formal). We look different – my hair is too short and my clothes too black, Roland's hair is too long and he's too pale and skinny. His T-shirt has random swirls rather than a declaration of belonging. We might call our children 'angel' or 'pickle' but obviously only in the privacy of our own home.

The girls have already assimilated. Amalie has wisely realised she has the wrong kind of mother to pull off the 'bright white polo shirt with ribbons in hair' look seen at nursery and has gone for the 'active kid' style of tie-dyed T-shirt, denim shorts and sneakers. Josie knows that if you want to look cool you should copy your older sister.

So here we are, on a fine autumn day, in a woodland clearing in the middle of a capital city, waiting for The Clown. He is in the traditional mould, with giant shoes, baggy tartan trousers and painted face. Fonzie and his assistant are the only black people at the gathering. I'm sure I read that Washington DC is two thirds black but it doesn't feel like it so far. Fonzie does some warm up tricks with scarves. Now for the clever stuff.

'Children, say with me the magic words, I love the USA!'

'I love the USA!' they yell and Fonzie pulls a dove from his hat.

'I love the USA!' the children shout again and out comes another dove.

The kids go wild.

Are British magicians telling the children to shout 'I love Britain' instead of 'abracadabra' these days? Somehow I can't picture it.

The parents are trying to work out how Fonzie did the bird trick. The children don't care because they have been promised free cake and they can see it coming.

'The only thing I have noticed that has changed since 9/11 is the patriotism,' says Sally later as we watch the dog walkers go by from her porch. 'People used to just put a flag out for Memorial Day and the Fourth of July.'

Sally was born in Paris of American parents and came to the US by ship in 1933. She remembers standing on the deck with her sister and brothers to see the Statue of Liberty as they sailed into New York.

We look for some late flowers to pick as Sally talks about 9/11.

'The day before, I was gardening and the sound of planes took me back to 1939 when I was young. Jet fighters went over. I had never seen any before in 40 years here. They knew something was coming. When it happened I called friends and said, turn on the TV. I went to the grocery store just to do the normal thing. One was a bit shaky with the Pentagon hit.'

Everyone knows someone who had a narrow escape – a dad who had a cancelled meeting at the Twin Towers, a brother who headed into work late because of a hangover.

Pushing Josie on the swings near the public library later that week, I get talking to another mum. She is on her way to see her aunt and is sad at the closure of the nearby Baskin-Robbins ice cream shop. She was going to take some as a present.

'It's only just shut,' I volunteer, showing off some local knowledge.

Her little girl is in her best white and pink visiting outfit and we persuade them not to go in a muddy puddle today.

The mother's accent is unmistakably from New York City. She was at home in Manhattan when the Twin Towers fell.

'I went to the funeral of my ex-boss's husband – it was the saddest thing. You forget Manhattan is an island and they closed it down, shut off the bridges. At least it stopped my Mom coming over so we didn't have to work through her trauma as well as our own. I said, Thank you Mayor Giuliani!'

It is time for her to go to her aunt's and we say our goodbyes.

'Your Tony Blair,' she calls after me, 'we want him to be president.'

Tony fever is everywhere. Democrat voters appalled by Bush's rabbit-in-the-headlights reaction to 9/11 – and with the reputation of their former hero Clinton tarnished – have become instant Blairites on hearing his statement to the House of Commons a few days after 9/11.

'…let us unite in agreeing this: what happened in the United States on Tuesday was an act of wickedness for which there can never be justification. Whatever the cause, whatever the perversion of religious feeling, whatever the political belief, to inflict such terror on the world, to take the lives of so many innocent and defenceless men, women and children, can never, ever be justified. Let us unite too, with the vast majority of decent people throughout the world, in sending our condolences to the Government and the people of America. They are our friends and allies. We the British are a people that stand by our friends in time of need, trial and tragedy, and we do so without hesitation now.'

A neighbour, Bill, stops me in the drive. 'That was a good speech from your Tony Blair.'

In the park, a stranger hears my accent and comes over. 'Are you British? Blair is so good – did you hear his speech? You're lucky to have him. He makes a good speech like Clinton but Clinton was flawed.'

'Would you vote for him as president?' I ask.

'Sure would,' she says.

In the street we meet Sherri from down the road walking the dog in her jogging gear. 'Did you hear Blair?' she says….

And the soul-searching continues. 'Why does the rest of the world hate us so much?' Leah asks. 'What have we done wrong?' It is a sentiment expressed by many.

But life goes on. The YMCA is hosting a potluck family dinner. The sports and leisure club likes to hold these community events every so often where everyone just turns up with a dish to share. People are holing up in the 'burbs', keeping clear of downtown unless they have to go there for work. We are frightened that there is more to come. Children play different games in the nursery school playground – imaginary planes crash and kids 'die' or run away.

ABC News says that residents in Montgomery County, where I live, are asking firefighters to come to their homes to show them how to protect themselves. Now we should all have an emergency plan, a place to meet up outside the city, three days worth of water, canned food, batteries and torches. Some people pick a 'safe room' in their home with few doors and windows to the outside and get tape ready to seal off air vents in case of chemical attack. Me? I do nothing. But it bothers me that the Washington Metro, unlike the London Underground, still has rubbish bins and there is no unseen voice piped onto the platform warning travellers to 'beware of suspicious packages'. It would be such an easy target.

So today, two weeks after 9/11, we go by car. The afternoon sky is weirdly dark as I turn off River Road into one of the many garages. The children in the back are getting nervous and clamouring to go home. 'In a minute,' I promise. 'We just need to go to the garage shop first.'

The friendly assistant guides me through a baffling array of battery chargers.

'This one is real good,' he says, before adding, 'Ma'am, I love your accent!'

'Everyone says that,' Amalie tells him.

As I pay, we can hardly hear ourselves speak for the deafening sound of a torrent of rain crashing onto the roof (I even thought I heard hail, surely not at this time of year). We sprint the few yards to the car, fighting against a rising wind. With the windscreen wipers on high speed, I can barely see the road. Should I pull over?

No one else seems to and some cars even overtake so I keep going, in a sedate British way, cursing impatient American drivers. Turn into Little Falls Parkway and the trees are swaying alarmingly. Remember there being something on the radio this morning about a storm approaching but didn't expect it to be this bad. Pull into the driveway as the rain suddenly stops and the wind eases. But the sky is still black, almost greenish. Get the girls into dry clothes and they trot off to the basement playroom to rummage in the dressing-up box.

The phone rings. It's Sally.

'Do you know what to do in a tornado?'

'No,' I reply, surprised by the question.

'Thought not,' she says briskly. 'Go to your basement now. Bye.' And she hangs up.

I turn on the radio and discover that a tornado has passed through Virginia, crossed the Potomac River and is heading from DC into Maryland. That's us.

Sally may be being over cautious, but she has lived here a long time. I decide to follow her advice. I grab my cup of tea and the radio and head to the basement.

The tornado misses us, picking up force further into Maryland, leaving thousands without power. It touches down six miles away at the University of Maryland in College Park. Two sisters are killed when the car they are in is hurled over an eight-storey building. On the college campus, hundreds of trees are uprooted or snapped in half and 300 cars damaged or destroyed.

I read about the aftermath in *The Washington Post*. One man was talking to his neighbour while cooking hotdogs on an outdoor grill. They heard a low rumble, the sky darkened and they shouted, 'Basement!' People came back upstairs to find half their roof gone, carried away by 200 mph winds. Another described watching the top of a tree fly by.

Experts on the radio say it was a category F3 – strong enough to pick up and carry a portacabin or a car – and caused simply by warm air hitting cold. They agree with Sally that you should run to the basement (most people seem to have one). If you are caught in the car, the advice is to get out and lie in a ditch or on the road. I really hope I never have to do it.

I survey the fallen branches in the garden the next morning with Lena. 'We were very lucky,' she says grimly.

As Sally wanders over, I ask her for tips should another tornado come our way. She ponders before answering. 'A tornado cloud looks like fudge bubbling on the stove.' Right. I suggest that as she is always tuned in to TV or radio she could be my personal tornado spotter. She gives me a long look.

I have only just learned that there really is such a thing. The government's National Weather Service has a SKYWARN volunteer programme with around 230,000 trained severe weather spotters, 'part of the ranks of citizens who form the Nation's first line of defence against severe weather'. They watch out for thunderstorms, floods and the 1,000 tornadoes which occur across the US in an average year.

There are also 'storm chasers' who get off on the thrill of following a tornado. Followers can even go on a storm chasing vacation across 'tornado alley', starting in Oklahoma or Nebraska. Imagine a bunch of people with binoculars in a minivan with all sorts of geeks' accessories. I conclude they are the same kind of people who are interested in UFOs.

Since the tornado, life has got quieter, I tell a caller from home one weekday morning. Yes, the undercurrent of post-terrorism hysteria is still there but it can't go on forever can it?

A few hours later two men walk slowly and purposefully up the drive as I put out the rubbish. They look too clean cut to be storm chasers and I guess that they are Mormons. I am about to say, 'not today thanks', when the older one speaks.

'Good afternoon, Ma'am. FBI.'

They hold out their ID cards. A stab of fear goes through me before I collect myself. I haven't knowingly done anything wrong so why should I be worried?

They sit at my kitchen table. It is hot, warm enough for T-shirts and shorts, but they both keep their nylon jackets on and I can guess what is underneath.

My guests politely decline drinks. (Not allowed while on duty I presume. I might poison them.)

'Have you been here long?' the older one asks. He is fit-looking, probably in his 30s, with short, brown hair and that all-American look that firemen and park rangers have. His accent is from New York, I guess, and I have to follow his words closely. He watches my face intently. Well, I came here three weeks ago from West London, I tell him, although so much has happened that it feels like three months. No, I don't know who owns the house. No, I don't know who lived here before. We did everything through an agent.'

'Do you ever send faxes?' he interrupts.

'Well, sometimes.'

'Does the name Victor mean anything to you?'

'No, I can't think of anyone I know with that name,' I reply, confidently.

The eyes of the younger man, an African American who is silently taking notes, meet those of the agent asking the questions.

'Are you sure?' asks the questioner again. There is a long silence punctured by a loud crash from the next room where I have put the children in front of a video. We all jump.

Victor is obviously in big trouble, I think. He tries again.

'Does the name Roland Victor mean anything to you, Ma'am?'

Only then do I realise they are trying to confirm Roland's middle name. Standard FBI questioning technique, no doubt. I laugh nervously. 'Sorry, I thought I had to think of a first name.'

Silence. The other agent keeps writing, even though I'm saying nothing. Then he meets my eyes, watching my face thoughtfully.

I look away, distracted by some stray Panda Puffs still on the floor from breakfast. His shoes are so close he is sure to crunch them.

'Did you speak to someone in Virginia on the phone on September 12?' asks the older agent.

Did I? I don't know. Maybe. Yes, I did, the night after the terrorist attacks. It was a weary late night conversation with Roland during his long drive back from Florida. How do they know about that?

The note-taker smiles encouragingly. He doesn't speak, but his face says, *'Don't be frightened.'* I must be looking worried.

'Do the words "falcon one" mean anything to you?' asks his colleague.

I must have misheard. 'Could you repeat that please?'

But it still sounds like he is saying 'falcon', and that can't be right.

Patiently, he raises his arms to demonstrate a flying action and says, 'Like the bird, Ma'am.'

OK. 'No, they don't mean anything to me,' I reply. They have really got me this time.

It doesn't seem to matter. They appear to be winding up. 'We need to speak to Roland today,' says the older agent. 'He hired a car in Florida and stopped at motels along the route, right?' Right. I promise to call him at work right away, to tell him to stay there and that they are coming downtown to interview him.

They stand to leave. 'We have some other calls to make in the neighbourhood, so we'll come back round in ten minutes after you have spoken to Roland,' the interrogator says.

I watch them walk down the drive and turn the corner, out of sight. There is no sign of a car. Have they really more enquiries to make?

I pass on the message to Roland who laughs out loud, failing to appreciate the trauma of being confronted in my own home by two presumably armed men.

Exactly ten minutes later there is a knock at the door. The video has finished and my children glare sullenly, suspicious of these strange men, and hang onto my skirt. But the mood has lifted. The Feds are smiling, talking to the children.

Was ten minutes the time it took for my story to be confirmed on their database? Had they just been listening to my conversation with Roland? Or had they just surmised that we were unlikely recruits for Al Qaeda?

'We don't need to see Roland now,' says the older agent. 'We'll just call him. Can you make sure he is at home early tomorrow morning?'

They vanish into the afternoon sunshine as quietly as they had arrived. An hour later I switch on the radio.

'Police said today that terrorists involved in the September 11 attack may have gone to Britain first,' the newsreader says. 'There have been arrests in West London.'

A stranger's face flashes by the window next to the front door. I run to answer it but there is no one there. Down the street a man is getting into a mail van. Isn't it late in the day for mail? And where's our regular postman?

A helicopter passes overhead but this time it doesn't hover. Sirens wail in the distance, coming closer, but then fade. They aren't coming to get me yet.

The next morning, a Saturday, the phone rings at 8.30am. It's the Feds. After more questions, Roland learns that a vigilant and patriotic hotel receptionist in Georgia had become suspicious of a stressed Englishman, registered as Roland Victor Watson. He checked in late at night and was overheard speaking, in an unfamiliar accent, to someone on his mobile about the President's movements. He made rushed phone calls to DC, received faxes on the subject of missile defence and wouldn't let the towel-change man into his room. As if that weren't enough, the receptionist thought she heard him say something like 'Falcon thirty-one secure' into his phone.

Had he said something that sounded like it? (He has no idea what.) Had she watched one movie too many? Or was she so desperate to be seen doing her patriotic duty that she had made it up?

For us, it is a sharp reminder that, while our educated neighbours in the suburbs are interested rather than frightened by our English accents, to many Americans we are weird foreigners.

From now on, in this fevered climate, I am going to be careful what I say.

Chapter 3:
The Fear Factor

IT IS A LOVELY autumn day and we take a Sunday morning stroll through the park and along the trail into Bethesda. Whole families go by on bikes – nothing clanky or rusty, all shiny, new and in good working order. Rather like their owners, in fact. Families often ride in colour-coordinated sports outfits or model a white and beige theme.

These leafy, pothole-free, pristine paths which wind their way through Washington and its suburbs allow no motorised vehicles. They are for runners, walkers and cyclists with a neat line splitting the traffic going in different directions. Safety is paramount. Every cyclist wears a helmet (unless they have just arrived from somewhere in Europe) and it is agreed etiquette that anyone overtaking shouts, 'on your left!' as they go by.

The girls are inspired by the speeding cyclists covered in gadgets and gizmos, and pedal furiously until a muscle-bound rider shouts, 'on your left!' so loudly that they get a fright and career off the trail into the bushes. Distraction is provided by an altercation between two golden retrievers coming in opposite directions.

After a stop at the drinking fountain, which also has a special tap and bowl for dogs, we arrive in Bethesda. Here the leafiness ends, giving way to concrete high rise, luxury apartments with hotel-style facilities, a huge bookshop which opens until late and restaurant after restaurant – Tex Mex, Indian, Spanish, Italian, Thai, Mongolian, Greek, Chinese.

We pick the nearest place with hybrid cuisine and order lunch. Some British friends are with us for the weekend, paying the promised visit despite the high state of alert. Our parents are shortly to follow, fatalistic about being potential victims of global terrorism.

Just as the food arrives Roland's phone rings. The US has begun military strikes against Afghanistan. He gets a cab to the office. The rest of us don't feel much like eating now and head home to watch the news.

CNN reports the US and British have fired Tomahawk missiles against 'terrorist targets' in Kabul, Kandahar and Mazar-e-Sharif.

In a national address, George Bush says, 'More than two weeks ago, I gave Taliban leaders a series of clear and specific demands: close terrorist training camps, hand over leaders of the Al Qaeda network and return all foreign nationals. None of these demands were met and now the Taliban will pay a price.'

The Taliban ambassador to Pakistan doesn't see it that way, of course, and says, 'These brutal attacks are as horrendous terrorist acts as any in the world.'

The television Emmy awards ceremony, scheduled for tonight, is called off for the second time.

It is almost a month since 9/11 and the neighbours are again in sombre mood, shaking their heads and muttering about the threat of retaliation. With every missile the feeling of foreboding increases. Fear is in the air.

The day after the bombing starts, I see on ABC News that a photo editor in Florida has died from anthrax. Now there is reported to be a second case at the same tabloid newspaper offices. A special FBI bioterrorism squad is searching for clues. But Tommy Thompson, the Health and Human Services Secretary, goes on TV to reassure us that the victim was an 'outdoorsman' who had drunk water from a stream while travelling through North Carolina. 'There is no evidence of terrorism,' he maintains.

John Ashcroft, the US Attorney General, says nothing has been ruled out and suspicions mount. The anthrax is now thought to have either arrived in a package or through the ventilation system. Is it coincidence that the offices are close to an airfield used by 9/11 terrorists? There are a lot of unanswered questions but I take comfort that this time the action is a long way away in Florida. The next day *The New York Times* says reassuringly, *'Pulmonary anthrax is extremely rare in the United States, occurring only 18 times over the past century.'* But bioterrorism experts, dubbed 'germ warriors', are coming out of the shadows to lobby senators for billions of dollars to prepare the nation for a biological attack.

Should I be worried? I mull it over as I wait in a line of cars to drop off at nursery school, housed behind a white pillared and red brick colonial-style church. The bumper sticker on the car in front tells me to 'Trust in God'.

Later, we take the Metro downtown to show our British visitors the sights – The Mall, a swathe of green with The Capitol, The White House, the Lincoln Memorial around it. The city is deserted, save for police and a few office workers passing through. Mine are the only children on the Metro. So who exactly is 'putting their trust in God' and living normally?

I'm thinking that the place is now more secure than before 9/11. Surely with all the increased security terrorists will be forced to go for softer targets, like when IRA bombers abandoned London for places like Warrington?

The Washington Post reports an incident with a man on the Metro. *'He fires the gun and misses, but it's the spray bottle that seems most menacing. Is this a bioterrorist attack? The station is shut down for six hours; a hazardous materials squad shows up in yellow spacesuits; passengers are stripped and hosed with bleach. The bottle, it turns out contains cleaning fluid.'*

Am I being a bad mother? I ask moms I meet along the way, 'Would you use the Metro now?' and get a unanimous 'No'. But, on further questioning, I find none of them used it before anyway. The moms of the suburbs like the convenience of their car. They are not, like me, excited by their bright, clean, efficient underground transport system but listen politely to my arguments on congestion and pollution before jumping back in their 4x4s without a trace of guilt.

What frightens me is not the Metro but driving on the Beltway, the M25-style ring road around DC, where heavy duty people carriers weave in and out of four lanes, bumper to bumper.

Statistically, I am more likely to die in a road accident than a terrorist attack, particularly if I momentarily forget to drive on the right.

More anthrax cases have been found in New York. The newspapers say people are stockpiling gas masks and antibiotics.

Desperate restaurateurs try offering free desserts to pull in the punters. But they are thwarted when the FBI announces another high alert status. Downtown, *The Washington Post* finds some World War Two veterans holding a reunion and a predictably fearless British couple from Manchester. John says, *'The White House was shut, the FBI tour was shut. We're not scared but apparently somebody here is.'*

The mood from across the Atlantic is noticeably stoical. 'Of course we're still coming over,' say the grandparents, surprised that we asked.

Let's be sensible about this. Anthrax has just been found at media offices in Florida and New York, not here. But then one morning the radio tells me otherwise. It's now been found in Washington, in a letter sent to Senate Majority Leader Tom Daschle. Hundreds of Capitol workers are being tested for possible exposure and are taking antibiotics.

President Bush and his team have told the nation that if they see anything suspicious they should report it. Panic-stricken citizens have called out the crack hazardous materials (Hazmat) units for a series of false alarms. Suspicious powder has, rather inevitably, turned out to be sugar, flour and dust.

I eye up other peoples' trolleys in the Giant supermarket. Do they usually buy that much water, tinned food and batteries? I get an extra box of Graham crackers (like digestive biscuits) and some longlife chocolate milk on special offer. I already have some water in the car in case I break down on the Beltway and pass out through heat or stress. Should Armageddon come, who wants a glass of warm water and a cold can of condensed soup for their last meal?

There's been a run on Cipro, the antibiotic used for anthrax. Adverts promise the drug can be shipped to you in 24 hours. Dozens of websites have sprung up to sell it but how do customers know they are getting the real thing? The authorities warn, 'consult your physician', and not to take it if you don't need it.

'I have enough for the whole family,' another mother confesses matter-of-factly. 'You've got some too, right?'

'Actually no, seems like over-reacting to me,' I reply. Hope she doesn't prove me wrong.

Across the capital of America, post is being opened with gloves. Secretaries are donning surgical masks. Endless reporting on anthrax incidents is finally getting to Roland. Until now, he thought the extra precautions were only for the paranoid but tonight he refuses to bring the post inside as usual, removing letters from the outside mailbox and sitting on the garden steps to open them. Sally gives him a wave as she takes the air with her dog. She doesn't need to ask why he is opening envelopes next to the hostas. But there is no need to panic: it's all lawnmower advertising, pleas to help the destitute and too-good-to-be-true credit card offers. Corporate America is still in business, that's for sure.

I clear up the kitchen and cook some chilli-bean casserole for dinner. A psychiatrist on the radio says, 'I think we're in a state of high anxiety.' White powder on a lift button on Pennsylvania Avenue near The Capitol earlier today turns out to be the sugar frosting from a jam donut.

With more anthrax found on Capitol Hill and workers testing positive, 100 people in the area have turned up to a hospital emergency room asking to be tested or put on antibiotics. From Wisconsin to California, schools are cancelling trips to Washington. So much for solidarity. A survey says that 60 per cent of Americans are praying more.

The sound of my accent in the supermarket or the park is a trigger for anyone who has ever been to Britain to talk about their trip.

'I love your country – the people were so nice.' (I'm not convinced we were but they generously decide that the national reticence was due to shyness and modesty rather than grumpiness). 'I couldn't get iced tea anywhere in London and I had to *ask* for ice in my water. It was so funny.'

'People in the Lake District seem to *enjoy* walking in the rain. You know that's why English women have such good skin, it is all the rain.'

'We drove an RV (camper van) but we couldn't even get it down the street in Oxford!'

There is great interest in the clear plastic rain cover I still have attached to the buggy. 'Excuse me, what is *that*?' I say that everyone has them in Britain, you just pull it down over your child to stop them getting wet. So what do Americans do when it rains? 'We stay home or go by car.' Oh. There is also great interest in our buggy board, attached to the back so the older child can stand on it. I explain it's very handy for the bus or train as you can detach it and carry it with a shoulder strap when you have folded down the buggy. My new friends show polite interest but wouldn't dream of doing it themselves. Instead, they favour wide double 'strollers' in which both children can sit in comfort and which fit into the back of a people carrier with ease.

Two postal workers in Washington have now died from inhaled anthrax. Therapists are recommending that, to lower stress, people should avoid the news just before going to sleep. Elaine from round the corner and I think that Sally is getting overanxious with her almost round-the-clock monitoring of TV news and radio. 'It just makes her worry,' Elaine says. She herself is philosophical, a New Yorker with Irish roots who watches mafia drama *The Sopranos* because it reminds her of home. We are kindred spirits, secretly preferring charity shops to shopping malls. We also have a dark secret – we are vegetarians. And she got a knock on her door from the FBI after 9/11 too (they didn't come in though). Sally introduced us over tea from a china pot. 'I thought you would get along,' she says cheerily.

Later, I am in the local post office, a trip which I dread as I always seem to be in violation of some minor regulation. As usual, there is a long queue but in these times, nobody has the heart to complain. When we glance at our watches we do it surreptitiously, not pointedly like usual. An elderly lady with powdered face and bouffant hair smiles sympathetically at a counter clerk. 'We feel so sorry for you at the moment,' she says. We all nod in agreement. The reply from the young woman is polite but matter-of-fact, 'Don't, Ma'am. We're fine.'

The parcels are weighed and stamped, insurance is bought, boxes are thrown into skips and wheeled into the sorting office behind the counter. The queue is inching along.

Suddenly, a swarthy, possibly Arabic man rushes in and tries to open a side door leading to the back of the post office. 'No, Sir, not that way,' the same counter clerk shouts.

The man looks agitated, stressed, and quickly goes back outside. The clerk runs out of sight into the sorting office but we clearly hear her say, 'I need help, urgent.'

A burly co-worker appears with a bunch of keys and locks the side door.

There is silence except for the sound of parcels being stamped. 'Will that be all, Ma'am? Have a nice day.'

'Thank you sir.'

The dark haired man arrives back with parcels under his arm and joins the queue. We turn and look and he smiles weakly, confused as to why are we staring at him. He looks at his watch, probably late back for work and thought he might be able to avoid the line.

'We have sold out of Stars and Stripes and Statue of Liberty stamps, Ma'am,' announces the Latino clerk apologetically.

I head over to the toddlers' music session at the bookshop. We kick off with *If you're happy and you know it*. We clap our hands and stamp our feet with gusto. Right now, you have to appreciate the little things. The music man finishes with some Dylan for the parents. 'The answer my friend, is blowing in the wind.'

Anthrax bacteria has now been found at a post office on Wisconsin Avenue. This is just down the road from the Friendship Heights post office that I sometimes use. It's getting closer.

I look up the disease control website run by US government scientists to check the facts for myself. Anthrax is an acute infectious disease mostly found in wild or domestic cattle, sheep, goats and other herbivores. Humans can get it if they are exposed to infected animals both dead or alive. The infection comes in three forms: cutaneous (skin), inhalation and gastrointestinal. Symptoms, depending on the type, include a black centred ulcer. It can also feel like a common cold followed by breathing problems, or nausea, vomiting blood, abdominal pain and fever.

The scientists say those who should get vaccinated are: those who work with the organism in a laboratory; those who work with imported animal hides or furs; people who handle infected products from high risk countries (not the US); military personnel in areas with a high risk of exposure to biological warfare.

So, it has been pretty rare in America until now. I idly search for anthrax online. The January 6th, 2000, edition of *The New England Journal of Medicine* pops up. It says that, during World War I, German spies carried out a covert programme of biological warfare using anthrax. It was directed against horses and mules waiting to be shipped across the Atlantic to work for the army. From 1915 to 1917, their US mastermind was the American-born Anton Dilger. He imported cultures from Berlin and 'grew them in an improvised bacteriology laboratory in his suburban Washington DC dwelling'. Humans weren't directly targeted, but reports of cases increased.

I wonder where this lab was and do another search on Anton Dilger. Turns out he and his brother Carl set up their home lab in the basement of a rented house in Chevy Chase. Well, fancy that! Anthrax production in my neighbourhood.

Sally waves at me as I unload the shopping from the car. 'I'm just back from the hospital,' she says breathlessly and shows me her thumb, swollen with a dark patch. 'It started happening at the time we were being told to be careful opening envelopes. I saw dark at the cuticle on a couple of fingers on my left hand. Then I woke up this morning and my thumb was swollen and aching. I went to hospital immediately. They were very concerned.'

Both Sally and the hospital staff feared it was the cutaneous, most common form of anthrax where bacterium enters a cut in the skin. It's the agricultural related type that comes from infected animals or their products. How on earth could Sally have got it? But, as mysteriously as it appeared, the symptoms vanish before she even gets to the specialist.

Tonight, November 8, 2001, George Bush is giving an address to the nation. It is two months since 9/11. He says, 'We are a different country than we were on September 10, sadder and less innocent, stronger and more united...' I'm not convinced about the last part.

Later, he says, 'Our people have responded with courage and compassion, calm and reason, resolve and fierce determination. We have refused to live in a state of panic – or a state of denial. There is a difference between being alert and being intimidated – and this great nation will never be intimidated.' This is not how it feels from the white picket fence. People are frightened and anxious, staying near to home and avoiding planes and trains.

The President continues, 'Too many have the wrong idea of Americans as shallow, materialist consumers who care only about getting rich or getting ahead. But this isn't the America I know.' Actually, this isn't the America I know so far either. When I mess up the electronic credit card machine for the third time in CVS (a cross between Woolworths and Boots) the assistant says, 'It's alright, Ma'am, I'll help you.' When I waltz into a mechanics' workshop to pay for petrol, the boss kindly tells me, 'We pay at the pump in the US. This your first time? I'll come and show you what to do.' Desperate for adult conversation in the park, I not only get a chat but a phone number and a new friend.

Yes, there is a national obsession with shopping. The huge mall car parks are always full at the weekend but so are those for the churches and synagogues.

And George Bush has more on his agenda. He wants us to become a volunteer, to serve in our community (pronounced 'cumYOOniddy'). Become a hospital or fire service worker (this option is a good one as it automatically makes you a 'hero'), mentor a child, join neighbourhood watch or Crimestoppers. I wander off to put the washing on, wondering if I am tall enough to join the US fire service.

The next day I sit in line with other mothers outside the new ballet class. We are all from somewhere else but I am the only foreigner. We placate the younger siblings with snacks while their older sisters cavort in floaty costumes with a very thin lady in a leotard. My snacks are sugar-free (because of tooth decay and diabetes), theirs are fat-free (so their kids don't get obese like the trailer trash). We talk about our new home town and how it compares with our last. One previously lived in the mid-west. 'I really don't feel settled here. I miss small town America. I was never so happy as then. There was nothing there – my husband couldn't wait to get out – but I had such a community.'

I read the rest of the Bush address in the paper. I missed the bit on anthrax. *'The second attack against America came in the mail. We do not know whether this attack came from the same terrorists; we don't know the origin of the anthrax – but whoever did this unprecedented and uncivilized act is a terrorist.'* How can he even make a possible connection with 'the same terrorists' when all the indications are to the contrary? Conspiracy theorists whisper that it is to George's political advantage to keep the public and the media compliant through the threat of the Islamic fundamentalist bogeyman.

The core message is simple. Americans value life, education, women's rights, free speech and religious freedom. The new enemy is a ruthless killer who forces women to stay indoors, brutally punishes those who speak out and dictates the form of worship. It's black and white, right?

This is all starting to feel oppressive. We need to get away from here, take a break, but this is not the moment for an activity holiday. Somewhere warm and relaxing, away from all the stress and paranoia. Perhaps the Caribbean. I look at the adverts in *The Washington Post* and try a few travel websites. There are some good deals to the Dominican Republic and the Florida Keys so I take down the details.

Soon it is Veterans' Day, when Americans remember those who have fought for their country. This year is more poignant than most with US soldiers fighting in Afghanistan and the political message that every US citizen is under attack. The situation is both a nightmare and a dream for George Bush. How on earth does a leader deal with a national disaster on the scale of 9/11? But at the same time, no opposition politicians or journalists are daring to criticise him for fear of appearing unpatriotic. He is untouchable.

Many working parents have the day off but Josie's playgroup is still on. It is boot camp for the under threes – running, jumping, throwing balls and climbing through hoops in a red brick community hall in a local park. The facilities are simple but pristine – no litter, no graffiti, no weeds. The dads are out in force today, in their white sports socks and college T-shirts. 'Go Macy!'

'Good job Buddy!' 'Yeah – that was awesome!' I manage a meek, 'Well done, Josie,' and smile encouragement to a tiny, curly-haired boy who keeps getting left behind. His dad whoops and shouts, 'Go, go, goooooo!'

Time for a water break. Josie leads me over to socialise with the other parents. She is fast realising that if you are aged 2, look like a cherub and have an English accent, nine out of ten Americans will swoon. Today, she is trying out a new improved version which sounds uncannily like the Queen. 'She is so cuuuute!' says one mother. 'I just love the English accent.' She pauses. 'I am so sorry that you had to come to America at a time like this.'

On the drive home, I flick the radio on for the news. A plane has crashed in Rockaway, Queens, New York. More than 250 people on board are feared dead and at least six local residents are missing. Please, not another terrorist attack. This is an area where police, firefighters and office workers live – the community lost at least 70 of its own two months ago on 9/11. I don't want to listen any more.

By the evening, CNN reports that investigators suspect 'a catastrophic engine event' as the likely cause for American Airlines flight 587 to fall out of the sky. It was on its way to Santo Domingo in the Dominican Republic. It is completely illogical but somehow I don't feel the same about going there on holiday anymore.

Stories of security incidents get passed around daily. 'Did you hear about the guy who was lining up for a plane out of New York carrying a bottle of Coke?' a neighbour asks. 'Security men surrounded him and refused to let him on the plane until he had drunk it in front of them. It's getting crazy out there.'

A day trip to the countryside is what we need. I wade through my leaflets and guidebooks and pick out an old-style working farm with an equestrian centre.

In less than an hour's drive, we are there, wandering among wooden Dutch barns and livestock. Horse boxes and pick-up trucks are everywhere. The smell of hot dogs mingles with the aroma of horse poo.

There is a competition going on which the announcer describes as 'western-style'. The riders come out into the ring resplendent in cowboy hats and suede-fringed trousers. The shirts are brightly coloured and studded and some of the women wear diamante chokers. A nearby van sells horse shampoo and other riding accessories. The riders' families set up chairs and vast supplies of food from giant cool boxes.

A woman rider sits down nearby to watch the competition. 'Your children are adorable,' she says as they prance around pretending to be horses. 'Where are you all from?' Kelly has long, bleached, permed hair, burgundy fingernails and lives in rural Pennsylvania with her husband and 12 horses. 'I used to live in Washington and Baltimore,' she says, 'but there was so much crime. It was always on the news. I like it much better with my horses in the mountains.' What would she have done if she had still been living in Washington on 9/11? 'I would have left town,' she says simply.

An old-fashioned yellow school bus pulls up next to the horse boxes. African American city kids tumble out and run shrieking with delight to see the horses and goats, stroking them and feeding clumps of grass. Then they spot two baby calves and crowd around. A little girl of about six looks up at her teacher and asks, 'Is that a horse?'

Her friends don't laugh, clearly not sure either.

As the onslaught on the Taliban continues, I read that there are an estimated 60,000 Afghans in the North Virginia and Washington DC area. Decide it might make an interesting article for the British press and head to the Afghan Market in Alexandria, Virginia, to interview some customers. I find it behind the 7-Eleven and the Car Wash Express, near Burger Delite. The aroma of spices, strawberry molasses tobacco and tea welcomes customers inside and they greet each other in Farsi. A few miles north is the home of the CIA which has plotted the rise and fall of successive Afghan regimes.

Yousaf Khan, who wears a baseball cap, jeans and a 'Together we stand' badge, is happy to talk. He has no criticisms of the US bombing campaign and the work he has found in the 7-Eleven and

Wal-Mart makes him enough money to send some back to his family in Pakistan. 'The immigration, the local authorities – I love them!' he says. 'The US is very giving. They give to many people.'

Here are exiles from the pre-Taliban, Soviet-backed regime, academics, entrepreneurs and musicians, all hoping that the war will bring freedom of speech, womens' liberation and music in the streets once more. There is universal gratitude to America for taking them in but also hope that one day they can go home. Market owner Rafi Habibi sips tea from a crystal glass and talks of his countrymen. 'They are good people and they need us.'

The sun is up and we head for the park. Another mother, Claire, sympathetically listens to my lament about the lack of daily drop-in playgroups for toddlers like the ones I used in London. 'You need to sign up for some activities,' she says. 'I'll give you all the numbers.' I have found myself a volunteer lifestyle guru.

A few weeks later we are sitting on high stools at her kitchen counter discussing the merits, including cost, fatigue and fun factors, of toddler and pre-school gym, ballet and soccer.

Her friend Sonya is here too. Both are stay-at-home-moms, ex-lawyers, liberal, Jewish, and, in my eyes, perfectly groomed and super-efficient. This, I am discovering, is a common combination in the Washington area. My toenail paint is chipped and my hair is sticking up but they really don't seem to mind.

We drink 'soda' (caffeine-free diet coke) with ice from the refrigerator dispenser, as I scribble down numbers for kids' clubs. I'm desperate for a cup of tea but decide against asking in case the only kind Claire has is Lipton's, which is not tea as we know it.

We compare notes on the mornings our eldest children spend at nursery school. 'At the schools here you get strep throat, foot and mouth and head lice all the time,' Sonya advises cheerily. As the noise around us reaches a crescendo of crying and shouting, she leans over and says under her breath, 'I'm going to sell my frigging children to the circus.' This is the first time I have heard an American swear after months of living here and I am seeing encouraging signs of a sense of humour. (The pressure to be on best behaviour in public is such that recently arrived Brits are known to hold clandestine get togethers where they can swear, drink and smoke away from the critical eyes of puritanical American society.)

Back in the kitchen, the conversation comes round to the stresses of life post 9/11. 'My husband is in New York on business but I persuaded him to take the train instead of flying,' Claire says. Airport security is so tight now I had assumed it must be the safest way to travel. I decide it isn't the right moment to announce I think the next big terrorist incident will be on trains.

I try out my argument for going downtown. 'You have some of the best museums in the world, all for free, and they are deserted. Terrorists are not going to try and attack there now because of all the security. You can always drive if you are worried about the Metro.'

They listen thoughtfully but not completely convinced. 'If there is more to come, isn't a soft target like a shopping mall more likely?'

Now I feel awful, I hope I haven't made them frightened to go to the mall.

This morning the radio is tuned to National Public Radio (NPR) as I pour out the Rice Krispies. Suddenly the voice stops abruptly and gives way to a continuous, penetrating alarm noise. What does it mean? Are we under biological attack? Do we need to evacuate? It seems to go on forever, then stops as abruptly as it started. An announcer's voice says, 'This is a test for the alarm warning.' Shit. Does someone think we need one?

Chapter 4:
Food Poisoning

'IT WOULD BE easy for bio-terrorists to contaminate a reservoir,' an expert says on the radio.

'And what about the security threat to nuclear power stations?' asks the interviewer. I switch off.

The local authority in Montgomery County is getting 300 to 400 calls a day about bio-terrorism. Local emergency leaders say to pack a bag with essentials – the usual list of water, torch, batteries, radio, canned food and a change of clothes. It is unclear where we should go, what happens when we run out of petrol or the fate of those without a car.

It is well into October now but along the main arteries which link the city centre to the suburbs – Massachusetts, Connecticut and Wisconsin Avenues – US flags are still flying. Hand-painted 'God Bless America' signs have been erected by the road and the churches have notices for prayer vigils. Yellow school buses go by, a symbol of apple-pie America, but today they are full of kids who will soon be in therapy if their parents don't get a grip.

So how are people coping? Some, say media reports, are indulging in a bit of social drinking (not that you would ever know, it is not the very public, debauched kind you see in Britain).

In the months since 9/11, a New York hypnotherapist says she is seeing more people whose eating patterns are out of control. They sit in front of their televisions stuffing their faces with junk food while watching the latest doom-filled news. Is it any wonder they are depressed?

Amalie keeps getting tummy cramps and now she is throwing up. Josie is whiny and then she joins in the puking. Now it's me. Roland shows no symptoms, safely locked away in a sanitised office downtown. The rest of us are on the suburban front line. We go to the post office, speak to the postal workers (who must now be wondering if it would have been a better career move to join the army) and mingle with neighbours with suspected cutaneous anthrax.

The good news is we definitely don't have the symptoms of the usually fatal inhalation anthrax – a common cold followed by severe breathing problems.

But what about intestinal anthrax? Government scientists say initial signs of nausea, loss of appetite, vomiting and fever are followed by abdominal pain, vomiting of blood and severe diarrhoea. It results in death in 25 to 60 per cent of cases.

We haven't got to the 'vomiting of blood' yet but the first symptoms are there. I pick up the phone to the doctor, apologetic. 'It's probably just a tummy bug.' I never went to the doctor in Britain over a bit of throwing up. It is just that, since arriving in America, the unthinkable keeps happening.

The doctor's receptionist doesn't think I'm crazy, giving the impression that most mothers have been on already, and schedules an appointment that afternoon. Children don't go to GPs here, they have a paediatrician. Ours, on the list covered by the health insurance scheme Roland's employer uses, is in a gleaming tower block, above a post office. Everything is sparkly, new and clean, quiet and carpeted.

Cartoons are on the TV, there are books without any pages missing and wooden bead toys. Everyone has a seat and no one seems to wait for more than ten minutes. We are the lucky ones, those with good health insurance, sitting companionably with the white, middle class moms dressed in J.Crew and Banana Republic. What happens to those on the other side of town with little or no cover? I'm getting my information from the responsible news outlets – NPR, BBC World, *The New York Times* and *The Washington Post*. What about the mothers whipped into a state of terror about anthrax by the TV news and the hoards of right-wing, sound-bite radio stations? Do they just turn up at the hospital accident and emergency and worry about the money later?

'Amalie and Josie?' asks a beaming nurse in teddy bear print overalls.

In a sunlit room decorated with patchwork quilts, I go through a list of questions. In between tests and the arrival of the doctor we read *The Cat in The Hat*. Anthrax is quickly ruled out but I am not ridiculed. Right now we have a viral infection. But the stomach cramps before that could be down to something else.

'I want you to change your diet for a few weeks, cutting out peanut butter and foods with nuts in them,' the doctor says. 'Watch the additives too. Your bodies need to adjust to a different kind of diet here.'

So, America is giving us tummy trouble.

The Giant supermarket, or 'grocery store' as they say here, flies the American flag. It always seems to be open. If I can ever get my head round the club card scheme, the special offers and the two-for-the-price-of-one deals, I could probably save a lot of money. This week's star buys are lean beef, soda, Lucky Charms cereal, salted crackers, lunch meats and deli macaroni 'salad'. There are more cereals, snack biscuits and fizzy drinks than I have seen in my life. A quick glance at the ingredients and you see the same list of E numbers found on many British supermarket shelves. But something else that I haven't seen before keeps popping up – 'corn syrup'. Drinks, cookies, jam – there it is again, including some products with the 'healthy' or 'organic' label. High-fructose corn syrup, HFCS, is a thick liquid made from corn starch, I later discover, and appears to be a common ingredient in the US. (Nutritionists say its increased use mirrors the rise in obesity but the government's health watchdogs don't seem to have acted on this.) I swing into the next aisle with my shopping trolley ('cart'), which is disguised as a car. The girls are whooping with delight but the pleasure is short-lived – the way they are sitting designates a 'safety hazard', according to a passing shop assistant. We reorganise and proceed to the baking section. Suddenly I understand why I have heard mothers stress that they have made cakes 'from scratch'. There are mixes for everything – sponge cake, muffins, pancakes, cookies. Just add vegetable oil, or an egg or just water. At the end of the shelf, a few bags of flour are left for the purists.

I flick through the catalogue at the bakery department. This is where, I've been told, you buy cupcakes for school events. They are guaranteed peanut-free – baking at home is high risk if there is a lawyer parent in the class whose 'junior' is prone to spasms. (Asthma and allergies strike one in four Americans, says the Asthma and Allergy Foundation of America. Food reactions are more common among children, with nuts, milk, eggs and wheat often the cause.) Pile on the additives but hold the nuts, is the general message.

And what an exciting array of brightly coloured goo is on offer. How about a religious occasion cake with 'God Bless You' on it, one with a little golf cart in the middle for Dad, or one based on the Yu-Gi-Oh! card game for the lads?

The staff are a friendly lot, patient with the 'seniors' fumbling with their change, sending me back to fresh produce to get my free watermelon. They are called Al and Bob and like to talk about last night's game with customers. While waiting for them to pronounce on the play of the quarterback, you can gaze at the supermarket tabloids, the cheap magazines which one week proclaim that a Hollywood star is anorexic and the next that they have cellulite. They are displayed alongside the recipe magazines – 'fifty, fabulous chocolate desserts!' – and the diet books – 'lose 10lbs a week and still eat candy!'. The messages are so mixed it's no wonder some people give up and eat for America.

Safeway is similar to Giant, but the local one is smaller and closer so has a core of regulars, like Sally, who like to be recognised when they go to the store. They have the same chilled cookie dough in a can and vast array of milk – lactaid, low-fat, no-fat – and DIY meal kits. They also have an impressively large choice of indigestion medicine and laxatives, many 'as seen on TV'. A whole industry is based round the American gut. The pharmacist kindly identifies the red marks on the back of Josie's legs as 'classic heat rash'. 'All the little kids get it from sitting in their car seats.' He sells us some cream. I remark on the large selection of off-the-shelf medicines. 'We need a quick fix so we can keep going to work,' he says matter of factly. I have noticed it is less acceptable here to 'take a sickie', and two weeks annual leave is not unusual. Then there is the cost of health insurance and all the extras which aren't covered by it.

Many Giant and Safeway customers have probably never set foot in Wholefoods. If you can shop here on a regular basis, you have made it. It is an expensive, guilty pleasure with breathtaking arrays of fresh produce from California and Washington State, pyramids of oranges, star fruit, avocados, and strawberries all year round. Skip breakfast and you can taste your way round on pitta bread and homus, chips and salsa, fine cheeses and Jewish apple cake. The deli counter is stuffed with meats and exotic salads and the chill section has ten different kinds of tofu. Alongside are endless cheeses, Amish, French and English. And for the finale, gourmet bread and cake to taste. French-speaking Africans tend to work here and long lines at check-out are unheard of. Like the lower end supermarkets, the assistants pack for you but here there is an automatic choice between paper or plastic bags. More assistants are on hand to wheel your heavy trolley to your car – even though it is parked just outside – and they don't take tips.

At weekends, the demand for the Wholefoods experience is so great that stewards in florescent waistcoats direct you into your parking space. For a while, even the local police did it. Some shoppers thought this was great, they wanted an armed man in uniform to tell them to turn right onto River Road while the garden centre opposite was busy. Me, I was frightened of getting shot for driving on the wrong side of the road. Or for accidentally stealing an organic carrot.

I am also frightened of some of the other customers, who expect perfection and life on their terms at all times. They bark at the ever polite assistants for not having the right fresh herb in stock for their power dinner party and glare at children helping to push the trolley or choose the fruit, presumably because they should have been left at home with a nanny.

There is one grocery store I can actually walk to – woo hoo! Only trouble is, it is along a six-lane road and involves crossing a junction next to the fire station. And the fire engines go out a lot these days. After several near death experiences with emergency vehicles, people carriers and pick-ups I decide to drive.

Trader Joe's is the poor man's Wholefoods and a favourite with West Coast types and Europeans. I like it because it has a sense of humour. Italian food is labelled Trader Giottos and Spanish dishes Trader Jose's. They sell British muffins named after prime ministers. It is not part of the corn syrup conspiracy and you can get gluten free, sodium free, soy, kosher and low fat with ease. Rest assured, the seafood suppliers are not involved in seal hunting and genetically modified ingredients are not on the menu. Here, I do not suspect that the 'meatless meatballs' really have meat in them.

It is quiet today, after lunchtime and before school is out. The assistants in Hawaiian shirts chat about this week's shifts as they stack the shelves. Bet they all know how to surf and skateboard. The cool dude at the check-out sees us coming. 'Wanna help me?' he says to the girls. They scan and pack, bursting with pride. 'Thanks girls. Help yourself to a balloon.' They are so overcome they forget to argue about who has the last pink one.

At Trader Joe's, a child such as mine can knock over an entire cranberry display and be instantly forgiven ('It's ok, you're a kid'). No one will shout at them, except, of course, their British parents.

This afternoon, an assistant blocks our way to the lift which goes to the lower car park. He looks nervously at the children. 'I'm just checking the elevator,' he says. He whispers to me, 'Someone thinks they saw a mouse.' The girls prick up their ears and start crawling around calling, 'Here, mousey mousey.' We check on each floor.

'Mummy, perhaps it went to the golf shop.'

'Maybe it is in the liquor store.'

In the end, there is just one conclusion to be drawn. 'I think it went to Wholefoods. They have more cheese.'

Keeping fit feels like a priority with so many more culinary temptations and fewer opportunities to walk. There are local outdoor pools, but once they shut for the winter it's a drive to take a swim. We sign up at the YMCA and head into the female communal changing area. An elderly woman opens the neighbouring locker. She has bleached blonde hair, grey at the roots, wrinkled skin, and an all-over tan. She is completely comfortable in her nakedness so I guess she isn't American. The puritanical streak brought by the pilgrims lives on and the natives have either retreated behind the curtains of the private changing rooms or have towels wrapped tightly around them. 'You should go in the outdoor pool,' she suggests, 'it's so warm today. Have you been over from England long?' Her accent is American but tinged with something else. She can't contain herself any longer. 'What *is* our government doing bombing Afghanistan? It is madness.' Although the US has been her home for decades, she is German-born. 'I know you will understand why I don't like it, as you are European. The Americans think I'm being unpatriotic.'

Later we are at the children's dentist for our first check-up and I am worried that the low fat but high sugar American diet will have taken its toll. The surgery is another modern, gleaming office block with its own parking lot. A pile of forms about health history awaits. A quick look in Amalie's mouth and it is decided she needs a tooth removed. It is the broken baby tooth which our NHS dentist in London told us to 'keep clean and let it come out naturally'. They are not interested. 'It *must* come out, Ma'am.'

I am going through the paperwork that parents must read prior to tooth removal. There are all sorts of litigation and insurance clauses, so neither the dentist nor the nurse can be held responsible for their actions. Then some of the nitty-gritty. 'Has your child got HIV? What are your child's hobbies?' I really can't see the relevance of the last one. Will they buy her a new football to make up for the brain damage? Next is a section on the mental state of the parents. I am tempted to write, *'worsening by the minute'*. Then a list of side effects for the tooth removal drugs are detailed. The word 'death' is used more than once.

My dentist in London comes to the phone straight away. His parting words a few months previously were, 'American dentists are more interventionist than European ones. Call if you are worried about anything.' I explain the situation and hang on the line as he looks at her last x-rays. 'Honestly, if it doesn't hurt, I would leave it. She's only four.'

So, I pay up the amount not covered by health insurance and do a runner from the death-by-tooth-removal dentist, ignoring their letters and phone messages. My friend Leah sympathises. 'Go to ours. You get bubblegum flavoured toothpaste and your nails painted.' Now that's more like it. This dentist, in another gleaming tower block, takes our health insurance and says the tooth can stay.

Now, I don't consider myself paranoid, but something peculiar is happening to my head. Every time I try to read, the words blur at the edges and I am getting spots before the eyes. The logical explanation is I need glasses. Better go to one of the many one-stop eye shops and get a test. The optician peers through her instruments looking for clues and gets me to read out a list of letters.

'There is nothing wrong with your eyes,' she concludes.

'So why am I getting blurred vision?' I ask, having already chosen some stylish frames. 'Am I ill?'

'No,' she says, reassuringly. 'Your eyes are sensitive to the intensity of the sunlight here. You have always lived in England, right? You are used to more cloud. Just wear shades more, even on days when the sun might not be completely out.'

I am hoping I don't need those huge wraparounds favoured by the little old ladies who hang out in chichi Friendship Heights. The look is completed by bouffant hair, lots of makeup and a Cadillac style car which is too big for them to drive. But after a few weeks of wearing regular sunglasses, the spots gradually disappear and the blurred vision eases.

For such a God-fearing country, Halloween, which dates from the Dark Ages and looks to the dead, devils and ghosts, seems an unlikely date to celebrate on such a grand scale. Giant, Safeway and CVS fill their aisles with huge packs of candy, sugar-loaded, orange-wrapped sweets, lurid costumes and improbably large pumpkins.

At nursery school, the Halloween songs are being sung in earnest. 'One little, two little, tree little witches, flying over haystacks, flying over ditches, sliding down moonbeams without any hitches, hey ho Halloween's here.'

'Usually we take a hayride to the pumpkin patch,' a mother at Time for Twos storytelling in the library says. 'You drive out to a farm and they take you on a tractor and trailer to pick your own pumpkin. It's so neat. The kids love it.' She pauses. 'I don't know if we will do it this year. It doesn't feel right to be celebrating right now.'

What about trick-or-treating? 'We like to make a little home movie of them knocking on doors in their cute outfits. I guess we'll still do that but we'll only go to close neighbours,' she says.

Everyone says the build-up to Halloween is much quieter this year. There are rumours that terrorists will poison sweets. Warnings circulate on the radio that children should not take anything unwrapped and not touch anything that looks homemade.

Kids can traditionally dress up as anything – not just witches and devils – and this year there is a run on US military fatigues and firefighter uniforms.

When the night comes, Amalie is struck down with her first dose of the dreaded strep throat (streptococcal infection) and lies moaning in bed holding her head. Josie, in rabbit pyjamas and a witch's hat, opens the door to the few souls who refuse to let Osama Bin Laden spoil the party. They grab fistfuls from the candy bowl before heading off down the street to find the few other houses that have a lit pumpkin outside. An angel says she only likes Hershey's Kisses and the Grim Reaper asks if we have any Reese's Peanut Butter Cups.

At nursery school, a teacher confirms it isn't normally like this. 'It was very quiet. I only got kids I knew this year, no strangers. I guess the parents are afraid.'

I wonder if they still celebrated in Tombstone, Arizona, or Cape Fear, North Carolina, or Skull Creek, Nebraska.

The girls are modelling play dough with some new American friends in our basement and their mother asks what they are all making. The others say 'a flower' and 'a bunny'. Mine say 'wine' and 'beer'. I sense this is not a good answer. In Britain, I considered myself a moderate drinker but here I feel like a lush. Having a glass of wine over weekend lunch is apparently living on the wild side. It is dawning on me that many Americans don't think their kids should see them drinking. Is this why liquor store purchases are disguised in brown paper bags? Are the dog walkers looking in horror at the number of bottles in my recycling box? Leah, who likes a glass of fine wine after her baby and toddler are tucked up in bed, advises, 'Wait until it is dark and slip a few bottles into your neighbours'.' I wonder if I will bump into anyone else doing the same.

A new weekend treat is breakfast at The Pancake House. It's diner style with black and white tiles, red-seated booths and autographed photos of local TV presenters and American footballers on the wall. It has 'cheap eats' awards and gives 15 per cent of sales to charity once a month. Everything is in abundance. An omelette can last you three more meals, your spare pancakes two more breakfasts. The teenagers at the next table have huge pancakes piled high with chocolate chips and whipped cream. The clientele is a noticeable ethnic mix and, despite the portions, it isn't filled with overweight customers. They just all take doggy bags.

Today I speak to Jared Fogle for an article about the efforts by overweight Americans to eat better. No one has heard of this cheery young man in Britain but here he's a national hero after losing 17 stone. His diet? Eating nothing but Subway's turkey and veggie sandwiches for a year. He is now their advertising figurehead. So how did America become such a fast food, fat nation? 'I think it is partly our attitude,' Jared says. 'We are a nation of plenty. Everything is big here.' The debate has been fuelled this year by Eric Schlosser's book *Fast Food Nation* which looks at 'the dark side of the all American meal', but the outlets are still plentiful and busy.

With evangelical enthusiasm, Dr Neal Barnard, president of the Physicians Committee for Responsible Medicine, wants Americans to go vegetarian. The grandson of a cattle rancher, he used to eat 'enough meat to sink a ship'. But now he has seen the light. 'In America, meat is a religion,' he says. 'But although we are more out of shape than ever, we also know more about nutrition and obesity than ever before.' More than half of all US adults are overweight but Dr Barnard isn't despairing. 'There is a sub-section of folks across the age spectrum that have become interested in changing their diet,' he believes.

These Americans certainly know how to do optimism.

Chapter 5:
Happy Holidays

'FALL' IS A favourite time of year here. The temperature changes quickly and with it the colour of the leaves. The newspaper travel sections talk about where to find the best 'fall foliage', the richest reds and the deepest oranges. Expert 'leaf peepers' say you have to go to Vermont but the mountains of West Virginia have their charms. For me, the blaze of colour on every tree-lined road nearby is spectacular.

The end of November also brings Thanksgiving, marking when the pilgrims first feasted with the Native American Indians. It's the most important time for families to get together in America, in the same way that Christmas is in Britain.

Thanksgiving is the time for counting your blessings, eating too much and wearing embroidered jumpers. Turkeys are ordered and traditional dishes allocated to different members of the family – brussel sprouts and nuts, sweet potato with marshmallows, pumpkin pie.

Scraping the flesh from the inside of a pumpkin takes hours and goes on into the next day. I use my new Halloween pumpkin cutter kit, which has a scoop, with chisel and tiny saw. It must taste good for Americans to make this much effort, I conclude. The pulp looks wet, stringy and squishy but I carry on with the recipe anyway, hoping the cinnamon will take away the awful smell. Even warm from the oven, served with fresh cream, it is quite disgusting.

I share my experience with mothers in the park and at toddler keep fit. They are polite but surprised. 'I'm sure it was delicious.

You could try Martha Stewart's recipe next time.' Then Leah tells me the secret to a perfect, smooth filling. 'Anne, we just get a can of pumpkin puree from the Safeway.' Oh.

Josie and I find another library storytelling and craft session. This week the theme is Thanksgiving – a story about the pilgrims, another about furry, woodland animals storing food for winter, then songs of apples and leaves (with lots of actions to demonstrate them falling from the trees). The first librarian wears a black pilgrim hat for the occasion and a brown knitted cardigan with embroidered fall leaves on it. The second goes one better and has leaves *and* turkeys embroidered on hers.

'Now we are going to do a fun craft activity for Thanksgiving!' I am baffled as to why we are being told to draw an outline round our hand and cut it out. To Josie it is perfectly clear. The thumb is the turkey's head and the fingers are its feathers. Just stick on an eye and some coloured paper and say 'gobble, gobble'. Fabulous.

We are flying to the Florida Keys, the strip of islands that forms the southernmost tip of the US, for Thanksgiving weekend. It is my first time at an airport since 9/11 and it feels like a very different place. Before, it was a relaxed affair with a gratuitous security check. Now, we are met by soldiers in full combat gear holding machine guns. Josie's tiny pink rucksack has sent security staff at baggage x-ray into a panic. We are told to stand next to one of the men with a machine gun as they search it. Out come the plastic Dalmatians, the cuddly sheep, the pencils and paper, a rubber ball and newly acquired stickers which say 'good job!' and 'you rock!'. The security woman won't meet my eyes, her face grim, her demeanour tense. Eventually they let us go. Now we are late but dare not run with so many jumpy looking armed men around.

Safely on board, and the pilot announces a new rule – only one person can wait outside the bathroom at a time. But the Southwest Airlines slogan – '20 years of luv' – is still all around us and the further we get from Washington DC the more relaxed the mood.

We wake at 8.00am, the sunlight flooding through the palm trees into the hotel room in Key Largo. Just time for a quick swim before breakfast. The sound of pulsating Motown music gets louder as we approach the pool. Must be some young all-night partygoers finishing their session, I guess. But turning the corner, a very different vision awaits us. Rows of deeply tanned pensioners are pushing dumbbells into the air to *Jimmy Mack*. Most sport huge wraparound black shades, with baseball caps or flowery swimming hats. The few men, wearing heavy gold chains, sit out of some exercises, basking in the sun with the air of people who know how to appreciate life. The women do everything with gusto, undaunted by the already hot sun. The instructor, whose age is difficult to determine because of the dyed hair and taut look from cosmetic surgery, cranks up the volume of *You Can't Hurry Love* for the water aerobics finale. Then it's all over. Participants don luxurious white towelling bathrobes and flip flops, jump into huge Cadillac-style cars and speed off to their next engagement in paradise.

Later, we head to a sea life centre for the much hyped dolphin show. Under a brilliant blue sky, next to crystal clear water, the tourists gather, Americans in their logo T-shirts and baseball caps, cameras at the ready, we Brits scruffier, pinker skinned and devoid of bright white clothing. We take our turns to stroke the dolphins and let them give us a playful splash and clap enthusiastically as they flip through the air. The Disney-style musical accompaniment fades and an unmistakably patriotic song starts up. Around the lagoon comes an all-American beauty – blonde hair, tanned skin and a perfect physique covered by a full body wetsuit. She rides a dolphin through the surf while the strains of *God Bless America* fill the air. As the dolphin swims to where the crowd sit expectantly, the trainer rises up, holding aloft an American flag. The crowd goes crazy, whooping and cheering. We clap politely. There is no sign that anyone else thinks what we have just witnessed is over the top.

After some messing about on the beach, time to relax and watch as the sun goes down at the waterside Cuban restaurant. The young waitress brings black bean soup and plantain. She stops to chat, remarking on the children's command of English. 'I am worried about my kids,' she says. 'They are one and three and just speak gibberish. They are not speaking proper Spanish or proper English. I am half Cuban and half Puerto Rican but I want them to be real Americans.'

'Why?' I ask.

'Because there are so many opportunities for them here,' she replies. 'They can do anything.'

A boat full of partying young Americans holding beer bottles pulls up at the jetty and she goes outside to take their order.

Key West is an old wreckers' town 90 miles from Cuba. You get to it over a thin stretch of land and miles of sea bridges, past pristine white beaches lined with palm trees, past the 'hurricane shelter' and 'hurricane evacuation route' signs. Hemingway wrote here and it has long been a magnet for backpackers, hippies and divers.

Feeling the heat on arrival, we head into an air-conditioned shopping mall in search of ice cream. Almost immediately, a smiling, avuncular, bearded man wearing a Hawaiian shirt approaches. 'Guuuuys! I love your accents. You have to be from England, right? It's my favourite country. I just love all the history and the people.' The multi-coloured parrot on his shoulder is similarly friendly. 'Hi guys,' he says before letting out a loud squawk. 'Have you just arrived?' asks the owner. 'Why don't you take a look at our nature centre on the top floor. There are some cool films of the reef.'

Why not? We step inside and read some details about the sea life, accompanied by amateurish, hand drawn graphics. Then we move into a corridor filled with a re-creation of the local vegetation, huge green leaves, exotic flowers and parrot noises. 'Mummy,' Amalie asks, 'Why is Jesus in the jungle?' Sure enough, partly hidden between the leaves, is a black and white drawing of the Son of God. Cosmic music is coming from the room where the 'films of the reef' are supposed to be showing. When I put my head through the door a lone, spotty teenager gives me a wave. I distinctly hear the word 'God' coming from the sound system. The way out is through the cinema with the exit firmly shut, the way back is past another big bearded man in a Hawaiian shirt. But this being a mall, it has to have a fire exit. We find it and escape from God's own nature centre back to the brightly lit shops selling Slush Puppy iced drinks and Key West keyrings.

Over at the Sunset Festival by the water, hippies in tie dye with no teeth wander about and the palm readers have headphones and mics. A shaven-headed unicyclist is the star busker. 'I've seen him before,' announces Josie casually, with all the certainty of a two-and-a-half-year-old. It turns out she really has. 'Yeah, I was performing in Covent Garden six months ago,' he confirms in estuary tones afterwards as we all admire the sunset at the end of America.

Back in Key Largo, we sit down to our first Thanksgiving dinner at a hotel buffet with holidaying American families who didn't want to cook and rich Cubans dripping in gold. New arrivals fill up the last seats, little girls in huge taffeta and velvet dresses, dads in their church suits who lead grace before the eating begins. From tables laden with a vast feast, we all sample dishes with cranberries, turkey and sweet potato, pumpkin and key lime pies, washed down with complimentary champagne. Eventually we admit defeat and leave our eating companions at their tables (have they all been fasting for two days before?) and lie under a tree on the beach to recover.

The next day I come face to face with the hardest woman I have ever met. (Definitely tougher than the teenage boxing champion who threatened to kill me when, as a junior reporter, I wrote about her latest conviction for violence.) Shelly works at an alligator farm in the Florida Everglades. She is a solid mass of muscles, combat clothes and tattoos and her bleached hair is pulled back so tightly into a pony tail that it would give anyone else a headache. She has a buff, male Latino friend armed with a big stick who follows her around in awe. He is supposed to help Shelly if a gator goes for her but she shows no sign of needing him.

With an expression which says, 'don't mess with me', she wades into the water and pulls a five-foot-long gator out by the nose. She keeps hold of it while talking in a gruff, southern voice. 'You cannot train them. They live by instinct and their brain is the size of this fingernail.' It hisses menacingly as she stands astride its back, prizing open its mouth to show us its teeth. Motionless gators are all around her, lying in piles like logs washed up by the tide.

Shelly comes out of the gator enclosure with her minder and clanks the gate shut. She is holding a baby one, mouth firmly taped shut, for us to touch. Now it is feeding time and she marches into the alligator cage with a bucket of raw chickens. One, which looked like it was asleep, suddenly darts closer and with lightning reflexes Shelly kicks out with her army issue boot. Gators are now slowly, menacingly climbing out of the swamp, smelling the dead meat. She hurls the last chicken and gets out just as a gator comes within inches of her leg.

Outside the gator farm, black agricultural workers pick fruit in the fields near the swamp. Pick-up trucks drive into the trailer parks where American flags fly and prisoners at the Dade County Correctional Institution parade through the yard, shut in by metal and wire like the alligators.

The Washington suburbs now seem a bit tame.

'I just couldn't believe it when I heard about Iain Duncan Smith winning the Tory leadership. Of course none of the candidates were any good. My mother says everything has changed.' I swap notes from home with another British mother outside the ballet class. We crane our necks to see what costume the dancers are in today (looks like Little Red Riding Hood). Britain, we have both been hearing, is going to the dogs with knife crime and road rage on the rise. Transatlantic phone calls reveal everyone is also convinced that London will be the next place for a 9/11-style terrorist incident. So which is safer, London, where we are travelling to in December, or Washington?

I spot an ad for a children's version of The Nutcracker ballet near Washington and fix it up for the next day. We walk through the Virginia town of Alexandria in search of the venue, past a toy shop with frothy fairy costumes and numerous ice cream parlours. The Georgian-style houses aren't so old by British standards but are carefully maintained with manicured frontages. There is no litter, no grime, no dead plants. We arrive at the column-fronted hall where the show is to take place, wrapped up against the cold in woolly hats and comfy clothes ('children sit on the floor, adults stand at the back,' the ticket seller explains). As we wait for the doors to open, a huge, shiny new jeep pulls up and two small girls in organza, velvet and gold braid dresses clamber out, patent black shoes first. Their hair is improbably blonde and pulled back with enormous bows. The mother comes next, also blonde and wearing a tight tweed skirt and cashmere sweater with pearls. She carries the same dainty, ballet-themed clutch bag, or 'purse', as her daughters. No one wears a coat, they seem to know exactly when the doors will be opening and presumably expect to be collected at the door. More similarly attired children and mothers are being dropped off in a convoy of increasingly large, gleaming vehicles. The more practically dressed contingent, who parked up the street, took the Metro or walked, are in danger of being outnumbered by these frighteningly styled creatures. Inside, my girls dive for a spot on the floor as I stand behind, sweating with a bundle of jumpers and coats. They are surrounded by stiff, puffed-out skirts that take up way more space than is practical. Amalie gives the beautifully coiffured child to her left a long, incredulous stare. 'Her dress is sticking in me,' she whispers loudly. I glance at the mother, wondering if she has a diamond-encrusted revolver in her ballet bag, but luckily she is too busy talking to someone called 'honey' on the phone. The organiser makes the children promise not to go over the white line and the show begins. They can almost touch the ballerinas, teetering by on their points in elaborate tutus, and gasp in delight. All goes well until the last 15 minutes when the big-skirted contingent begin to fidget and wail. The hairstyles are being pulled out (the big bows turn out to be false ones attached to clips) and the velvet and organza is getting hot. Skirts encroaching onto neighbours' legs are being pushed away as the ballerinas dance back on stage in the nick of time. Then it is all over and the big skirts are whisked away in their waiting limos to another kind of America.

The vacant plots on Wisconsin Avenue are a mystery. All around them, every inch of empty land gets snapped up, as do the old brick houses, to be demolished and replaced with fancy new models. Except for these two empty spaces. Now something is happening there. Huts are appearing and a giant, inflatable snowman. There are clusters of college boys with straggly hair, jeans and hoodies. Then truckloads of Christmas trees, erected in straight lines in size order. The boys busy themselves with chopping and trimming and strapping the giant conifers to buyers' car roofs. They work until late at night, under the fairy lights in a woodland grotto, as car after car pulls up.

The line winds down the leafy path which leads to the elephant house at the national zoo, but I promise the girls it will be worth the wait to see the newborn baby. We are marshalled to the fence, behind notice boards to make sure no one queue jumps or blocks access for the elephant keeper. A large family are in front, discussing the weekend's suicide bombings in Israel which injured 200 people. 'Wasn't it terrible?' the mother says to me. I agree. 'We have friends and relatives there,' she says. 'It is such a relief that no one we know has been hurt.' Her generous descriptions of Israeli friends all have three things in common: each is 'a wonderful person', 'has an amazing house' and 'loves to shop'. They also cook Jewish speciality dishes for charity. We are now inside the elephant house, having inched past the hippos who are getting decidedly smelly. Our conversation on how nice so many people are and how sad it is that there cannot be peace in the Middle East is abruptly cut short when the mother shouts, 'Cameras out! *I can see it*!'

Christmas is coming. Skimming through the pet section of the local *Gazette*, past the adverts for dog walking services, is one for a pet barn somewhere out of town. It says to bring your pet along for a photo shoot. They will pop some antlers and bells on its head before taking your pet's picture with Father Christmas. By taking part you will help raise $2,000 for 'the community'.

The shops are full of shiny gold decorations with red velvet bows and towering displays for pre-wrapped 'holiday gifts'. But there are no Christmas cards, nor nativity play at nursery school, just a Santa puppet show.

The candlelit Menorah for the Jewish holiday of Chanukah is erected near the 'holiday tree' in the shopping mall. Chanukah, like Christmas and anything religious, stays outside the school gates. But there are plenty of churches and synagogues to chose from. A quick check under Chevy Chase in the phone directory lists just some of them: North Chevy Chase Christian Church, Christian Science, Church of Jesus Christ of Latter Day Saints, All Saints Church, St John's Episcopal, Chevy Chase United Methodist, St Paul United Methodist, Ohr Kodesh Congregation

Synagogue, Temple Shalom. Driving by, they all seem huge, prosperous, immaculate and busy.

Waiting in the car at the lights on Wisconsin Avenue, I read the bumper sticker on the white saloon car in front. 'No Jesus, no peace; know Jesus, know peace.' On Massachusetts Avenue, the message on the people carrier ahead reads, 'We have a friend in Jesus'. A tradesman's van goes by with the message, 'Why worry? God's in control'. I glimpse the driver as I pass by in the next lane – just an ordinary looking bloke in a baseball cap.

The invitations to pre-Christmas embassy parties that foreign journalists usually receive have not materialised – public partying looks insensitive after 9/11 – and with them goes the chance of voyeurism into another world.

I settle for a French haircut. Hopefully a Parisian will be less baffled than American hairstylists by a short haircut on a woman.

Pierre, who arrived from Paris two months ago, struts out of the cutting area in his black and white uniform, his eyes lighting up at the sound of my voice. But it is not my accent that interests him. 'Aaah you are British? Do you like football?' he asks. ''Ave you 'eard of Chris Waddle?'

I am his first client in America who has heard of the former England and Marseille player and he is beside himself with excitement. 'I will do you a beautiful French crop cut. These American stylists – what have they done to your 'air? They can only do 'air like Monica Lewinsky!' I volunteer as much chat about the Premier League as I can while he shimmies round the salon.

'See that lady over there,' he whispers. A heavily made-up woman, aged around 50, is walking through the salon, her newly dyed hair wrapped in pieces of silver foil. She wears flip flops while her shiny burgundy toenails are drying and carries a pair of six inch heel snakeskin stilettos.

'She is an ambassador's wife. All the ambassador's wives come 'ere,' he says with pride.

'So they are still going out to parties?' I ask.

'Yes,' Pierre confirms. 'But they say they are smaller and more exclusive than last year because of the security.' Then he adds kindly, '*You* would 'ave more fun watching the football at the sports bar in Dupont Circle.'

'Hi Annneee!! You have won the sweepstake!'

I think there has been some mistake, I tell my new friend Bob when he calls on the phone. 'I never enter things like that.'

'It's no mistake Annneee – you're a winner!'

Oh dear, I realise too late that he must be trying to sell me something. It turns out to be magazines, but not just one, a subscription to a whole host of titles for all the family, from kids' TV cartoons to golf 'for him' and 'a more beautiful you' for her. I say, really, no thanks, we might not be here that long and frankly I have enough trouble reading the newspaper every day and this really isn't a good time to call. 'Thank you, bye.'

The next day, at a different time, Bob is back. 'Annneee, how are you?' Then the next day, I ask a mother at nursery for advice on how to deal with this. She gives me an incredulous look. 'Just leave the phone on voicemail or hang up. There's no need to be polite.'

It's a chilly weekday afternoon in December and we have driven further out into the suburbs to a kids' gym full of brightly coloured crash mats, ropes and rings. The 4-year-old trots off to the mini gym with a group of energetic boys while Josie and I wait for the mother and toddler group to start. But there are no other small people to be seen. I enquire at the registration desk. 'Looks like Josie is the only one down for this class,' she says, looking at her watch. 'It's two o'clock and most kids her age will be taking a nap right now.' So that's why the playground is always deserted then. I have also started to notice that many mothers refuse to move from their homes during sacrosanct 'nap time'. This has come as a shock to someone whose child abandoned any daytime sleep a year ago. No snatched snoozes in the buggy or the car for these American two and three-year-olds. So what happens to the wide-awake ones? The answer stands before us. A beaming, muscle-bound man with gold earrings (think Mr. T from *The A-Team*) shakes Josie gently by the hand and says, 'Hi honey, you got yourself a personal trainer.'

Half an hour later we are still going strong. 'Go Josie! Through the tunnel, along the balance beam – good job! Now Mommy's turn!'

Christmas is a whirlwind trip visiting relatives and friends in rainy Britain. 'What a time you have had!' people say, as we recount tales of terrorism, the FBI and anthrax. 'Bet you're tempted not to go back.'

'Yes,' I reply.

'No,' says Roland.

A few weeks later, we are driving through Dupont Circle in DC when a flurry of snowflakes comes down. The four men playing chess under the trees don't notice. An African American, a Hispanic, an Asian and a white man, they are wrapped up against the cold in woolly hats and scarves, steaming coffee at their side, engrossed in the game. It is late January now and the snow virtually guaranteed here every winter has not yet arrived. But tonight the local TV news channel is predicting several inches. The camera pans to shoppers buying sledges, salt and snow shovels. I look closer and realise it is our very own Strosniders Hardware. The next shot is at the Giant where there is a run on milk and batteries. We laugh at all the fuss. These Americans, what are they like?

The next morning I am forced to eat my words. Snow is falling hard and we have no sledge. Fifteen minutes later I am at Strosniders, hoping they haven't sold out. I'm in luck. Shoppers are crowded round an array of old-fashioned wooden ones, aero-dynamic long ones and round ones in neon colours. I ask a woman in running clothes and a furry hat with earflaps which one is best. 'The little ones like the round ones but my boys want something fast.' Now she is on her mobile. 'Hey, I'm at the hardware store. Got you a sled that looks real fast. It's a torpedo, yeah, a long one. It's tie dye.' I am caught up in the fever of sledge buying, squeezing past the other customers to check out the goods. 'Hot pink or tie dye?' a woman in a Yale sweatshirt asks her daughter. A small boy jumps up and down and yells, 'I want that one!'

'Sure, bud,' his Dad replies, no time for a tantrum before heading to the office. I buy a tie-dye torpedo and a hot pink round one to avoid fights.

Head to Trader Joe's for bread and milk. The assistant is from California and is as excited as we are. None of us have seen much snow before. 'How do you drive in it?' he asks. I don't know either. Very slowly, we decide, after some discussion. Outside, gritting lorries and snow ploughs are roaring past. Back in our street, neighbours are clearing driveways with snow shovels and making paths along the pavements outside their homes. I opt for trying out the sledges in the park instead. Sally is the only other person who hasn't cleared her steps. I ring up to get reassurance that it doesn't matter. 'They are worried that it will turn to ice,' she says. 'But this isn't a big storm. The sun will be out tomorrow and it will all melt anyway.' And so it does.

I queue up for tickets at an outdoor ice rink. Then line up for boots. Finally we are ready to make our entrance onto the ice, under the fairy lights and to the sounds of *Love Me Do*. But the voice on the tannoy tells us we have to 'clear the ice' immediately. What is going on? A machine, a bit like a mini combine harvester, is reversed out of the shed. Agonisingly slowly, it moves onto the ice, spraying water and smoothing the surface, the driver in his 'rink guard' bomber jacket looking for nonexistent ruts. The machine drives round and round, not missing an inch. Finally it leaves the ice and we get ready for our big entrance. But we are not allowed back on yet, oh no. The rink guards have to test it. On they come, speeding by, showing off their backwards moves and spins. An hour later, the rink still looks perfect but the same process happens all over again. The American guards would be horrified by their British counterparts who give the ice a quick squirt of water in between sessions then let the skaters back on before there is a riot.

Saturday morning, sunny and crisp, perfect for a bike ride along the trail into Bethesda for coffee and bagels. The seats outside the bookshop are crowded with families as cyclists pass through. Suddenly I see an unattended fluorescent blue rucksack leaning against a litter bin. No one else seems to have noticed. In London I would report it – especially four months after a major terrorist attack. Why is nobody else concerned? A few minutes of watching and it is still there. I decide to walk over and ask people around if it belongs to them. As I near it, a little girl with a blonde pony tail walks past with her bike, picks up the rucksack and swings it onto her back. She rides off down the trail after her parents, the 'bomb' bouncing on her back.

The sales are on at the shopping mall. Fergie, taking advantage of the American obsession with British royalty, smiles out from giant advertising posters amid the gold and musak, extolling the virtues of the branded shopping experience. It is a Roald Dahl kind of world, a manufactured shopping nirvana where the temperature stays the same no matter how hot or cold it is outside. The teenage girls in tight jeans trip into Abercrombie and Fitch for crop tops while their moms trawl the department stores for the 'two-for-the-price-of-one' bargains. In the Victoria's Secret lingerie shop, hoards of overweight women are snapping up 'for him' basques in red with black lace. The kids are being pushed around in shopping trolleys made to look like cars or fire engines, placated with giant cookies and bagel bites. By 4.30pm they are all crying and screaming anyway, desperately trying to be heard above the musak.

It is a weekday morning and the lights are red at the junction between River Road and Little Falls Parkway. Everyone is in a stupor, on their way to work or school. Before the lights change to green, a roller skater comes from nowhere, dressed in a boiler suit, woolly hat and mirror shades. He ignores the pavement and the cycle path, speeding straight through the lines of traffic in the centre of the road and disappears out of sight. An environmental activist protesting at the overuse of cars? Or just someone suffocating from the pressure to be conventional and conservative?

'We will, we will rock you!' belts out on the sound system, mixed with the latest dance tracks. Pom pom waving cheerleaders in skimpy tops do their routines. The job requirement seems to be long, glossy hair and white or honey-coloured skin. This is the build up to a Washington Wizards basketball game at the Metro Centre in DC. We get astonished looks when we ask if we are allowed to take food to our seats. Everyone has game food on their laps – ribs, Cajun, Chinese, pizza and fizzy drinks or beer. The DJ cranks it up as the players run out onto the court, all giants among men, and with them the legendary Michael Jordan.

Trophy wives and girlfriends in gold jewellery with gangster rapper types in even more gold jewellery are courtside. We're off, and the noise is deafening as the DJ/compère and the video screen tell us to shout 'defence!' every time the opposition advances. There are frantic runs then pauses for 'time out', the seconds filled by music, dancers and trampolinists. Your eyes cannot rest for a second. 'Make noise,' says the video screen. Play stops again and a roving camera goes round the crowd, landing on unsuspecting people who are then told to kiss on screen. There's a prize draw for free pizza. Two volunteers put on giant Wizards hats and have a tricycle race to win tickets to the Caribbean. The crowd goes wild. Now a man in a blue superhero suit and mask runs into the arena to a rock anthem and starts firing T-shirts into the stands. The crowd goes even wilder.

The next cause for celebration is almost here. Giant hearts are everywhere. Hechts department store has a Valentine's Day sale and the card shops are bursting with 'I love you' merchandise. The supermarkets are stocked with Valentine's 'candy', heart shaped sweets and chocolates and boxes of cartoon character cards for children to give. Every child at nursery school is expected to give to all the others in the class. You can labour over homemade affairs, but all they really want is the sweets. Happy Valentine's Day.

Chapter 6:
Behind the White Picket Fence

IT IS 8am on a fine spring day and the dust carts and recycling trucks thunder through the neighbourhood. Behind the wheel and hauling the dustbins are mainly black workers. Filipino nannies walk by, delivering children to school, pushing babies in buggies. Pick-up trucks pull up and out jump Latinos to re-build houses and landscape the gardens. Their wives and sisters come off the bus and walk to their cleaning or childcare jobs. More African Americans arrive to install cable TV and fix power lines. Later, just before the yellow school buses start turning into the neighbourhood, the mail van comes round driven by smiling black postal workers.

You can't help but wonder, 'Where did all the black neighbours go?' After all, we are in the suburbs of a city whose population is nearly two thirds black. The answer is, African Americans just don't tend to live here.

Haamid is a Nigerian Muslim cab driver, here in the land of opportunity to save money for his masterplan – to give a good education to his children, build a house back home and become a local politician there. 'What do you think of Iain Duncan Smith?' he asks as we are putting on our seatbelts. 'Have you met Owen Bennett-Jones (the BBC World Service presenter)? I *love* OBJ!' Round the clock he listens to National Public Radio, BBC World Service and American politics on C-Span. Passengers who don't engage in conversation probably assume he is an African American in his jeans and baseball cap. Post 9/11, there are no clues in the cab about his religion, it's safer that way. He's part of a legion of cab drivers, mainly African, who keep this city moving. This is another job that white people don't do and many of the non-native Americans don't have Haamid's perfect English. You can't help but wonder about the lives they left behind. Did the Afghan who picked us up at the airport used to be a heart surgeon? Was the Somalian at Union station a former college lecturer?

Waiting outside dance class, Anju tells how she arrived from India a decade ago. She took a nannying job and liked it so much she brought her husband over. 'One day, I hope my daughter and parents can come,' she says. 'There are so many opportunities here.' She is happy living in a modest flat and spending money on frequent calls home. What doesn't she like? 'It is so materialistic,' she sighs.

Back at our house we sip tea and she notices the cricket books and the Indian wall hangings. 'It feels like home!' she laughs. Adjusting the cushion behind her back, she realises it is made out of the same material as her wedding sari.

When the first European settlers arrived in Montgomery County 300 years ago, they found a rich land of rivers and forests where deer, buffalo, bear and wild turkey roamed. They named the area after an Irish-born, British army officer Richard Montgomery who never came here.

Later, the life story of a Montgomery County plantation slave, Josiah Henson, became the model for the main character in the novel *Uncle Tom's Cabin* and, in turn, a focal point for the anti-slavery movement. Although Maryland was a slave state, it did not join the Confederacy in the Civil War like neighbouring Virginia. But the county had divided loyalties. Maryland is below the Mason-Dixon Line, on its border with Pennsylvania – the symbolic divide between North and South, between freedom and slavery. No one would dream of flying the Confederate flag here but technically, Maryland is The South.

Schools were officially desegregated in 1954. But it wasn't that simple. Race riots, provoked by the assassination of civil rights leader Martin Luther King, rocked Washington DC in 1968. Sally still remembers the tension. 'You could feel it when blacks and whites walked past each other in the street.'

Today, Montgomery County's neighbours, Prince George's County and Washington DC, are both 60 per cent black. The city's North West is predominately white and affluent. Montgomery County is around 70 per cent white (similar to America as a whole) with the rest black, Asian or Hispanic.

Within each county, people traditionally gravitate to neighbourhoods dictated by ethnicity and economic status. Rich blacks and rich whites are in their own enclaves, poor blacks and poor whites in theirs.

Sally mulls over the question of race while sipping on an old-fashioned bottle of Coca Cola (she doesn't like cans) and smoking a cigarette. Before moving to Washington from Atlanta in the Sixties, she saw people with Ku Klux Klan hoods and baseball bats. It was so intense that one night, before going out to support a civil rights protest, she left her will on the mantelpiece.

'It always was segregated here. I cannot think of any black family in the neighbourhood. Indian or Muslim, yes, but not African American.' The occasional international, mixed race family moves in before their next posting but that's about it. Yet, statistically, this part of town is Democrat voting, liberal minded (by American standards) and church or synagogue going. Is this unofficial segregation dictated by the residents or the realtors (estate agents)?

I speak to Winfred Rembert, one of the last survivors of lynching in America, for an article. His brush with death happened in his home state of Georgia in 1964. Now an artist in Connecticut, he is making an emotional journey to Atlanta for the opening of *Without Sanctuary*, a harrowing collection of lynching photographs. It drew record crowds in New York but in the South few were prepared to give it public backing. Critics in academia tell me that both blacks and whites are in denial. It is still too painful for many to face the fact that close relatives were murdered or that their loved ones were the killers.

These days, in the homes, restaurants and shops of Montgomery County and Washington DC, different races appear to get along just fine. And at least the Ku Klux Klan aren't around anymore.

But a race hate monitoring organisation suggests otherwise. Even in traditionally liberal Maryland, they say there are three Ku Klux Klan groups, a couple of Neo-Nazi organisations and two black separatist groups. Neighbouring Virginia is awash with Neo-Nazis, the Ku Klux Klan, Neo-Confederates and other hate groups.

Over a cup of tea, my Australian friend Lacie prepares me for the worst. When she went to the local authority office in charge of admitting international children into state school, she was reduced to tears. The official said her daughter would have to undergo vaccinations all over again because her paperwork was one day too old for the regulations. 'No shots, no school, Ma'am.' Arguments that this might not be good for the child's health were dismissed.

Now it is my turn. Amalie and I sit on the chair outside the interview room, armed with a folder full of documents: passports, birth certificate, a proof of employment letter, medical records, house rental agreement. Everyone else seems to be Latino. 'It's mostly Mexicans round here,' says the lady next to me. 'That family is from Ecuador.' She points to a frightened looking young couple, carrying a screaming baby and toddler, two older children trailing behind. We are called in. Behind the desk is a smiling young Asian woman. Opera plays in the background and she invites Amalie to help herself to candy from the M&M machine. The official briskly checks through the paperwork, firing questions at regular intervals. Finally the rental agreement.

'There is a page missing, you will have to come back,' she says.

'Are you sure it isn't all there? You've got the pages confirming the agreement with our signatures,' I protest.

'No, I need the page with part 14 (iii) on it. You'll have to come back.'

We trudge down the corridor to the health room. At least maybe we can get that over with. The noise grows louder. The narrow room is filled with some 30 Latinos and the sound of tired, bored children. A cartoon is on the TV. There are no seats left, so we sit on the floor next to the leaflet stand which warns us about child deaths from firearms in Maryland. We are in a zombie state, like everyone else, when our turn finally comes.

'She'll need hepatitis B,' the official says.

'But isn't that optional?' I ask.

'No, you have to have it to go to school in Montgomery County,' she insists as the needle goes in. 'She'll need two more, you'll have to come back.'

At the weekend, I get chatting to a heavily pregnant mother at a kids' party. I ask when she is due. 'I'm booked in for a C-section at 10am next Friday. My Mom is looking after Johnny and my husband will be off work at the weekend. Then I can get straight back to work.' I am astonished. 'Really, it will be fine, it's what I did the first time.'

Another perfectly groomed mother-to-be chimes in. 'I have my C-section booked too. It's so much better for your schedule. I have facial, manicure and pedicure appointments the week before.'

'What if the babies come early?' I ask, but before they can dwell on this inconvenient thought the cake arrives and we all start singing.

I call another mother to fix up a playdate with a new three-year-old friend. I haven't met her much as the child is more often with the babysitter (nanny) but she seems to welcome the call. 'Sure she can come over. But she cannot eat egg, kiwi or pineapple.' I assure her this is no problem. Then, an unexpected question. 'Do you have a gun in the house?'

I pause in shock, before spluttering, 'No, I'm from Britain, only farmers and gangsters have them there.' This seems to be an acceptable answer and she moves on to confirm the time and directions. I feel the need to ask, 'What would you have said if I did have a gun?'

'I would have asked you if it was kept locked up,' she calmly replies. 'If it wasn't, I would have cancelled.'

The next day, I ask around to see if this is normal.

'I've never been asked that,' says Sonya.

'No, never,' says Leah.

But then another local mother admits to asking the gun question routinely before letting her child go to a new home. 'Y'know, this is America.'

We are overdue for the post-birthday check-up at the paediatrician. It's easy to get an appointment and we only have five minutes of cartoon watching before a nurse in a Mickey Mouse tunic takes us through the routine tests. When the doctor arrives we are almost done, just some questions on diet, sport and school. To finish up, the doctor says, 'Five is a good age to talk about firearms safety.' I nod nervously. 'This gives you some information.' She hands me a '5 years' safety sheet from the American Academy of Pediatrics. It recommends: 'Get the helmet habit!' when cycling; learning to swim; and using safety seats and seat belts in the car. Then comes a section entitled Firearms Hazards. 'Children in homes where guns are present are in more danger of being shot by themselves, their friends, or family members than of being injured by an intruder. Handguns are especially dangerous. It is best to keep all guns out of the home. If you choose to keep a gun, it should be kept unloaded and in a locked place separate from the ammunition. Ask if the homes where your child visits or is cared for have guns and how they are stored.'

I read up on statistics compiled by academics from government information, journals and institutions. In 2001, last year, there were 29,573 gun-related deaths in the United States – about 80 deaths per day. The firearm death rate among US children aged 14 and younger is nearly 12 times higher than the combined rate in 25 other industrialised nations. In 2001, 35 per cent of adults in the US lived in a household with a gun.

But surely not here in suburbia? I spot Sally on her porch, taking the air with her cocker spaniel Jasper. She thinks for a moment. 'There was that neighbour who drank. Then he went in the garden shooting his gun in the air.'

I ask Elaine. She thinks for a moment. 'You wouldn't necessarily know if your neighbour had a gun,' she says. 'They wouldn't talk about it round here.'

I ask around. No one knows of any (or at least they are not telling) until one lets slip of a known gun owner in her street. The next day I overhear a dad tell his son to stop 'goofing around' in someone's driveway. 'They're armed in that house,' he warns. Is he joking?

Montgomery County may have the reputation for being full of progressive Democrats, but right now it still has 16 shops which are licensed agents to sell guns. When I check state records, I find more than 60 in Maryland. They include sports and hunting shops plus the big retailers Wal-Mart and Kmart, a 15 to 20-minute drive away up highways which could be anywhere in America, lined with petrol stations, tanning salons, McDonalds and Starbucks. Their products range from air rifles to handguns. One Maryland company advertises machine guns, claiming 'an average citizen' can own one providing they complete the appropriate paperwork and pay the fees.

I have just stocked up on summer T-shirts at Old Navy (Gap meets Urban Outfitters only cheaper) and have ten minutes spare to browse in the book shop before nursery school pick-up. I skim through *Time* and *Newsweek* before moving on to the glossy travel section, filled with white wooden beach houses at the edge of the ocean. Then the words 'Man-sized magnum' catch my eye, followed by 'Double the fun!', 'SXS Rifles'. This is the firearms section, in the US equivalent of the local Waterstones or Books Etc. Here is what I find:

The Complete Book of Autopistols

GUN Buyer's Guide, 'Varmint Rifles', 'New breed comsat handguns'

Eastman's Hunting Journal (mule deer issue)

Tactical Knives, 'The Cutting Edge of Survival'

Hunting

Whitetail

Big Bucks

Rifle Shooter

American Handgunner Annual

Shooting Times

Auto Loaders

Small Arms Review.

Well, what did I expect in a country with an estimated 200 million privately held guns? I am living here on a temporary visa with no right to vote, so I just have to accept it. And the right to bear arms, enshrined in the constitution, would still be there if Al Gore was president.

Now that events have calmed down, it really feels like we are settling in, I say to Roland on the phone before he returns from a work trip to China. But when he gets back he doesn't seem well and inexplicably loses his balance. We realise we know nothing about the American health system other than that we are lucky enough to have insurance. The nearest kind of doctor to a GP refers him to an ear doctor. The ear doctor sends him for tests, diagnoses an incurable inner ear condition called Ménière's Disease and puts him on a low sodium diet. But he is getting worse. The neighbours are concerned. 'He is getting so thin.'

I ask everyone if they know a good doctor. Have you heard of anyone with these symptoms? What did it turn out to be? Everyone looks worried.

Acupuncture helps but doesn't cure it and we resort to therapies practised by crazy hippies from the West Coast (one pops out to the shops when he falls asleep mid treatment). Medical websites are mainly frightening and phone calls to more specialists advise a long wait before the next free appointment. They all say plane travel could make the symptoms worse, so we can't even go home for an NHS opinion. Then it slowly dawns that we may need to try a different approach in America. Instead of telling doctors' receptionists he can't 'walk', we try saying he can't 'work'. Bingo!

'What! You can't work? That's terrible sir, we'll see you right away.'

He gets an appointment at the renowned Johns Hopkins Hospital in Baltimore. Neighbours spring into action so I can drive Roland there. Lacie takes the girls for breakfast before driving them to nursery. Then a ride back with a friend's nanny, a playdate and more neighbours on standby if we run late.

I drive along the Beltway and the I-90 in torrential rain, Roland with his head in his hands because the windscreen wipers make him dizzier. Juggernauts roar in front of me and pick-ups overtake. Why doesn't everyone slow down? The radio talks of 'wrecks' across the area's roads. We finally arrive and walk into what could be a hotel lobby, manned by people in uniform oozing calm efficiency. Taking the lift to the right floor, we reach a reception desk run by women with sleek hair and impressively long, lacquered nails. They hear our accents and shriek with delight. 'Listen to that! It's like having The Beatles!'

We leave with a new diagnosis (a chronic migraine-related condition) and medication, hopeful that we finally have a cure. It has taken weeks of hustling, asking questions, filling in forms and paying top ups, and that is with full health insurance. I pity the 40 million people out there without any who have to choose between illness or debt.

We get the elevator down to the parking lot. There are five of us, a couple chatting casually about their visit and a young woman in a black suit speaking into her mobile phone. 'I pray Lord, that he will be healed,' then a pause and, 'Amen brother! Amen!' Emotion now seizes her. 'And the good Lord will heal! Yes he will!' There are tears in her eyes as the lift stops and the other people get out, still talking as if nothing unusual has happened. As we walk in the same direction to our cars she finishes the call. 'Goodbye brother, goodbye sister, God bless you all.' She has just been taking part in a conference call prayer meeting in the lift.

Chapter 7:
The Great Outdoors

I SIT ON THE front step in my pyjamas with a cup of tea, enjoying the quiet of the early morning. The odd dog walker passes by, giving me a neighbourly wave. Then a few cars, drivers clutching giant silver coffee mugs.

The sound of pounding feet breaks the silence, 20 running shoes on Tarmac racing round the corner from the park. I soon discover you can time your watch by them.

This is boot camp, suburban style. Not an unruly teenager in sight. An early visit to the park finds the 'platoon' groaning through a punishing regime of press-ups and sit-ups. This is about getting the 30-something men and women who take part to the peak of physical fitness.

Rain or shine, morning after morning they stretch, bend and run before I have even had my Cheerios, a pack of chattering enthusiasts in leggings and T-shirts out for an 'integrated full body workout' with military trained instructors wearing sergeant's stripes. As Sgt Fitness makes clear in his adverts, 'I'm not selling personal training...I'm selling results.' At least you don't get sent to Afghanistan.

Strange things have been happening in the local park for decades, according to historians. At the turn of the century it became a US Department of Agriculture experiment station where government scientists investigated animal diseases, including anthrax. A laboratory and stables housed cows, horses, hundreds of guinea pigs, rabbits, mice and silk worms. The USDA apparently used to burn cows on the site that is now the home of the outdoor public swimming pool.

When the King of Abyssinia gave President Theodore Roosevelt a zebra, it was sent to the research station and mated with a local mare to create a 'zebhorse'. The zebhorse project was abandoned after five years.

When more houses were built nearby in the Twenties and Thirties, there was a not-in-my-backyard campaign against the smells and flies from the farm. The residents eventually succeeded in shutting it down and turned it into a park.

Today, if you are lucky, you might catch a dog birthday party – the best time is early evening. This is an opportunity to sing happy birthday and hand out doggy treats. There used to be a dog bakery in nearby Bethesda. The cakes looked so delicious that first timers, including me, would go in to buy them for themselves. The assistants said it happened all the time. You can still get a 'doggie bagel' at the bagel shop for 99 cents ('not for human consumption'). The water fountains along trails have dog bowl attachments and dog friendly shops put pet drinking bowls outside.

A whole sub culture is out there with members identified by the name and breed of their dog. Borrow a neighbour's for an hour and you get to be a temporary member of the club. 'Good to see you! You're looking great!' They mean the dog.

Early on a weekend morning and dusk on any day of the week, they gather in the park. While the dogs run and play, the owners talk and stroll, stopping to break up the odd fight or amorous liaison.

In workaholic Washington DC, people often complain that 'you are what you do'. Wander out into suburbia and you are what dog you own.

'Hey Bo, how are you boy?'

'Great to see you Buddy! You *have* grown!'

It is early on a Sunday morning and Sherri is in the park with her elderly dog, Buster. She is a couple of minutes' walk from home. Now, the rule is that dogs must be kept on a lead. But it is 6am, the park is deserted, no children are out and Buster is too old to run, so Sherri takes it off. It is a beautiful time to be out, the sun is coming up but it is still cool, just a deserted playground, an expanse of green grass and the odd early jogger. Then, who should appear from nowhere (undercover behind a large oak?) but the park police, demanding to see ID and slapping her with a $50 fine for the lead violation. 'I didn't have anything on me,' Sherri said later. 'It was 6 o'clock on Sunday morning! I just couldn't believe it was happening.' You just never know who is watching.

While investigating canine culture, I spot what might be the social event of the dog calendar. On the 'precious pets' advertisement page of the newspaper, under 'pet events', interested parties are invited to a 'bark breakfast' to raise money for a dog charity. Treat your dog to the pets' room service menu while enjoying a buffet and hearing tips on grooming, fashion and healthcare. 'Costumes are encouraged.' It is not clear if this is directed at owners or dogs.

There is no need to feel guilty about going on a dog free holiday here. While the owner is away, the animal can go to the Pet Resort Day Spa and Hotel for Dogs and Cats, with 'plush suites', swimming pool, dog day camp and state-of-the-art salon. The pet's holiday accommodation could easily turn out better than the owner's.

Sally's dog Jasper hasn't been around for a while. He last bounded over a few weeks ago and did a poo under the hostas. Then Lena phones to tell us the news. The black and white spaniel mix, with no tail and curly hair, died today. Early in the morning, Sally found him collapsed under a bush in the garden. She called her neighbour Dennis who climbed over the fence still in his bathrobe to carry Jasper to the car. They drove straight to the vet but it was too late. Neighbours are invited to the burial in the back garden. The girls are already upset so we tell Sally we will come over later and put some flowers on the grave. Then we do what suburban Americans do when there is a death, a birth or an illness – we bake. Today it is Sally's favourite – brownies. As we walk up the steps, a fellow dog owner sits on the porch, come to pay his respects.

Summer is on the way and the grass is growing at an alarming rate. A manual mower comes with the house rental but it is long, sweaty work and the mosquitoes are starting to bite. Is it worth buying one for while we are here? On the next block, a gardening team in beige uniforms and a liveried truck sweep across the lawns and flowerbeds creating order out of potential chaos. They look expensive.

I see Lena as I put the rubbish out and she sympathises on the length of the lawn. 'We use Ricardo's Boys. They are cheap, you don't have to get them every week and they can just do the grass.' Sherri agrees it is money well spent.

The appointed day arrives and a pick-up truck screeches to a halt outside. A gang of Latino desperadoes in mirror shades, baggy trousers, pork pie hats and bandanas swarm up the drive. Armed with power mowers, cutters, trimmers and blowing machines, they roar into action, fanning out across the front and back gardens in a well practised pincer movement. Then, as suddenly as they came, they are gone, on to the next house with the sound of mowers and blowers getting fainter.

I decide they are worth it every few weeks for the spectacle alone. You pay with a fistful of dollars in person or put a cheque under a stone on a neighbour's top step. Ricardo himself comes to the door to finalise the deal, a solemn middle-aged man who claims the women in the street nag him like his wife. He tells a parable about a cow. The moral is about sharing work.

The outdoor party season has begun and back gardens give way to bouncy castles, clowns and magicians, and this mysterious object called a piñata which is new to us. The excitement is palpable, kids running round in all directions shouting 'the piñata, the piñata'. It turns out to be a mould decorated with coloured tissue paper and made to look like an animal, a cartoon character or a sports ball. The piñata is hung from a tree and the children line up to whack it with a baseball bat. The inside is packed with candy and when it is hit hard enough the sweets all come pouring out for the partygoers to pick up from the ground.

The biggest and strongest child inevitably gets the pleasure of breaking it and the pushiest children come out of the scrum with the most bulging candy bags.

The first time is the most traumatic. My plaintive calls of 'make sure you share' and 'help your sister get one' are drowned out by parents shouting 'good job!' and 'Hey Bud! Under the tree!' Josie is rescued from the pack by her sister, bringing the triumphant news 'I got one!' (Luckily she doesn't notice that the boy next to her has about 30.) Amalie, now aged five, says loudly and indignantly, '*That* boy was pushing *babies* out of the way!' The apologetic hostess attempts to redistribute stash from the successful to the crying losers but the damage is done. A British dad and piñata veteran watches his shy daughter dissolve into tears over her empty collection bag with sad resignation. 'It's survival of the fittest,' he concludes.

There's a strange stillness in the air tonight. Neighbours out walking their dogs stop to say hello as I put the recycling out. 'It's a beautiful evening but it feels like a storm might be brewing.' That night, winds fell nearby trees and a tornado wipes out La Plata, a small town in Southern Maryland, taking off roofs and throwing a house into a ravine.

It is three and a half hours' drive over the Bay Bridge to the Atlantic coast of Delaware. You pass farm shops selling pyramids of tomatoes, flat open fields and white wooden houses with signs advertising 'Ferrets for sale'.

The main road along the coast is crammed with discount shopping outlets, chain restaurants, motels and holiday homes. It's hard to get a glimpse of the sea from the road. Many stretches of sand are private, reserved for those owning or renting a holiday home, and you need a pass to park the car and get on the beach. College kids earnestly check accreditation and enforce regulations, the police force of the future.

The public beach is just like *Baywatch* with teams of lifeguards in regulation red hoodies and shades, working on their baggy sweats look. These are superfit college kids doing press-ups in the sand before their shift. As it hots up, they work on their tans and, from their chairs on stilts, randomly blow their whistles at the kids in the surf. I wonder when I will witness my first rescue and hope it isn't for me.

An hour or so up the coast in New Jersey, it is sunset on the beach, a holiday weekend in chocolate box Cape May. Nearby are candy-coloured Victorian bed and breakfasts, boardwalk motels, ice cream parlours and T-shirt shops. The bronzed lifeguards have climbed down from their white wood chairs, leaving sunset swimmers at the mercy of the ferocious Atlantic surf.

Holidaymakers, families in shorts and baseball caps, gather for the flag lowering ceremony. An older man, a veteran, leads the proceedings, gathering some of the children to help him slowly bring down the Stars and Stripes. Cameras click as the sun dips into the surf and he flicks on a tape recording of God Bless America, '...from the mountains, to the prairies, to the oceans white with foam, God bless America...'

The woman next to me has tears in her eyes.

The little kids are distracted, kicking about in the sand. 'Stand still and shush for a minute,' I hiss.

'Oh, sorry,' says my five-year-old, 'I thought they were playing a Disney song.' I can see her point.

The football World Cup has begun and we sit on the sofa in front of the TV with England flags, a pot of tea and Spanish commentary. We get wildly excited when the USA beats Mexico but the country barely notices. After much asking around, die hard sports fans Fraser and Eddy seem to be the only ones who stayed up to watch it, at home on their own in suburbia. It just about made it into the paper. Then the US gets knocked out by Germany in the quarter finals and that is that.

The outdoor pools are open and the college kid lifeguards are taking their jobs seriously. They may look like slackers – the girls in short shorts and bikini tops with pony tails, the boys with grunge hair and baseball caps – but don't be fooled. They've got a whistle and they are not afraid to use it.

Babies: No nappies in the big pool and plastic pants must go over the top of swimming nappies.

No rubber rings. One day I attempt to violate this rule with Leah's toddler son who hates armbands. The whistle blows.

'Why can't he wear it?' I protest.

'You can fall through,' is the steely reply from the Britney Spears look-a-like. She ignores my reasoning that there is absolutely no chance of him falling through, his plump tummy jammed in tight like Winnie the Pooh in a honey pot. The manager isn't around so I give up before we get banned.

The whistle again, then a tannoy announcement. 'Children must leave the pool for fifteen minute adult swim.' So now we have to sit on the side, in 90 degrees, as a handful of adults swim lengths of the vast pool, just as they had room to do before the children were kicked out. Forty-five minutes later it happens all over again.

There is no diving except in a designated diving area. Otherwise it is feet first only. There is no eating except in a designated area. Then a distant rumble of thunder and the whistles blow again. The voice over the tannoy announces, 'Everyone must leave the pool!' Sometimes a ferocious storm follows but more often than not you are left to walk home in the sunshine.

Early evening is a special time when the water is still warm and, still in your swimsuit, you can call up and order a takeaway pizza to be delivered poolside. There are picnics and barbecues on the grassy area and kids are turning up for the swim team practice, the teenage veterans fine-tuning their speed turns or hanging out, chewing gum. The day of the trials is scarier, with stern faced parents holding stopwatches at the end of the lanes.

'Go Daniel!'

'Good job Natalie!'

Even if your kid only makes it to the B team, expect the area 'meets' to have volunteer parents acting as referees, timers, starters and turn judges. This is serious business.

Living in the right street gives you automatic membership to a private neighbourhood pool with its own swim team, guest list and, probably, a record holders' plaque. The scene is similar to the public one but everyone here has to be local and that means from the same social, economic and ethnic background. It's a readymade summer social scene of parties, kids' activities and barbecues. A postcode country club financed by 'town taxes'. Similar ones, hidden up leafy side streets, provide the same scene for a membership fee. It means the whole summer is taken care of in between camp and the beach house. I think the local council's pool is fantastic. Suppose it depends what you are used to.

It is late on a Sunday afternoon and it's a scorcher – still 98 degrees on the field. The amateur league college boys are limbering up in improbably tight trousers. Onto the centre of the ground walks a teenage girl, in skintight jeans. She wears a crop top and a bandana over her hair. She holds a microphone with attitude. Everyone else knows what's coming. They're all on their feet. The old boys take off their floppy hats and put down their score sheets. Dads whip off baseball caps, never mind that there's no shade and its nearly 100 degrees. All the school age kids instinctively put their hands on their hearts. 'Oh say, can you seeeEEEEE.' This one is a tough note to hit. Even tougher if you have feedback on your mic. It seems that singing the national anthem at ball games is where wannabe *American Idol* entrants earn their spurs. But here there are no judges. As long as you hit the last line of this 1814 war poem with some oomph, everyone is happy. 'O'er the land of the FREEEEEE and the home of the brave.'

At professional games you not only get the national anthem but a song written in 1908 called *Take Me Out to the Ball Game!* It is an unofficial anthem, traditionally sung during the seventh-inning stretch, and everyone seems to know the words:

'Take me out to the ball game,
Take me out with the crowd.
Buy me some peanuts and Cracker Jack,
I don't care if I never get back,
Let me root, root, root for the home team,
If they don't win it's a shame.
For it's one, two, three strikes, you're out,
At the old ball game.'

This league game is where the college boys do their apprenticeships before a chosen few make it into the professional league. They wear collarless shirts and baseball caps (obviously) and many sport goatee beards.

The young boy next to me wears a team hat and T-shirt. 'It's safest at second base,' he tells me, quickly realising I need some instruction. He then adds excitedly, 'You can swap foul balls (ones which go out of play) for baseball cards.'

British indie pop and US oldies are pumped out of the sound system between plays. Then a rap song comes on and the F word is clearly audible. The family crowd is shocked, murmurs of indignation sweeping through the stands, and complaints are flying before the song has even finished. The announcer comes on to apologise profusely. Thankfully a distraction is at hand. The announcer is beside himself with excitement. 'The pizza has arrived! And don't forget folks, you can also get popcorn, dogs and ice cream, yeah!'

Someone dressed as a bear goes round the crowd giving high-fives to kids. My programme says I can get in free to future games if I wear a Hawaiian shirt or an Elvis wig. Worth bearing in mind.

Suddenly there is action on the pitch. A player writhes on the ground, injured. Onto the pitch runs the medic, in tiny white shorts and T-shirt, blonde pony tail bouncing. She leans over him for a few moments taking things from her first aid bag. The player soon gets up. I think he was faking.

Today is a 'red day' in Washington DC and its suburbs, says the radio, and it is going to be 'hot and unhealthy'. Temperatures will be in the mid 90s but the humidity will make it feel over 100. Buses are free. Leave your car behind, the authorities ask, and don't fill up with petrol until evening. If you can, stay indoors. Most at risk are the old, the young and those with asthma.

I consult a neighbour, Haley, who has lived here for 10 years. 'We never used to get this, just the last few years – it must be the ozone.'

Lena warns me to be prepared for power cuts. She says it often happens when it is this hot as so much electricity is being used to keep people cool with air conditioning and refrigeration.

Haley is confused with the colour coding. 'It seems to be the same code they are using for the terrorist alerts. I never know if I should be worrying about terrorism or the weather.'

The next day the weather code is orange. Only asthma sufferers need to stay in.

Chatting to the local handyman, I say how nice it is that at least the kids can cool off in the paddling pool. He pauses, looking worried. 'You're not leaving the water in overnight are you?' Why not? 'Mosquitoes breed in standing water,' he says firmly. 'And they spread West Nile disease. You need to empty it out.'

It is the Fouth of July, when the neighbourhood goes red, white and blue. At the local parade, a man dressed as Uncle Sam sits on a convertible, driving sedately towards the park, pumping out patriotic songs on the sound system. Behind him ride children and babies, bunting and flags on their bikes and buggies. The kids' races begin – running, sack and three-legged. It could be an English village fete but the refreshments are iced water and watermelon rather than warm tea and cake. This year it's a hot one, 100 degrees and humid. It doesn't put off the contestants in the who-can-stand-on-your-head-the-longest contest. A superfit local cyclist wins, coming down after about 15 minutes when everyone else has given up. 'I've never been beaten,' he confesses.

We Brits yet again look like overripe tomatoes and the mosquitoes have totally ignored the fact that we are sprayed from head to toe in repellent. Home for a cold shower and itch cream.

The afternoon gives way to backyard barbecues and parades on the TV with floats and marching bands from the mid-West.

We join Elaine and Dennis to share cold beer, bug spray and cupcakes with stars and stripes on the icing. There are too many of us to fit indoors so we sizzle outside, comparing notes on keeping cool – 'stand still and breath deeply' – and thinking up excuses to go inside for a blast of air conditioning.

Since 1777 in Philadelphia, Independence Day has been celebrated with fireworks. But we're in Chevy Chase, Maryland, one of 16 states with a fireworks ban. You can go to a big organised extravaganza. But if it's a few rockets in your back garden you're after, forget it. (Although nobody can stop Maryland commuters buying at a roadside stand, a few minutes away over the DC line.) So we have to make do with writing our names in (permitted) sparklers.

It is only an hour and a half drive to the nearest part of West Virginia but it could be another planet. Lean men with goatee beards, baseball caps and jeans sit outside their trailer homes next to pick-up trucks and stare as we go by. Old timers watch from white wooden porches, surrounded by kitsch china animals and pot plants. But like most of suburbia around the Fourth of July, all have an American flag outside. Sunday morning, and the church car parks are packed. The only other sign of life is at the 24-hr Wal-Mart superstore. At the diner, the waitress cannot understand what we are saying but seems to like us anyway. A gang of bikers are just leaving. No one wears helmets, just bandanas and shades. One models a T-shirt saying, 'if you can see my back the bitch must have fallen off'. You can buy fireworks and guns everywhere.

Back home, an educated east coast neighbour is horrified. 'You didn't go there did you? It's the armpit of America.'

We wake up to find an American flag stuck into the ground at the end of the drive. Where did that come from? I look down the street and they seem to be at the end of every garden. Word goes round that the flags are from the local neighbourhood association, but they deny it. An estate agents eventually owns up, saying it is an 'anonymous' donation, a show of solidarity post 9/11.

Another red alert weather day in DC. It is 100 degrees all over Maryland and Virginia. I think I could cope with the heat if it wasn't for the bugs. They are silent stalkers, after your blood.

I got my first bites while looking round the garden of a possible house rental. It was overgrown and damp – mosquito heaven. Within minutes I had itchy red lumps all over. The estate agent dropped me off at the CVS chemist and the pharmacy assistant took a look. 'Oooo come and see this,' she said to her colleagues. They crowded round sucking in breath. 'They bit you *bad*,' one of the women in white coats concluded. This was the first of many trips to the chemist, the supermarket and the hardware shop on a relentless quest for the ultimate itch cream and mosquito repellent. I need one that works, doesn't make me come out in a rash and doesn't smell disgusting. I have market tested them all. From natural citronella and peppermint to chemically fuelled 'high DEET' types for 'woodsmen'. The chemical name for DEET is N,N-diethyl-m-toluamide, a government-approved ingredient. On the shelf the products look like they mean business with brand names like 'Off!', 'Deep Woods' and 'Enforcer'.

A neighbour has heard that the best way is to spray the hardcore, high DEET kind ('not suitable for children') onto clothes. Unfortunately this has an extreme chemical reaction with Josie's favourite tie-dyed T-shirt. Sherri swears by Avon's non-DEET Skin So Soft. Europeans favour the natural, lemon eucalyptus varieties. The latter don't stop my family getting bitten but they do make us smell nice.

For the army issue version, I have to go to the kind of hunting and survival shop where I suspect potential mass murderers hang out. The 30 per cent DEET repellent (issued to combat troops deployed in jungle terrain) is apparently great 'whether you are at a barbecue or on patrol'. And even better, the greenish container 'won't stand out against your camo in the woods'.

I try it out in the jungle of Chevy Chase where the camouflage bottle is too dull a green to blend into the bright lawns. I think I might have fewer bites but I still get some. Sometime soon I fear there will be scientific research on the harmful effects of the ingredients on the human brain.

In the heat of summer, gardens, parks and woodland are bug party venues. They hide in bushes, breed in standing water and have menacing names like Asian Tiger. Government health advisors say that 'prime mosquito-biting hours are usually dusk to dawn' and recommend spraying skin and clothing ('skeeters' can bite through thin fabric) with a repellent containing DEET, even if outside for a few minutes. At dusk many parents around here admit defeat and herd the children inside, slapping insects as they go.

But there are some locals, like Sally, who never get bitten. This is lucky as she is in the high risk over 50s group for developing severe and potentially fatal West Nile virus. It is spread by infected mosquitoes and the symptoms are like the flu.

But Sally sits on her unscreened porch in the heat of summer without a single itch. 'We used to say in the South, they only bite you if you are sweet and sexy and I'm neither!' she says. She is baffled that I can't even walk up her garden path without a new bite.

The phone rings. 'Hello, it's me.' Sally sounds excited. 'I just heard on the radio that if you tuck a sheet of Bounce in your belt you won't get bitten.' (The fabric sheets are normally used in the tumble dryer to stop static).

I give it a go. After several days of more bites and people saying 'excuse me, Ma'am, you have something caught in your belt', I give up.

Sally is disappointed but not yet beaten.

She leaves a magazine on my doorstep, the pages turned to 'garden gadgets'. For $400 I can buy a propane-fuelled trap which uses a scent to lure blood-seeking insects into the capture chamber. For under $50 you can get a portable 'bug zapper' which attracts mosquitoes with ultra violet light and 'eliminates' them. Then there is the 'Stinger' or the more romantic but less dramatic repellent lantern. All nice ideas, but if your neighbours don't have one, what is to stop the mosquitoes flying over the fence? Nothing.

How about getting a mosquito-eating bat, someone suggests in the community newsletter. I check it out but discover bats don't eat enough mosquitoes to control them significantly. And a bat bite can also give you rabies.

Early one morning, I follow Jeannine through the woods, doused in the kind of repellent which claims to repel black flies, ticks, mosquitoes, chiggers (the biting larvae of a mite), deer flies and stable flies. Should the worst happen I have anti-itch cream plus tweezers and oil (to get off the ticks) in my bag. I am on mosquito patrol with the Maryland Department of Agriculture, cruising the suburbs of Washington DC, for an article on West Nile virus.

Jeannine, who has superhero status in my eyes, has set traps to gauge how bad the mosquito menace is going to be this summer and to test what diseases they are carrying. We see it in the shadows of the wood, framed by bulb-light and steaming dry ice to attract the insects. Jeannine draws in breath. 'There are a hundred mosquitoes in there, just from last night – this is bad.' The black buzzing mass is repeated at the children's playground, the garden dump and the river. Passing a backyard, Jeannine spots a tarpaulin over children's play equipment. It is full of puddles. 'If that water is left there for a week, several hundred mosquitoes could breed in that.' It is enough to make you paranoid.

Tonight, I carefully prepare, with a concoction of repellents, for the barbecue. This is how people like to eat during the hot months in suburbia, with meat or fish on the outdoor grill, steaks, hot dogs or ribs. I always seem to be the only vegetarian at the barbecue. 'But you do eat fish and chicken right?' an interested guest volunteers tonight. This is not the first time I have had this question. I produce some tofu sausages from my bag and explain the definition of the diet. The crowd is educated, worldly, but this is new to them (an estimated 2.5 per cent of Americans are vegetarian). They listen politely, baffled.

'What *do* you eat?' another enquires, looking me up and down for signs of starvation.

'Extra firm tofu works nicely grilled,' I say, trying not to sound like someone seeking converts for their cult.

A hundred degrees in the shade again, and DC Emergency Management Agency have set up 'cooling centres' across the city where people can relax and sip cold water. Outdoor kids' summer camps are forced to spend time indoors. Electricity grid operators report a huge increase in demand as everyone puts on the air conditioning. But so far, we haven't lost power. Signs outside car parks say an engine idling for longer than three minutes is illegal in DC.

Reports are starting to appear in the media about what to do in case of biological attack. Is there any evidence it might happen? No one volunteers any, but suggestions include staying indoors, turning off the air conditioning and stockpiling water, batteries and tins. Here we go again.

There are deaths from West Nile virus in Louisiana and the first case has been found in the DC area. Dead birds have been infected. Health advisors warn the public not to go out of the house without sunblock and bug repellent. 'Living round here in the heat is like being under house arrest,' a neighbour complains.

We escape for a weekend to the Blue Ridge Mountains of Virginia, immortalised in the song and film *The Trail of the Lonesome Pine*. They are part of the vast Appalachian range, between Shenandoah and the Great Smoky Mountains of Tennessee, the home of early settlers, mountain folk and bluegrass music. We drive past white-painted houses, roadside stalls of sweet corn, tomatoes and watermelon. There are more and more bikers as we get near the mountains. I have never seen so many Stars and Stripes bandanas. Over breakfast at our lakeside lodge, you can't help but notice that they all pray before eating their morning grits, hash browns and bacon.

Later, a father and son pull up in a pick-up for a Coke. The boy, no more than 15, with a brace and pimples, jumps out from behind the wheel. He wears a Confederate T-shirt and proudly says it is his third driving lesson. They have come up to the mountains especially. Nearby, a group of girls, dressed like their mother in long pinafore dresses with plaited hair, try some fishing by the lake. It could be a scene from *The Waltons*.

When the sun sets over the lake the children, a mix of Virginians, Vietnamese and British, gather to feed the fish. After much discussion, they decide to give them a half-eaten hamburger to see which they like best – the bun, the burger, the ketchup or the cheese (it's the bun). The mothers sit on the bank and watch the entertainment. 'If only life could be this blessed,' remarks an American mother, 'all nationalities getting along together.'

Further along the Blue Ridge Parkway, people gather by the lake for Sunday lunch, sitting round picnic tables cooking barbecues with their church groups, some still in their Sunday best. One crowd is white, one African American and one Latino, everyone happily sticking with their tribe.

A friendly gang of teenage boys on a trip from Richmond, the Virginian state capital, want to know where we are from. They haven't heard of Britain or London and swim off laughing.

A little girl with bunches sidles up to the girls in the water. 'Are you from round here?' she asks sweetly. Her brother, who looks around eight and has no front teeth, bounds through the water and says fiercely, 'No! They are strangers!' Then he adds darkly, 'They are from Minnesota.' I step in to correct him. Anywhere but Minnesota seems to be fine and he splashes off singing, 'It's raining, it's pouring, Mama is snoring, she went to bed and bumped her head and couldn't drink beer in the morning.' His mother sits in a deckchair on the beach laughing, cool box of beer by her side.

A month before the anniversary of 9/11, the city and the suburbs have the jitters. The need to escape the August heat and head for the coast is intensified. And so to Ocracoke Island on the Outer Banks of North Carolina, the windswept barrier islands known to sailors as The Graveyard of the Atlantic. The last leg of the journey is on a little ferry with dolphins swimming either side.

Here the motels have hammocks on the balconies and you can watch the sunset over the fishing boats from the beach bar. Lightning flashes across the sea before the rain comes. The natives are descendants of pirates and some even have black beards (it was here that the notorious pirate Blackbeard met his death). The original houses were made of driftwood from wrecked ships.

Holidaymakers drive their jeeps and pick-ups over the dunes and park up at the waters' edge as if their car were a beach towel.

Every business venture, down to a table in the garden selling fruit and veg, has its own roadside sign and locals have their names on the gate. Outside the wood-fronted general store, a man sits on the porch playing *This Land is Our Land* on his banjo. Next to him on the notice board is an announcement of a recent birth. Mother and son work behind the old-style counter keeping up with local gossip on the phone.

As it gets dark, the power goes at our inn. The receptionist says, 'It could be salt on the line or a storm on Hatteras Island. The whole of Ocracoke Island is out. We'll bring round flashlights if it doesn't come back on soon.'

The next day, with the power back on, a new friend Janet shows me the cereal on special offer at the general store. We meet again on the beach and she hands out chocolate Oreo biscuits to the kids. Her top tip on mosquito repellent – only the army one really works. Her family has been coming here from Columbus, Ohio, since 1968. It's a 14-hour trip but they take it slowly over a few days. Grandma says we should check out the local talent show – she never misses it. We promise we will.

On Ocracoke, the islanders double up on jobs. The pool aerobics teacher turns up as the hostess at a local restaurant. The swimming teacher is also a waitress at a café round the corner.

At the outdoor theatre, the band plays bluegrass – country music from the rural southern mountains – under candlelight and fairylights, surrounded by mosquito netting. A husband and wife team play while their teenage daughter takes the tickets and does the interval drinks. Roy, born on the island in 1921, tells tales of hurricanes and shows off his extraordinary yodelling talents. The potter Wes plays the banjo, while the owner of the hammock and sweet shops sings. It's a country jam session under the stars with the sound of the ocean in the distance.

The next afternoon, as the kids all play Marco Polo (where a swimmer shuts his eyes and has to find the others by the sound of their voices), I notice rows of eyes watching from the balcony. A line of girls, aged ten and younger, look on, hair in plaits and dressed in long, cotton flower print smocks. They run and hide when they are seen. Later, as it gets dark and the pool is empty, they creep in, wearing shirts and trousers, looking out for prying eyes. The girls look like they have come from another time in history, detached from modern America. I've seen families like theirs before, in quieter parts of the countryside or coast, living without material trappings. I guess they are Mennonites or Amish, choosing a simple life through their religion.

Back up towards the mainland at Rodanthe on Hatteras Island, sand crabs and jellyfish litter the beach when the waves go out. There are remnants of bonfires. Wooden houses on stilts, built too close to the retreating coastline, have been left to the mercy of the sea. Inside the Chicamacomico Life Saving Station, active from 1874 to 1954, guide Miss Lucy tells us of the black crew who 'demonstrated exceptional bravery' on the stormy Atlantic. They didn't get awards until they were dead. An old island family runs the convenience store (groceries, bait, beach clothes, gifts and petrol). Lightning storms streak across the beach at night and torrential rain comes close to blocking the only road. At the beach bar, Angie plays acoustic guitar and the burger eating contest is in full swing. A group of Irish lads are going to get the trophy.

Back in suburbia, the weather has cooled and thoughts are turning to the local leaf collection.

To prepare for the big event the gardening crews pour in with motorised and hand-held leaf blowers. Other homeowners invest in their own noise machines while the rest of us just rake. The aim? To get every last leaf off your lawn and make the biggest pile possible. Between November and mid December 'Lost cat' notices are pulled down and flyers announcing the dates of the street leaf collection are stapled to telegraph poles. You hope that high winds won't come and blow every leaf in the street back into your garden.

The day arrives and a giant vacuum cleaner on wheels (think the Noo-noo from the *Teletubbies*) chugs through the streets to suck up the unsightly leaves. The first time I see a leaf collector I think there has been a biological attack. He is dressed head-to-toe in a hooded white suit with a surgical mask – just like the hazmat teams who were called in during the anthrax scare. But I am reassured by his workmates, some of whom only wear the face masks. Perhaps the hazmat man is allergic to leaves.

The important thing with an impending leaf collection is to follow the rules. Here is advice from the Department of Public Works and Transportation:

Leaves should be placed in piles or containers on the grass or behind the curb. Placing leaves in streets or alleys can disrupt traffic and surface drainage, hamper snow removal operations or pose a fire hazard to automobiles parked over them. (Apparently heat from a parked car can set the leaves on fire.)

And for goodness sake keep your wood separate – *sticks, branches or coarse garden debris should be placed in containers or tied in bundles not more than four feet long.*

The local fire station's roadside noticeboard helpfully reminds, 'Never park on leaf piles'.

Why do we bother? Well, there is a practical reason. If the huge quantities of leaves block your drains and gutters before heavy rain, your basement gets flooded. It is also fun to jump in an enormous leaf pile, preferably before the local dogs have peed in it.

I do it because everybody else does. It's suburbia. I want to fit in.

Chapter 8:
School and Snipers

AT THE TALK for upcoming kindergarten parents, some voice concerns that two and a half hours of school a day is too long for four and five-year-olds.

I'm glad it isn't the custom here, as in some British schools, to dress children barely out of nappies in uniform and force them to walk silently in straight lines, but it strikes me the kindergarteners might actually like some numbers and words by now.

'Are they ready for this?' asks one mom in the kind of pink and green floral trousers which would never sell in Britain.

'Do they get a snack?' asks another.

'How much time do they have on the black top (playground),' says an immaculately groomed mom who looks like she has rearranged a business meeting for the occasion.

The parents are reassured that there will be lots of emphasis on the block corner (building things with giant blocks of wood) and the housekeeping corner (a mini-kitchen). As we leave the classroom, I notice that a lot of dads have attended but I don't remember any of them opening their mouths.

At school orientation, a getting-to-know-you morning for newcomers, the kids have their photo taken and are whisked away to plant a seed and eat some animal crackers. Meanwhile, the parents get more briefings. The counsellor says she is always on hand to help. 'A child will be very upset when they lose their dog. We work it through.' Now we fill in forms detailing our child's strengths and weaknesses. I end up with slightly more in the weaknesses column – the teacher will know what to work on. I notice the mother across the table has left the weaknesses section completely blank.

The supplies list has caught me by surprise. I assumed that at state school all the materials would be paid for by the council, but apparently not. This is a job for a favourite shop of mine, Bruce's Variety, purveyors of stationery, haberdashery and miscellaneous items, a throwback to 1950s America. From granny's hairnets to paperclips to lace, it will be here. Going past the plastic party favours, I meet another mother clutching a list. Heading up the ribbon aisle, there's another. My task is to find the following:

*12 glue sticks (they must be the bland kind which don't work, presumably to avoid poisoning and/or lawsuits)

*liquid soap (anti bacterial)

*paper towels

*white paper plates

*felt pens (thick and thin)

*play dough

*Post-its (all sizes)

*white or coloured index cards (of specific measurements)

*stickers (including 'dime size' dots)

*wool

*three of the following: magnetic tape, gameboard games, plastic bins, baskets, tongue depressors, book binding combs, silver book rings, plastic ziplock bags, brads, wooden clothes pins, Velcro strips, alphabet or number puzzles.

I don't know what a brad is and I'm anxious to learn what the tongue depressors are for. While I'm distracted by the list, Josie has seized the moment to rearrange the button display. I let out a wail and from behind the fabric paints a middle aged man, who seems to run the place, comes to my aid. He calmly takes the list and basket from me. 'You get the baby and the buttons, I'll find what's on the list,' he says helpfully.

I wonder what happens in areas where parents cannot afford a $70 list per child. Do their children have to wash their hands without anti bacterial soap and settle for an education lacking in 'dime size' dots?

It is the first day at elementary school. Ahead of us on the walk to school is a sea of giant backpacks jangling with key rings. There is no official uniform but everyone looks the same in T-shirts, shorts and training shoes. Crossing the road, we meet the safety patrols. These earnest 10-year-olds, wearing yellow straps to show their importance, are stationed at each quiet suburban corner on the route (the main road has an adult lollipop lady equivalent, dressed in brown like a park ranger).

The etiquette is simple. Do not cross until the patrol has looked both ways, walked into the centre of the road and beckoned. As you cross, they say, 'Have a nice day!' and smile. It is a job done with such pride that I hear two boys stationed at the same crossing squabbling under their breath about whose turn it is to take the next child across.

As the yellow school buses pull up at the entrance, more patrols escort younger ones to the line outside their classrooms. Here, the baton is passed to the kindergarten helpers who keep their charges in an orderly queue, budding camp leaders using games to keep everyone quiet. Others will help in the library and the office, instilling the spirit of volunteering for the community at an early age. The American flag is fluttering outside. At home time, the 5th grade honour guards will lower it and fold it up for the night.

I feel safely liberated from forms, having filled in a stack for the county and the school before day one. They included more than six on health, which make sure injections are up to date (you need to prove your child has had them), TB and lead poisoning tests and past illnesses. I thought that was finally it, but I was wrong. Now I have to fill in cards – four, identical – for emergency contacts with lists of names and numbers. Then a pile of information sheets to read through on parents' night, a school community picnic, the fundraising fun run and food allergy issues.

Josie is starting at a small nursery school in an old park building which I used to think was the public convenience. It is a co-operative and parents have to take on jobs and be the teachers' helpers every few weeks. Other Europeans have been attracted by the friendly informality of the place. But at the parents' meeting, we soon learn that no organisation escapes Montgomery County and Maryland regulations. Before we can be a classroom helper we must take a TB test. We have to sign forms to show that we have understood and agreed to a series of rules including washing kids' hands with water and liquid soap and drying them with kitchen towels. All health forms, with injections complete, must be in before the inspectors arrive. It looks terrifying. Kathleen, a nursery veteran, pats my arm and says, 'Don't worry. It sounds complicated but it will all be fine. Have a brownie.'

The first day of nursery school will be the first anniversary of 9/11. The helicopters are back, circling, hovering. There are more sirens from the fire station a few streets away. Our house is one of the closest to school and I agree, if anything happens, to bring home children whose parents may be locked in downtown and unable to call.

A sheet comes home from elementary school titled 'Remembering September 11: Tips for Parents', with suggestions 'to help you reflect with your children upon the September 11 anniversary'. The key points are to prepare them early for what they will see and hear on the media, explain the purpose of an anniversary and to listen and help them put feelings into words. As strong emotions are often difficult to express verbally, the guide suggests that parents 'model appropriate expressions for them' like 'I don't know where to begin. It seems like all my feelings are mixed up inside. Sometimes it seems too hard to even put into words. When I feel this way I…'.

After quizzing Amalie and Josie, aged 4 and 2 at the time, I conclude they have forgotten it all anyway and opt for the easier option of a media blackout until after bedtime.

It is September 10 and we are on 'Orange Alert' (for terrorism, not humidity). The radio says live anti-aircraft missiles are positioned around Washington.

September 11 2002, and just like a year ago it is a beautiful day with clear blue skies. The three and four-year-olds cycling round on tricycles in the nursery school playground are mainly American but their surnames are from other countries – Spain, Portugal, Germany, Poland, Korea, Ireland – and different religions – Judaism, Catholicism, Episcopal. They have a parent, grandparent or a history book to remind them of their heritage but America is home. Parents walking home from elementary school drop-off are wearing red, white and blue ribbons. Up the road the gardeners are mowing lawns and clearing the first autumn leaves with leaf blowers. George Bush speaks on TV from the Pentagon. 'This morning, I think I will go to church,' a neighbour says.

This is a Democrat stronghold and rival factions, vying to make their man the party's local candidate, are wearing T-shirts to get across their message ('Chris Van Hollen for Congress' or 'Mark Shriver for Congress'). Campaigners chat to voters in the street to argue the case for their man. Can't see much between them myself and privately think their energies would be better spent stopping Republicans getting any more seats in the rest of the country.

At school, the older children prepare for their political futures, campaigning for roles on the school council. Candidates for treasurer, president and vice president smile down from posters which list why they have the best qualities for the job. Endorsement forms are passed around and parents act as unofficial campaign managers, brimming with enthusiasm and pride. Voting follows campaign speeches. When the results are in, some younger pupils reveal that the boys went for 'the kid who said he would put more basketball hoops on the blacktop' and the girls favoured 'the one with the ponytail who wants more jump ropes at recess'.

'What does the president do anyway?' one boy asks.

'Oh, he just switches off the lights at the end of school,' says his friend with authority.

It is Back-to-school-night, when parents are invited into school. The ones who you don't normally see in daylight hours are out in force in business suits. The hall is packed, anticipation mounting before the presentation from the head teacher. We begin with uplifting music and slides with inspiring quotes about the concept of school. The main message is it's 'not just school' but a 'learning community'. I wonder what this means. The touchingly enthusiastic moms who run the Parent Teacher Association are modelling T-shirts publicising the forthcoming fundraising fun run. I notice that on the budget sheet it is listed as PTA 'Inc'.

Thousands of dollars are raised from the fun run, bake sales and book sales with the money spent on classroom books, the library, social events, the school directory (a list of classes with parents' names, addresses, numbers and e-mails) and a myriad of extras for teachers and pupils. I feel like a small cog in a big corporation and wonder if children in state schools with poorer parents have any books at all (the answer is 'yes' but often not enough unless a charity steps in). Meanwhile, a parent cheerleader urges, 'We need you to join the PTA, to make the suggested donation and to volunteer to help – sign-up sheets are outside your children's classrooms! Do it tonight!'

I study the volunteer sheet nervously. The 'Room Parents' organise parties and end of term gifts. This sounds too important. For each party, there are lines for every category: bring cupcakes, bring juice cartons, supply paper goods. Can I remember to bring Valentine's Day cupcakes in six months time? I am still dithering when a familiar mother, who has children the same age, comes to my rescue. 'Let's put down to help at the Halloween party. It will be fun. We'll just leave early to get back to nursery school.' Later, sitting on the step and looking at the stars, I wonder if this small act of volunteering makes me an official member of the 'learning community'.

School is shut today for the Jewish holiday of Yom Kippur. People are pouring into the synagogues in Chevy Chase and Kensington as I drive by to try out a new shopping mall at Wheaton. It is a chain mall but has a different feel to its sister one a few miles away. The Latino community is dominant and women are chattering in Spanish next to their stalls, selling plastic flowers, light-up crucifixes and pictures with moving waterfalls.

The novelty has worn off after the first few weeks of kindergarten and a mother is physically tussling with her reluctant son at the school door. 'I don't *want* to do the Pledge of Allegiance!' he shouts. Every morning, pupils stand before the Stars and Stripes and recite, 'I pledge allegiance to the flag of the United States of America and to the republic for which it stands, one nation under God, indivisible, with liberty and justice for all.'

Later, I ask Amalie, aged 5, about it. 'Oh, yeah we do it. You have to put your hand on your heart and there is a flag. I can't really remember what you say.' I explain that, as she is a British citizen, she doesn't have to say it as long as she is quiet while the others do. She looks puzzled at the notion of non-conformity in the classroom and wanders off to shoot some basketball hoops.

After school, we head over to see some Australian friends. The mothers settle down on the sofa with a cup of tea while the girls hurl themselves around the trampoline outside.

Lacie has something to get off her chest. 'I got called into school today about Edie,' she said. 'She is refusing to say the Pledge of Allegiance. The teacher says she will fail the kindergarten curriculum if she doesn't do it.'

'I didn't know it was possible to fail kindergarten,' I reply. 'Isn't it just learning-through-play?'

'That's what I thought,' Lacie says.

I bump into her the next day. 'Any news about the pledge?' I ask. She has just been to see the principal at the fee-paying school and a compromise has been reached.

'She doesn't have to say it,' Lacie says, relieved. 'But she must stand respectfully and not be distracting to her classmates.' (We wonder if she had been pulling faces and inciting a riot among the impressionable youth of America.)

I learn that 35 states, including Maryland, require schools to include recitation of the Pledge of Allegiance during the school day. Around half of these updated their rulings after 9/11. Another five encourage recitation and some, like Texas, also have a pledge to their state flag. Most make it optional for students with religious or other objections.

See Lacie on the way home from school. We stop to talk and realise we are blocking a line of buggies and dog walkers because we have naturally paused on the left of the path instead of the right. Once the queue has gone, she tells me the news. 'I got called into school again about Edie,' she says.

'Oh no,' I sympathise, 'not the pledge again.'

'No, not the pledge,' Lacie replies, unable to suppress a smile. 'She ate a glue stick!'

Later, while Edie tucks into her third bowl of pasta, I ask her why she did it. 'I was just sooo hungry,' she says. 'And it tasted delicious!'

It is my turn to be the teacher's helper at nursery school and so far it is going well. I have cleaned the loos, checked the liquid soap supply (it is the approved 'anti-bacterial'), swept the classroom and laid out materials for the art project. Now the children have gone outside to play in the park leaving the helpers to wipe down the tables and put a birthday cupcake at every place. The phone rings and I break off to answer – probably another parent calling to see if we have any vacancies. But it is the mother of a current pupil asking to speak to a teacher. I explain they are already outside with the children, it's such a beautiful day. She pauses before saying, 'Five people have been shot in Montgomery County...the authorities are saying that schoolchildren must stay inside.'

I run out and see the children are already being lined up to come inside. Leah is there too. 'I heard the news on the car radio and came right over,' she says quietly. The children are briskly herded back inside, speeded on by the promise of cake. The Latino and Filipino nannies in the park don't understand what is going on but they seem to know 'go home'. Someone mimes a shooting.

As we sing *happy birthday* the phone keeps ringing with more news.

'It was a man mowing a lawn.'

'Someone got shot at a gas station.'

'A guy got killed in a grocery store car park.'

A woman has been shot cleaning her van in Kensington, less than four miles away.

'So this is America,' another parent says grimly as we clear up the bathroom. I glance out of the window, checking for a gunman on the loose. The park is deserted and he is probably in hiding by now. But what if the worst happened? I decide the children would have to lie down under the tables or, if there was time, go into the store room.

The teachers are calmness itself and the children haven't sensed a thing. Maureen sits on a white, wooden rocking chair in a glittery scarf and floppy hat from the dressing up box 'eating' pretend food that the children bring her. 'We're fine,' she says calmly. 'It puts things in perspective.'

Montgomery County has ordered 'Code Blue', which means staff and pupils at state schools are locked in with the windows shuttered. I call elementary school to check if we still collect at the normal time. 'Everyone is safe,' says the school secretary. 'The children are just getting on with their day. But you cannot pick your daughter up without photo ID.'

No one is late for nursery school pick-up today. 'Can we go play in the park, Mom?' is met with a firm 'no, we need to get lunch' or 'you need to take a nap'.

As we walk home across the park I see a lone mother with her daughter. 'Have you heard the news?' I ask.

'No,' she says, a look of alarm spreading across her face. Her daughter is listening. She glances at her and says, 'Is it T-E-R-R-O-R?'

'No,' I reply, 'someone with a G-U-N.'

'We have to go home for lunch now, honey, Daddy might be back soon,' she says to her daughter and rushes off into the autumn sunshine.

It's been in the back of my mind for a while – how long can we hide away from America's gun crime? In the privileged bubble of white Washington suburbia, you could almost forget it exists. I feel sick and I want to go back home to a country with real gun control, where the shooting of a policeman still provokes national outrage.

Going home time at elementary school, and cars line the road to the entrance. Usually, most people walk as there is nowhere to park. Dads I have never seen before have left work early to collect their children. The classroom blinds are down and grim-faced teachers stand guard at the locked door.

I see Lacie, who has four children at three different schools, looking uncharacteristically stressed. 'This feels worse than September 11, it's so close to home,' she says, before pulling herself together. 'But you have to get on with your life. There's still more chance of dying on the Beltway.' We agree that, today, the tighter gun laws of Australia and Britain make a lot of sense. 'How can it be your right to have a gun?' Lacie asks with exasperation.

The next day, the gunman is still out there. Five people are dead in Montgomery County and there's another possible sniper victim in DC. Driving to school doesn't seem like a rational solution as I'll never get parked anyway. And the walk is on quiet back roads. Already the gunman has a pattern, keeping to main roads with a quick getaway. Police say he may drive a white van, so best keep a look out. Many parents and pupils are still on foot and we try to act normally. People move to the leafy suburbs to get away from the mean urban streets of the other Washington DC, where children get shot for being in the wrong place at the wrong time. Now those worlds are colliding.

At the school entrance there is an armed, uniformed policeman talking into his radio. The head teacher stands next to him, smiling and welcoming the children, hoping they will notice her instead of him. Then an older boy asks loudly, 'Why are the police here?' We move swiftly on. Amalie has already noticed that police routinely carry guns in America so one at the school gates is no big deal.

That afternoon there is another shooting, a woman at a shopping mall car park, but this time it is 50 miles away in Virginia. Doctors think she will make it.

A few days later, most people are still avoiding taking the kids to the supermarket or the petrol station but we are starting to relax a little. No one has been caught but there have been no more shootings over the weekend. Josie and I take a leisurely walk from elementary to nursery school. She stops to stroke a cat – looks like Meow from down the street – while I wave at a neighbour going past in her car.

As we head towards the park, my mobile rings. It is Roland calling from work to tell me there has been another shooting, a 13-year-old boy injured going into school. Shit. Even children now, this is horrible. I take a deep breath and try and be rational. It happened in Bowie, 20 miles away in Prince George's County, and it would take the sniper at least half an hour to drive from there to here.

I get to the nursery school and the kids are playing outside, riding 'big wheel' bikes and making chalk drawings. Parents and teachers are happily chatting – they haven't heard the news yet. It seems a shame to spoil the idyllic scene but I start passing the news around. We speak in hushed tones but some of the children sense the change in mood, crying and clinging to their mothers. They are whisked in and the door shuts before it gets worse.

'I was going to go grocery shopping but perhaps I'll leave it until another day,' says a mother with a baby.

I meet a European neighbour on the way home. She has just heard the news. 'Americans don't know terror,' she says. 'We have lived with bomb threats all our lives – they have had nothing before 9/11.' In the street and outside the schools gates we used to talk about our children, what activities they were doing, the weather, or George Bush's latest idiocies. Now we talk about guns. I remember the public outcry and united movement for tighter laws after major gun crimes in Britain. Maybe some good will come out of it, I suggest. But they shake their heads sadly and universally conclude that here, there will be calls for more guns.

One translates it into politics. 'Ehrlich will get in now.' Robert Ehrlich is the Republican challenger for Maryland Governor. His opponent is Kathleen Kennedy Townsend who favours tougher gun laws.

In the queue at the Giant, I talk to another shopper. 'I am against them but my ex-husband thinks everyone should have the right to own a gun,' she says.

I commiserate. 'At least he's your ex.'

'Are you letting your kids play in the yard?' Gail, a mother of three children aged five and under, asks down the phone. 'I don't know what to do. I'm scared to let them out but they are going crazy stuck indoors.'

'I am,' I reply. 'No one has been shot on a quiet suburban street like this and the girls keep to the back garden which you can't see from the road.' A police patrol car drives by as we talk. I have never seen one in our street before. She doesn't sound convinced. Later, I hear of mothers going to the doctor for anti-depressants.

'So, is it Al Qaeda?' asks the man at the check-out in Safeway.

'I think he is home grown,' I speculate, 'some ex-army loner, estranged from his family. We get the same type in Britain, they just don't usually manage to get hold of a gun there so they have to make do with a knife.'

'I still think it's Al Qaeda,' he replies. 'And the Feds never caught the guy who mailed the anthrax.'

As I drive back, I notice a lone Latino woman standing at the bus stop at the end of my road, most likely a cleaner or a nanny. She looks really scared. I have ten minutes before school pick-up. I pull over and ask if I can give her a lift to the Metro. But she doesn't understand me and I don't know the right words in Spanish. Now she looks even more worried (am I blocking her view of passing white vans?). She sees her bus coming and, relieved, waves goodbye.

Today, as well as an armed policeman, there is a police car with flashing lights at the school entrance. More and more sirens go off in the distance. 'You used to think it was a fire or a car accident when you heard that,' says one mother grimly. There has been a shooting in DC, someone just heard on the radio. Could it be connected? Or just another drug related crime on the wrong side of town, the kind that no one used to take much notice of?

'What did you do in school today,' I ask Amalie on the way home, trying to keep things normal.

'We did a poem about how to dial 911 in an emergency,' she replied.

'What else?' I ask.

'We made a puppet of a fire chief out of a paper bag. And we wrote a book called Blue Land about a place where everything was blue.'

Police chiefs in Prince George's County, Montgomery County and Washington DC have asked for Federal government help. A killer is still on the loose and the world is watching.

The radio says schools in Montgomery County, Prince George's County and Baltimore County are in lockdown. Afternoon kindergarten is cancelled. Parents of children being picked up must have photo ID.

It is day seven and there have been nine shootings and six deaths – in shop car parks, at petrol stations, a bus stop, and the school gates. One victim was mowing a lawn. Just normal people going about their everyday lives.

The older kids have had to give up the coveted job of crossing patrol for now. Today, parent volunteers stand on the corner of every road on the route to school, like a guard of honour. More parents than they needed have offered, one of the dads says. Other volunteers will be helping in the classrooms, providing extra distractions for restless kids.

'I kept my kids at home today,' Gail later confesses on the phone. 'I can't stand it.'

The next day, a man is shot at a petrol station in Virginia. It is like being an extra in a psycho killer film. Two days later, while the girls are safely locked in school, I interview customers at petrol stations for a newspaper piece. Flowers are at the spot where Lori Ann Lewis-Rivera was killed while vacuuming her van on a weekday morning. Everyone is trying to be rational. 'When your number is up, your number is up,' the customers say. These are the brave ones, but even they are crouching behind their cars and glancing over my head, looking for white vans. No one wants to talk for long. Chatting to mechanics in a garage shop down the road, pictures flash up on the TV of a new shooting at another petrol station in Virginia. Another death. They shake their heads and get back to work.

'It's a good job you and the girls are all so short,' a friend from Britain says on the phone, trying to be supportive.

While our children hurl themselves around Leah's secluded back garden, she and I discuss whether or not it is responsible to take your kids to the petrol station. 'What if you make them stay in the car and lie down?' I suggest. We sit in silence for a moment, hardly believing we are having this conversation.

It is revealed that a tarot card was left at the scene of a shooting. It read, 'Dear Mr Policeman, I am God.'

A woman was shot dead yesterday evening as she loaded her car at a busy shopping centre in Northern Virginia. The gunman (no one suggests they could be female) escaped again.

The park is deserted. Parents and carers park their cars and briskly take the children to and from the nursery school door. 'I am scared,' says one nanny. 'I feel like I am being watched.' I know what she means. This, idyllic, open green space has taken on a more sinister feel.

Sally admits she is frightened now that there has been an incident in a crowded shopping area. 'On Sunday I went to church and the Safeway. An assistant asked me if I wanted help putting my groceries in the car. I didn't think until afterwards what a big gesture it was.'

'Do you blame the gun laws?' I ask.

'No, gun crime is bad in Britain and Australia too. It has been a right from frontier days to bear arms. DC, with no guns allowed, still became the murder capital of the world.'

Sally says she is putting her blinds down at night for the first time and is glad to have her new cocker spaniel puppy for company. Our sombre mood is broken when the little dog comes running into the room with the end of the toilet roll in her mouth and leaps, barking, onto the table in delight.

At the hairdressers there is talk of nothing else. 'I don't know 'ow the sniper can sleep at night,' says Pierre the French stylist. 'It couldn't 'appen in France, we 'ave gun laws. Of course you can get them on the black market but it is 'ard.'

Defenders of gun ownership like to cite Canada as an example, arguing that many citizens have firearms and crime is low. About two-thirds of homicides in the US involve a firearm compared with one-third for their neighbour. But there are more than 30 times more firearms in the US than in Canada.

Sherri down the street shakes her head, glancing at the empty trampoline which usually has children bouncing on it. 'It's like living in Beirut for these kids, locking them in,' she says.

At first we keep it vague in front of the kids. 'I expect the teacher said you had to stay in for recess because there was a storm coming.' But children talk. 'Do you know why we are locked in at school, Josie?' Amalie asks her sister. 'Because there's a bad man who wants to hurt kids.' At home they pull down the blinds and peak through, looking for the bad man. Later they chant, 'We are the spy kids,' over and over again. It can't be good for you, living like moles. But whose mental health is most at risk, the adults or the children?

A man survives a shooting outside a diner in Virginia. The sniper leaves another 'I am God' note. The letter also says, 'Your children are not safe anywhere or at anytime.' There are more tarot cards. He is clearly insane. Yet the combined might of several police forces and the FBI has failed to catch him.

Now a bus driver is shot dead in Aspen Hill, Montgomery County. It is getting closer again, eight miles away. It is day 21. Some police arrests quickly turn out to be a false alarm – illegal immigrants trying to get money. They have a footprint here and a tarot card there to go on. The police are trying to talk to the killer. It feels like a dangerous game.

At pick-up time, a policeman in a 'SWAT team' T-shirt races past the school entrance to his car to catch the radio. Another, in plain clothes, stands at the door watching. Do they know something we don't?

The children in the street say that if the 'bad guy' gets into their home he will kill them. I tell mine he won't get into ours. After school and nursery, we take it in turns for classmates to play at each others' houses – at least then they see a different back garden or a different living room. Now, no matter who comes, it is the same awful game. The children pull down all the blinds, turn out the lights and lie on the floor under the table in the dark.

The Montgomery County Public Schools website confirms that Code Blue security restrictions are continuing. There will be no outdoor recess or physical education. All field trips, regardless of destination, are cancelled. Schools will continue to keep exterior doors locked and monitor visitors. There are tips for adults on how to cope with cumulative stress. Severe signs to look out for are changes in relationships, health and personality as well as becoming housebound. A daily routine, healthy meals and exercise will help. 'Don't dwell on news of the crisis,' they advise. And remember, 'You are not alone.'

The school has suggestions for 'what children can do about terrorism'. These include, 'Make a fear box. Cut out pictures from newspapers and magazines about what frightens them. Write down their fears and put them inside.' Or, 'Put together a peaceful box. Ask kids to find toys, stuffed animals and pictures that make them feel safe and peaceful and keep these items in the box.'

On the evening news, pictures suddenly flash up of the FBI digging up a garden in Tacoma, Washington state, on the West coast. Later, an arrest warrant is issued for a former soldier and an unnamed young man believed to be with him. Police have also given a description of a blue Chevrolet Caprice. Not a white van then. Everyone is glued to the news, desperate for an arrest.

We wake up to hear that two men were arrested in a rural lay-by in Maryland during the night. The sense of relief is overwhelming. Everyone is smiling today, stopping to chat, savouring the chores of going to the supermarket and filling up with petrol. The children are ecstatic, running round outside like mad things, free at last.

Maryland has tough gun laws by American standards and a historical aversion to carrying out the death penalty, but will that change after the experience of the last three weeks, with ten people shot dead and three wounded? The face of Kathleen Kennedy Townsend, the Democrat candidate for Maryland governor, looks out from posters on many local front lawns. Will her tough stance on gun laws lose her what is already a tight race?

It's nearly Halloween and people are throwing themselves into it, post sniper, like never before. There are parties and parades at school, nursery and in the neighbourhood. Cake with lurid orange icing is a must. Mothers discussing menus shriek with delight when they realise their children all have peanut allergies. 'Who is your specialist? You must see mine, he's so good.' Costumes are bought (only sew it if you are tailor level), orange, black and white beads are collected for necklace-making and participants stock up on Halloween themed sprinkles for decorating cookies. The big day comes and cameras don't stop clicking. Even the teacher is an M&M.

At night, the neighbourhood pushes the boat out with houses decorated with carved pumpkins, fake cobwebs and skeletons. Spooky music is pumped out together with occasional chainsaw massacre sound affects. One man even hides in bushes in his front garden in a scary costume to frighten kids (is this normal?). A child's first Halloween usually means a particularly cute costume like a fairy or a white rabbit. Dad will be close behind in a novelty hat, filming their every move as they knock on your door and announce, just like last year, 'I don't like this candy, I only like Hershey's Kisses.'

The kids' football, cancelled by the sniper, is back on in the park. The three and four-year-olds charge around in oversized soccer T-shirts, trying to balance balls on their heads and bumping tummies. 'Good job!' shouts the genial young coach. 'Water break!' Never mind that there are only a few weeks left of the season. Just showing up and running around is enough to win them all a large, faux gold trophy at the end.

What with the sniper and Halloween, I almost forgot about the November mid-term elections. So, apparently, has Vice President Cheney who is reported to be pheasant hunting in South Dakota. The Republican Robert Ehrlich beats Kathleen Kennedy Townsend, ending the Democrats' 36-year hold on the state of Maryland. Would he have won without the sniper fuelling the gun debate? Local Democrats don't think so. To voters, more guns equals more protection.

We escape to the National parks of Utah and Arizona. It is a road trip of sunrise mountain walks, boat rides through dramatic gorges and rustic park lodges. At breakfast one morning, three generations of a family all wear bright yellow 'Grandma's 60th birthday' sweatshirts. Other stereotypes keep coming to life. At a run-down gas station in the middle of nowhere, a rusty Dodge pick-up truck pulls alongside us. Out get two identical looking men with ZZ Top-style long beards, mirror shades, baseball caps, jeans and check shirts. We both walk into the shop. I buy a bottle of water, they buy three boxes of cold Budweiser. Hunting rifles for sale cover the walls. The bearded men pick up a copy of a mule deer hunting magazine with a picture of a fierce redneck on the front. There is nothing else here but a boarded up motel and trailer homes.

Back home the day before Thanksgiving, and Wholefoods' car park is full of men in fluorescent tabards carrying two red flags each. You must park where instructed. 'Please don't argue with me, Ma'am, I am just doing my job.' Give an American a uniform or a tabard and they act like they are the official spokesman of their employer. Inside, there is a stampede for turkeys, squash, pumpkins and breads.

Bill and Lena have been given a special cinnamon apple pie by some neighbours from Michigan and let us have a taste.

Amalie proudly brings home her paper Thanksgiving turkey from school. I notice other kids have written 'I am thankful for my dog' or 'For my family and God'. After recently reading about the origins of man in a children's encyclopedia, she has written 'I am thankful for monkeys'. I fear this is controversial.

Chapter 9:
State of Emergency

'HOW WAS YOUR weekend?' asks Gail. 'We went up to the farm and cut down our own Christmas tree. It was really neat.'

Must be part of the American suburban experience – we should do it. So the next weekend we are at the farm where we are lent a shiny new hacksaw and told to drive up the track, following the signs. Wellies on, ready to tramp through undergrowth, hunting for the perfect tree in dense woodland, we come round the bend to reveal an extraordinary sight, row upon row of trees, planted an equal distance apart and in order of size, trimmed to a perfect cone. They have all had a haircut. 'It is so difficult to decide,' Amalie concludes after ten minutes of walking up and down rows. 'They all look the same.' Eventually we go for a medium sized model and start sawing. Three strokes with the shiny new blade and it is down, ready to be squeezed into a mesh bag to stop the needles making a mess. We pay in the farm shop, stocked with improbably large fruit and vegetables, and gape at the Christmas tree decorations – huge gingerbread men, shiny Santas and enormous red velvet ribbons. Our wellies are still spotless.

It's Chanukah, time for the Jewish kids to get some presents to make up for having nothing at Christmas. But for some, the sense of injustice is too great and they pick off the younger ones who still believe in Father Christmas and tell them the truth. 'Didn't you know? He's not real, it's just your parents, stupid.' Well, it had to happen sooner or later.

Weather forecasters are warning of early snow and it is the main subject of conversation. Will school close down? 'In Boston there is so much snow you go to school in blizzards, in Arizona it is so rare, there is a flurry and everything shuts,' says one well travelled mother. 'Here they shut because so many parents are lawyers and they don't want an accident.'

But a teacher has another explanation. 'They look at the whole area. The weather is worse in the more rural places where most of the teachers can afford to live.' The school crossing patrols have their ski jackets and fleece hats on in readiness. Now they say, 'Stay warm,' as well as, 'Have a nice day.'

The Nutcracker is on at the outdoor ice rink. It's a valiant effort in sub-zero temperatures with 'Clara' shivering violently in a thin red skate dress. The soldiers are too cold to concentrate and keep falling over. 'Smile,' hisses the teacher and the children all show their braces. The proud and devoted parents wear Santa hats with their offspring's name on, whooping and clapping to keep everyone's spirits up. On a stage nearby, a schoolgirl singing group rattles through seasonal Broadway numbers.

Today I get told off at the gym. 'We don't allow reading on the exercise machines, Ma'am,' says the young male instructor. 'It makes you stay on there for too long.'

'Nothing will make me stay on for too long,' I joke but he doesn't crack a smile. There is only one other person in the room, pounding away on the running machine, oblivious. 'No one seems to be waiting,' I add, but get no reaction. Perhaps it is time to go home anyway.

Time I had a dental check up (my British dentist said I might need a filling by now). I trawl through the list from the health insurance company and call the nearest. The next day, I am sitting in the dentist's chair as a bright young Asian woman with a gleaming smile says, 'Wow,' and, 'Look at that!' to her assistant. 'You need extensive root canal work and a crown,' she says. 'I will have to refer you to a specialist.'

'Goodness,' I reply, 'I thought I just needed a filling. This is all covered by insurance, isn't it?'

'No, it will cost at least $300, probably more.'

I wonder what the price would be with no health insurance at all. 'What do people do if they can't afford that?'

'Have the tooth out,' she replies.

'Or don't go to the dentist?'

'Yes' she says.

I decide to get a second opinion and ring round, looking for someone with experience of foreign clients. My new dentist is reassuring. 'I have seen this type of root canal work in many European patients,' he says. 'It will probably last you years but it is not the way we do it here – most American dentists would be horrified!' he beams.

'What did you do in school today,' I ask my daughter, now aged five and three quarters.

'Oh, Code Red,' she replies, twirling her plaits and taking a bite of toast. 'We had to hide in the bathroom and be very, very quiet. It means a bad man is *in* the school.'

'Let's hope it never happens,' I say.

'That's *just* what my teacher said.'

Montgomery County Public Schools defines Code Red – not to be confused with the government's terrorist risk index – as 'an alert status indicating imminent danger exists to all staff and students'.

Here is the drill:

*Lock all doors.

*Pull down window blinds and cover the glass on the classroom door.

*Turn off the lights.

*Gather the children away from windows and doors and take register.

*Children in the bathroom or corridor must report to the nearest room. They must identify themselves and the name of their teacher before being allowed in.

Code Blue is not so bad. Teaching carries on with the blinds down and the outside doors locked.

'Are you sad about the number of policemen killed or injured on duty?' the cold caller from a police society asks. 'Are you sorry and do you want to help?'

'Of course I am sad about it,' I reply crossly, 'but what do you expect in a country where citizens have the right to bear arms and burglaries guarantee a steady stream of weapons onto the black market. If you really care, your organisation should be lobbying politicians for tighter gun controls so that your members don't become a fatality which only merits a paragraph in *The Washington Post*.' I am ranting now. Must be all that pent up, post sniper angst.

There is silence at the end of the phone. His instructions on 'how to deal with difficult calls' don't appear to cover what to say when a potential donor launches into an anti-gun diatribe. The phone goes dead. I feel partly apologetic – it is just his job and he probably only gets paid commission when somebody donates – and partly exhilarated that I have made a fast talking cold caller hang up on me before I can do it to them.

I wait in line at the barbers on the maroon plastic chairs. The cutters come from all over the world – Europe, Asia and South America. Photos around their mirrors are scenes from home and portraits of children and grandchildren. There always seems to be someone from our street or school sitting in a gown when we arrive. Today the talk is of Iraq. On the overhead TV is the latest news from the UN weapons inspectors.

'I'm not sure about going in,' an elderly man says, clutching his *New York Times*.

'Me neither,' says a barber.

'Yeah, but they could be hiding Bin Laden and pointing their weapons at us,' a man in a check shirt with a military-style crew cut argues.

The boss switches to the sports channel where they are discussing last night's American football final, the Super Bowl, between the Tampa Bay Buccaneers and the Oakland Raiders. The mood lifts. 'So what did you think of the game? The Buccaneers did good, didn't they?'

On TV tonight, a forklift truck driver is pretending to be a millionaire looking for a wife. A pack of tanned, long haired women are vying for his attention at a French Chateau that they think he owns. Do they want him for his money or his personality?

Get talking to a Scandinavian woman at Trader Joe's who lived in South Africa before the US. How does it compare, I ask.

'People have the right values there,' she says. 'They don't in the US.' I am left wondering exactly what she means as I put the yogurt covered blueberries through check-out.

It's early Saturday morning and we lie half asleep watching the sun filtering through the blinds and listening to the girls playing in their room. The phone rings. Must be someone in Britain who has forgotten the time difference. 'Do you have the TV on?' the voice says. It is Sally, sounding agitated. 'The shuttle has exploded.'

Residents in Texas and Louisiana say they heard a loud noise and saw bright balls in the sky – burning space shuttle debris. NASA declares a state of emergency and flags at the White House and the Capitol are lowered to half mast. George Bush arrives in Washington from Camp David in a speeding motorcade to address the nation. 'Columbia is lost,' he says. 'There are no survivors.'

Everyone is shaken up by the loss of the shuttle and the seven astronauts on board. There's something quintessentially American about space travel. It is as if the neighbourhood had lost one of its own.

The snow is falling in huge flakes outside. The man ahead of me in the Giant, in a red fur hat and battered shoes, tries to get his food voucher card to work. Bob the check-out man and I try to help.

'We don't have these in Serbia,' the man explains.

'But you do have this weather, right?' says Bob.

'Oh yes,' he smiles.

'Nice hat,' I say as the card finally goes through.

Here we go again. Anti-aircraft guns are back around Washington DC and private aircraft are banned from a wide area around the city. It is February 2003 and we are again on Orange Alert. This is not the name of a new breakfast juice. It is the US government's colour code for categorising the risk of attack and it means 'high'.

Here are some of the recommended actions for citizens from the US Department of Homeland Security under its alert system:

Green (low risk): Develop a family emergency plan and practise it, create an emergency supply kit, consider becoming a community volunteer and taking a first aid course.

Blue (guarded risk): Complete the above, replace outdated items in your stored disaster supplies, be alert to suspicious activity and report it.

Yellow (elevated risk): Complete the above, ensure disaster kit is ready, check telephone numbers in family emergency plan, develop alternative routes to/from work or school – practise them. Continue to be alert.

Orange (high risk): Complete the above, be cautious when travelling, review your family emergency plan, be patient over delays and searches, check on neighbours who might need help in an emergency.

Red (severe risk): Complete the above, listen to local emergency management officials, stay tuned to TV or radio, be prepared to 'shelter-in-place' or evacuate.

New intelligence seems to have sparked the alert. The Attorney General, John Ashcroft, justifies it by saying that Al Qaeda is willing to use chemical, biological and radiological weapons. Fear runs highest in Washington DC and New York. There is talk of dirty bombs and smallpox. The CIA tells politicians of terrorist plans for surface-to-air missiles and underwater assault teams. The FBI says Al Qaeda wants targets with high symbolic value, mass casualties and maximum psychological trauma. Plotters might carry out surveillance as fake beggars. Softer targets like shopping malls and sporting events could be at risk.

There is panic buying of gas masks. Strosniders, the local hardware store, is rumoured to be selling out of the duct tape and plastic sheeting needed to seal a room. I head over and pretend to look at candles while watching to see if people really are buying tape and sheeting. They are – normal looking types throwing them in their trolleys without a hint of embarrassment. Sally goes in to get some tape for a dodgy electric lead. 'I was surprised at the sheer panic,' she says. The children practise emergency drills at school again and military helicopters circle over the neighbourhood.

Snow is falling fast and we go sledging in the park. It is deserted. An hour later we have only seen one dog walker. Have we missed the emergency warning? Is everyone else already safe in their sealed room? Back home I turn on National Public Radio (NPR) to check if a toxic cloud is heading for Chevy Chase. It isn't.

We start making Valentine cards and get covered in glue and glitter. At least we will die pretty.

Government Homeland Security officials recommend the following steps for households to prepare for a possible terrorist attack.

*Assemble a disaster kit with essential food, water and supplies for three days. This should include one gallon of water per person per day, a first-aid kit, blankets and non-electric can openers. Also keep an emergency supply kit in your cars and at work.

*Keep on hand a radio with extra batteries to listen to broadcasts from local authorities. It may be safer to take shelter at home than to take to the roads.

*Designate a room in your home where you can take shelter in case of chemical or biological attack. Have on hand a roll of duct tape, scissors and plastic to cover doors, windows and vents in the room.

*Talk with your family about potential emergencies and how you would respond, including what to do in an evacuation.

*Plan how your household would stay in contact if separated. Identify two meeting places.

*Pick a friend or relative out of the area for household members to call to say they are okay.

*Post emergency numbers by the telephone.

Kathleen kindly volunteers her friend's Virginia phone number to use as an emergency contact – 'You probably don't know anyone out of this area, right?' She is right but I decline, for now anyway.

I already have supplies of food and water in case we get snowed in (I also happen to know that Sally has some extra, though she has made me promise to tell no one how much). Torch and batteries are in the drawer for power cuts. Duct tape is not a problem. I already have enough to stick round the entire house thanks to my DIY Dad.

But honestly, do I really need plastic sheeting? A friend in the foreign military tells me not to bother. 'I've been on all the courses. Sealing off a room isn't going to do any good.'

Leah puts it another way. 'What would you prefer? Three days and nights in the same room with your family or taking your chances outside?'

A man in Connecticut has covered his entire 19th century farmhouse in 3,500 square feet of plastic sheeting.

It is the eve of my daughter's sixth birthday party. If the terrorists attack tomorrow I could end up with 18 children aged six and under for a mass sleepover.

More than six in ten people living in the area have taken precautions as a result of the terrorism alert, according to a *Washington Post* survey. More than one in three has discussed how to communicate with family members if separated, one in four has designated a safe room at home, and around one in eight has made plans about how to leave the area in a terrorism emergency.

Some of those interviewed simply put their trust in God. Others have stocked up on beer, ammunition and firearms.

Here is Sally's emergency plan: first, put the lead on the dog; then go downstairs to the basement where supplies of food and drink are kept. She would take her wallet, a tin foil blanket, dog food ('so the dog doesn't eat me'), woolly underwear and comfy shoes.

She wouldn't bother to ring anyone. The battery-powered radio would be on just in case. But she does ask the valid question, 'Would there be anyone on it?' Sally also decided after

9/11 that if there were ever an atomic bomb she would kill her beloved dog with a friend's gun.

I ask her if she would like a lift if we are told to evacuate. No thanks, she is staying here.

A few weeks later, and miraculously we are all still alive. And there is further cause for celebration. We don't have pus-filled blisters, ulcers, paralysis, bloody sputum, convulsions, vomiting diarrhoea or cancer (just a few of the symptoms to look out for after a biological, chemical or radiological attack). 'One thing I remember from all that crazy time is if there is atomic radiation you get in the shower,' Sally says. She pauses. 'Or do you get in the shower if it is biological?' I can't remember either. Oh well.

Walk through the snow to have dinner at friends' nearby. The blinds are all open at lighted windows, people watching TV and reading their books or looking out at the snowflakes. We eat Indian food and talk about world politics. The others are teachers, trade unionists and academics. One speaks in praise of British music. 'The Beatles saved my life,' he says. 'They gave me a reason to keep going through high school.' Most people in the US have a religion, and this gathering is Catholic and Jewish. We raise our glasses and make a toast to 'peace in our time'.

A foot of snow has fallen during the night and by midday it is still coming down. Lena says it has been ten years since a two feet dump around here. Fox News goes live to a demonstration on how to dig your car out of deep snow. They have already got 50 inches in northern Maryland and it keeps falling. It comes over the top of my $10 snow boots and the icy wind makes my skin feel numb.

This really is the big one. Maryland, Virginia and Washington DC declare a State of Emergency – this means they can use the National Guard. Airports are shut down and we are all advised to stay off the roads.

The shock news in the neighbourhood is that even Hechts department store in nearby Friendship Heights is closed. This is unheard of. Usually it's open every day until late and always has a sale on. It should be having its Presidents' Day sale right now. The Giant supermarket on Wisconsin Ave has managed to get enough staff in to open but apparently it is almost out of fresh goods. Usually there are six lanes of cars going up and down this artery between downtown and the Maryland suburbs. Today it is pedestrians only and shoppers are bringing milk home by sledge. I look out the window at the blanket of white and wave at a neighbour going past on cross country skis.

When it finally stops, everyone is out digging, shovelling driveways, then clearing the pavement outside houses, rescuing their cars. We don't even have a snow shovel, so borrow Bill and Lena's. I thought it was smart to leave the car in the road instead of at the top of the steep driveway. But I hadn't taken the council snow plough into account. As it forges down the street it leaves a 4ft wall of snow up against the car. The children valiantly hack at it with beach spades but it has turned to ice in minutes. Sally says she has everything she needs and intends to stay warm inside and wait for it to melt. An expectant father a few streets away clears his drive like a dervish, the thought of a home birth spurring him on. On some blocks, the gardening teams arrive in trucks, clearing drives and pavements with diggers and snow blowers.

We are getting nowhere fast and decide to go sledging in the park instead. Two hours later, the cold has penetrated ski clothes, jumpers and thermals and we sit in front of a log fire to defrost. The wood pile is disappearing quickly and the mountain of logs I bought from a Virginian in a pick-up, due to a cultural misunderstanding about quantities, won't last three years after all.

A few days after the big fall, icicles hang from the trees and the grit lorries roar up and down the main roads.

Now the local TV stations are whipping up hysteria about 'The Big Melt!'. The sun is out, the temperature is rising and the huge piles of frozen snow are turning to water. I know the drill from previous experiences of heavy rainstorms – move everything in the basement onto higher shelves or put things in plastic boxes.

But then I notice something else. A crack has appeared right across the living room ceiling. Above it, the roof is still laden with snow. I get on to our super efficient property agent who calls an engineer – 'He'll be with you as quick as he can.' A few hours later, a giant action man in jeans and check shirt appears at the door after battling through traffic from the other side of the county. He declines a drink, whips off his work boots and disappears into the loft. Ten minutes later he reappears. 'Your roof is *not* going to fall in, Ma'am,' announces the all-American hero. 'It is safe,' he declares, before pulling on his Timberlands and roaring off into the night.

Time to check out another American sport. The venue downtown is the same as for the basketball but it is a different crowd at an ice hockey game. Whereas basketball has a multi-cultural, urban audience with some sharp dressers, this is dominated by hulking white men in jeans, team shirts and baseball caps. They are blue collar, out-of-town supporters with goatee beards and some mullet haircuts. Everyone watches, quiet and motionless, until the Washington Capitols score, then they spring to life, jumping from their seats, whooping, dancing and flashing lights. You can buy cold beer and candy floss from your seat but there are no cheerleaders, no gimmicks, no men in super hero outfits firing T-shirts into the crowd. Just a few blasts of grunge rock.

Two shaven-headed men in black suits sit in glass boxes behind the goal. Most curious. When a goal is confirmed, three lights above them flash. The names on the backs of players' shirts point to ancestors from Scandinavia, Germany and Eastern Europe. At the end, the Caps fans hurl abuse and boo at the ref. This appears to be normal. Head home on the Metro to the station car park. In Britain this is called 'park and ride', here it is 'kiss and ride'.

The forecast is for even more snow and we compare notes at the school gates.

'I heard two inches.'

'No, the storm has moved, now it's six – do you think school will open?'

'Will school open late?'

'Will school shut early?'

'How was your basement last time? Ours had four inches of water. There were no carpet driers or pumps left at the hardware store.'

As I drive along Wisconsin Avenue, over the line from Washington DC, I notice the road is recently gritted. Montgomery County takes a pride in these things. Residents should clear the pavements outside county homes within 24 hours. This time, we vow to be prepared too. 'Have you got enough milk? How about de-icer?' everyone asks each other.

The children are not surprised by the snowfall. 'Well, Punxsutawney Phil did warn us...' Every February 2, at Punxsutawney in rural Pennsylvania, Phil the groundhog is coaxed out of his tree trunk to give the weather forecast. If he doesn't see his shadow, spring has sprung. If he does, like this year, there will be six more weeks of winter. The film *Groundhog Day* wasn't making it up then. *The Washington Post* reports it could be the worst winter in the history of Maryland.

It is steaming in the cramped dance school waiting room, remnants of snow in dirty clumps outside. The woman next to me keeps her long black coat on and baseball cap firmly over her face. Her phone rings. 'Yes, that's because he is missing me. I can't come now, your sister has a class...we will be coming in 15 minutes....I will call when we are in the car.' She rings off. A few minutes later the phone rings again. 'What? He is just staring out of the window? Put him on.' There is a pause. 'Hello Toby! Toby, it's Mommy here. I'll be home soon.' Another pause. 'Oh, he didn't listen? Take him upstairs to the family room. I'll be back as soon as I can.' There is loud barking in the background as she hangs up. I don't recall ever hearing anyone talk on the phone to a dog before.

I hear on the news that a seven-year-old girl has been accidentally shot by her ten-year-old brother in Washington DC. It is thought he tried to take the gun from her after she found it under her mother's bed. The bullet went through her hand and chest and she is in a critical condition.

Today, I discover a new religious website. You put your hands on the screen to join in the prayer meeting. Give it a go but it doesn't really do anything for me.

And now the talk is of war. 'Without the UN, I am worried that war with Iraq will set the rest of the world against us. I am so frightened of retaliation.' A Washington lawyer and mother, Nina, has thought it all through, rationally and emotionally. She didn't vote Republican, but never thought they would do this much damage. 'How can Europeans think George Bush is more evil than Saddam Hussein? It is diplomacy gone horribly wrong.'

As I drive round the corner I see two men in black suits walking up my driveway. Please, not the Feds again. I pull up and, with huge relief, see they are carrying Bibles. They are all-American boys, college age, football players with blonde, buzz cuts. 'We are Christian missionaries,' says the taller one in a southern accent. 'And we want you to read the Mormon Bible.'

After pausing to stare at his improbably white teeth, I reply, 'Lads, I am so pleased you are the Mormons. I thought you were the FBI at first! But I wouldn't waste your time on me – I'm from Britain.' They look nervously at each other and decide to make their escape.

'Well thank you, Ma'am, and have a nice day.' They head across the street to Sally's. 'She's Catholic but you might get a good theological discussion,' I shout after them. They change direction. 'Oh, not there,' I add, 'they're Jewish.'

The Washington Post brings out a 10-page Emergency Preparedness Guide. Subjects include 'Staying Sane in a Time of Lunacy', 'The Lowdown on Smallpox Shots' and 'Gas Masks: The Facts and the Risks'.

I am not about to get gas masks but am interested to see what people are buying. On one website you can choose from eight different kinds, ranging in price from $100 to $250. They have names like Advantage, Millennium and Panorama and come with accessories – drinking pouches, filters and spectacle kits (so people who wear glasses can use the mask). A mere $270 will buy a protective wrap for kids under-eight (the aged three to eight version makes the child look like a junior member of the Ku Klux Klan). But is the government even saying we need these? I check the US Department of Homeland Security advice and it doesn't recommend them for a chemical threat. It states:

*Improper use of masks and hoods, as well as creating a false sense of security as to their effectiveness, could pose a threat to public safety.

*For example, it is difficult to obtain a proper seal with the mask if you have facial hair such as a beard or long sideburns.

*Protective masks do not fit small children.

In conclusion, toddlers, bearded men and Elvis look-a-likes would be in trouble.

Never mind. I learn you can instead buy kid/beard-friendly protective suits (as used by the Israeli Defence Forces), a pocket parachute for $840 or some potassium iodide pills to pop after a radiological attack.

At nursery drop-off today, the subject of conversation is 'terror'. Someone heard a terrorism expert on the radio earlier. 'His daughter and grandchildren lived in DC and he said he was concerned for their safety and worried about terrorists. But he was actually more worried about drunken drivers and 19-year-old boys!' We all laugh, pondering for a moment on the evils of 19-year-old boys.

'Is that Vietnam vet still doing the siege downtown?' (A North Carolina tobacco farmer is holed up on The Mall for the second day. He sits in his tractor in a pond, claiming to have explosives and muttering about Waco as negotiators try to end the stand-off.)

'If he was an Arab he would have been blown away by now,' a mother says matter-of-factly. We all agree.

Saddam naturally scorns the Bush ultimatum to leave Iraq. Everyone is getting jittery. 'Do you have in extra food and water? I would stock up on batteries now and keep the car full of gas.' War feels ominously inevitable.

'I didn't know if anyone would come today,' says the ballet teacher. 'I thought people would be worried.' But most of us show up as usual. What can you do?

A *New York Times* piece says that 46 per cent of Americans consider themselves evangelical or born again Christians and 68 per cent believe in the devil. All feels a bit depressing so I put down the paper and switch on the TV. Nothing much to watch tonight except war specials and *American Idol*. Then a news flash – the sirens are going off in Baghdad. The 'target of opportunity' for US missiles appears to be Saddam himself.

The diner is quiet tonight, not the usual happy crowd of children in for a milkshake and a spin on the old-style fruit machines. War news is on the TV and I feel the urge to keep reading the subtitles. A man comes in for a burger and asks if he can watch the basketball instead. The waitress switches over to find the sports channel has abandoned its normal schedule and is running war news as well. 'Guess I'll have to watch the war instead,' he sighs. As we drive home, there are discussions on the radio about evacuation plans and emergency preparedness.

School sends out information on their emergency procedures. They are getting in extra water, snacks and torches. The Fox TV channel has gone to war, so *Married by America* (where viewers vote on which couple gets married) is put on hold.

At the weekend, we meet some friends at a council-run farm south of the city. It's near Andrews Air Force base and helicopters hover overhead. We stroke some ponies and chase a few chickens before asking when we can feed the animals and milk the cows. 'It is all cancelled,' the ranger says. 'We have been told not to do any activities today because of the war.' On the way back, we pass a bridge over the Potomac river between Virginia and Washington DC. There are two police cars at each end and officers on the bridge. Helicopters are overhead. They must think it is a terrorist target. The radio says US forces captured by Iraqis are being paraded on TV.

The cherry blossoms are in bloom and people pour in to nearby Kenwood park to admire the flowers and to take family photos. Little girls are in velvet dresses with bows in their hair, fresh from church, and the boys have their hair combed flat. Some lay out picnics and children set up tables in the street selling homemade lemonade. It's the same idyllic scene every year, a local tradition, a celebration of spring. The tulips and azaleas are coming out. Stars and stripes fly outside some homes, others have seasonal flags – flowers or beach scenes with lighthouses. But one thing is different this time: many of the trees have yellow ribbons tied to them for the soldiers in Iraq.

Drive a little further from home into Maryland or Virginia, and 'Support Our Troops' signs are outside every roadside restaurant.

Darryl Worley has stormed the country music charts with *Have You Forgotten?*, a song defending the war and invoking memories of 9/11.

'I hear people say we don't need this war
I say there's some things worth fighting for
What about our freedom and this piece of ground
We didn't get to keep 'em by backing down...'

Chapter 10:
Sisterhood

IT IS A BEAUTIFUL spring day, electric lawnmowers and grass blowers roaring in the distance.

Mothers in black lycra sit outside the bookshop with their soy lattes, lightly perspiring from running the trails behind their specially designed jogging buggies. The toddlers munch on bread from the nearby bagel bakery. The mothers don't seem to eat much but there is always the 'sport' bagel. This is the extra healthy option for those who exercise for America. Obesity isn't an issue for the educated and comfortably off. These are 'hold the butter', 'hold the mayo', no fat, no carbs kind of girls. It must make it so much easier deciding what to eat. As well as the 'sport', the nearby bagel shop sells: plain, poppy, sesame, multigrain, black and white, tomato basil, everything, pumperknickel, cinnamon raisin, onion, garlic, salt, blueberry, orange cranberry, granola, honey wheat, banana-nut, chocolate chip, egg. And that's before the specials like lemon poppyseed, coconut almond, apple cinnamon, raspberry cranberry or spinach and cheddar.

Then you have to decide what to have on it. Cream cheese with salad, smoked salmon or walnuts, pastrami, egg, peanut butter, jelly, swiss cheese – there's more – or a combination of the above, one toasted, one not toasted, oh, and make that one with the pizza topping.

The form is to know what you want, say it with conviction and shout to be heard over the noise of the kitchens and the street outside. To ensure understanding, never say 'blueberry', always 'blue*berry*'. If desperate, point and yell 'that purple one, please!'

Plain, poppy and sesame are the conservative varieties usually produced for a baby shower. Traditionally held before the baby is born (the superstitious do it after), this is a welcome opportunity for the exhausted mother-to-be to sit in state, nibbling at the freshly bought bagels and home baking.

A few days before such an occasion, I ask the hostess what I should bring. 'Oh nothing,' she replies, 'I've got it all covered.' But as I walk up the path, other guests are carrying trays of homemade cookies with baby motifs, exotic fruit salads and speciality baked egg breakfast dishes.

'Oh dear, I didn't bring anything,' I say apologetically.

'I *always* bake for a baby shower,' smiles the cookie lady.

They also carry something else I don't have, a shiny pastel-coloured carrier bag with a present, gift wrapped in colour co-ordinated tissue and ribbons. I have a small baby toy I wrapped at home.

Everyone else seems to be wearing bright whites, big floral prints and make-up for the occasion. I am in my T-shirt and jeans from dropping off at nursery school.

The food is proudly set down on a table already groaning with bagels, muffins and fruit, the catering size coffee machine gurgling in the background. The best china is out.

A nearby table is piled high with presents. Mine looks so sad and tiny I wonder whether to take it home again, but there is nowhere to hide it until then. I pop it on the table when no one is looking. Expect they will be opened later anyway, that's what kids seem to do at parties here.

I skipped breakfast for the occasion and am starving but no one else seems to be touching more than a few pieces of watermelon. I hope they won't notice how much I'm eating if I only have a little piece of food on my plate at any time.

I spot Gail walking in with a plate of food. She sympathises. 'Don't worry, Anne, it's really fine. Let me introduce you to some people.' The main topic of conversation is trauma of childbirth and I make a big impression on several mothers for having 'natural births'.

'No,' I correct them, 'I had pain relief.'

'Of course you did honey, but you didn't have a C-section like I did. We call that natural.'

All is going well when the host calls for hush. 'Now time to open your beautiful gifts, ladies.' The first is a head-to-toe outfit in neutral, unisex colours. 'It's adorable,' everyone agrees. More perfectly presented gifts follow. The softest blankets with embroidered motifs, more outfits and even more outfits. Then the mother-to-be spots a tiny crumpled ball on the table. 'Who is this from?' she asks. I own up. There is a hush as she opens it. Gail loyally breaks the silence with the words, 'Anne, it's adorable.'

After the excesses of the morning, I decide to buy lunch for the first homeless person I see. Only problem is, I can't find one. Even the Vietnam vet with a bad leg on Wisconsin Avenue (a neighbour claims he is a fake anyway) isn't about today.

My new tough love policy on baby showers is never to bring food – too much goes to waste anyway – and to give the present after the birth at a less public moment.

Weeks later, I finally find a homeless man outside the multi-storey car park who says he would love lunch from Chicken Out Rotisserie.

Our first school bake sale, and everyone is asked to contribute to raise money for school funds. I drop off some cupcakes made by the girls, a bit squished from the journey to school, in the designated room. It is a sight to behold – cake heaven. Brownies, individually wrapped and tied with ribbon, 'baked goods' piled high in wicker presentation baskets with bows and wrapped in coloured Cellophane. I comfort myself with the thought that no one will know who made what (don't think anyone saw me go in) and the kids will all buy the cupcakes because they have M&M sweets on top.

I bump into Kathleen in the corridor and compare notes. 'Don't feel bad Anne.' She whispers, 'What you don't know is who used a mix from the Giant and who got the babysitter to make it.'

I decide to bake a cake for a neighbour who has been in hospital. Yes, the sort of thing which a 1950s American housewife would do, but hopefully a welcome gesture. I walk up the steps bearing the still warm banana bread in a brown paper bag. At the same moment a car pulls up and the mom at the wheel directs her beautiful, rosy cheeked children to carry in 'the dinner'. The food (smells like lasagne) is in matching dishes, neatly topped with foil and looks like enough for several meals. I open the door to let them in – maybe my cake will do for pudding. But there is more to come. Carried triumphantly up the steps is a perfect, golden cake shaped like a heart. I just can't keep up with these women.

'What did you do before you had kids?' I regularly ask. The mother cleaning the loos at nursery school was a top flight lawyer. A helper at the Halloween party is a former CIA analyst. The soccer mom ferrying children in her people carrier was a television journalist. Many would love to go back part time but the workaholic American workplace doesn't make it easy. 'I tried to keep working after my first baby,' is a common reply. 'But they didn't like it that I couldn't still stay late every night.' Everyone seems to know someone who had a scheduled C-section and went back to work weeks after the birth.

So, how does an educated and talented former career woman fill her time when she is not looking after the children and baking? In suburbia, she volunteers. At school you can be a room parent, a reading helper, a field trip chaperone, organise after school clubs, fun runs, teachers' appreciation lunches, bake sales, book sales, international nights, book shop events, the fete, the drama production, picnics, 'sock hop' dances (so named because you used to have to take your shoes off in the school gym) or sign up for a sub committee. Sometimes there is a special date to celebrate, such as the school's anniversary. This ends with a 'hug around the school' (linking hands around the building and singing happy birthday). Then there is the local community, where a respectable number of men chip in some hours too. It needs 'block captains' to deliver flyers, organisers for social events like the Fourth of July, fundraisers for an even newer, even better playground in the park, members of neighbourhood committees, newsletter editors, planning watchdogs, tree planting organisers and sports coaches. And that's before any of the charities ('non-profits') in town have got wind of your skills.

It is Mother's Day and children are walking to school in 'I love Mom' T-shirts without a hint of embarrassment. I wonder how many moms have been given the lavish gifts advertised in previous weeks by the department stores – perfume, clothes, chocolates. A quick straw poll tells me quite a few. Someone even has a foreign weekend away and everyone seems to be going out to dinner. The nursery school kids are rehearsed to sing a mass version of *You are my Sunshine* to the assembled mothers before serving them a home-made tea. All a bit American and cheesy, I think to myself, before being embarrassingly overcome with emotion at the sight of a chaotic, ragtag bunch of children, whose ancestors came from around the globe, singing their little hearts out.

Later, I drive straight past my turning on Wisconsin Avenue, distracted by the bumper sticker on the car in front. It reads, 'Mommy. The most rewarding career I've ever had.' Other stickers on the giant 4x4 say 'Bush/Cheney' and the name of an exclusive Washington school.

Whoopee. We have been downgraded in the terrorism stakes from Code Orange to Code Yellow, 'elevated risk'. But why does a military plane keep flying very low over our house? I decide to stop having conversations with conspiracy theorists or to watch any more reruns of the *X-Files*. It is making me paranoid. Sally emails a piece she has found on the internet about dodgy CIA practices. As I read it, another military plane flies overhead. The CIA headquarters is only a short flight away, just over the Potomac River in Langley, Virginia.

It's early June and the end of school is approaching, the long summer holidays stretching ahead. The kids have pool parties, eat popcorn and ice cream, watch movies and play board games, bringing in T-shirts for classmates to autograph. Those who will be leaving elementary school this year have an official 'graduation' and write down their hopes for the future. Many of the girls want children, cats, dogs and a house in the suburbs. It's what they know, after all. But, encouragingly, they also want to be a doctor, an architect, an actress, a soccer player, a designer and the first woman president.

On the last day, the safety patrols give out candy and parents follow their kids down the street with video cameras. A Montgomery County letter comes home in the school backpack along with squashed artwork and leftover sweets. It tells us to prepare for bioterrorism. Apparently, we still need to be afraid.

The long summer holidays, from mid June until the end of August, have begun and for most kids that means camp. My first camp conversation was in January.

'So, what camps are you thinking of signing up for?' Claire had asked.

'Isn't it a little early to be planning the summer?' I suggested.

But apparently not. The schools and clubs running camps already had their websites up and the ads were starting to appear in parenting magazines. Time to do some research, before all the spots were taken. Overwhelmed by choice, I suggested to Claire, my trusted advisor on such matters, that maybe we could just opt out of camp. 'Sure you can,' she said cheerily, 'if you don't mind two and a half months of full-time childcare. Make that three months for pre-schoolers.'

For the over eights there are the sleepaway camps where kids get back to nature and brush up on their survival skills. 'Everyone comes home with head lice, ticks and mosquito bites,' a veteran camp mom, Elaine, tells me. Kids can go on wilderness expeditions, sailing with whales, rock climbing, water skiing, white water rafting or horse riding. The public library has books about children who don't want to go to overnight camp but end up loving it in the end.

For younger ones and the more faint hearted, there are daytime options. Non-stop sport – soccer, basketball, dodgeball, kickball, swimming, volleyball, softball, field hockey, lacrosse, baseball, basketball – or dance, cheerleading, drama, cooking and art. I rule out camps which include Bible Studies and gasp at the details of the modelling camp for the over fives. It boasts of 'instruction in modeling and fashion, social graces and etiquette, personal style and personal grooming... runway techniques... makeup application'.

All those exciting possibilities and what are we doing? The cheap, informal, multi-activity ones close to home that friends are doing, that's what.

It is the first day of camp and the parents are all congregated in the park with their offspring, waiting for the yellow school bus. The children are all dressed in shorts and T-shirts, with sun lotion and bug spray on, baseball caps, sports stuff and lunch in their backpacks. The camp counsellors, all-American college kids, check them off the list and give out enthusiastic high fives. For a lot of the five and six-year-olds, it's their first time and the parents wave and blink back a tear as the bus drives off to the activity centre. With this camp, though, they will all be back by three o'clock. Or even noon.

'What did you do yesterday?' I ask a neighbour.

'Oh, we had some Mommy time.'

This turns out to be an outing with just mother and daughter, traditionally cruising the shops together and doing lunch. Dads and sons have to stay out of this one, giving them the opportunity to shoot some hoops, watch the game on TV and eat junk.

It is a wet, windy afternoon and I'm sipping tea while people watching at a piano bar in Chicago, where we have gone for the weekend. A girl, I guess aged about nine, walks in wearing a grey, woollen coat and a beret. She carries a clutch of shopping bags, all with 'American Girl' written on them and a large doll. She is quite old for a doll, I think as I have a closer look. It has a brown bob, the same as its owner, and it is wearing an identical outfit. Another girl follows, with long blonde hair... the same as her doll. Behind them trip mothers with coiffured hair and heels. This must be high end mommy time, I conclude, and there is a whole industry built around it.

At the American Girl Place in LA, Chicago and New York you can dine at the elegant café, sitting your doll at the table in their 'treat seat', nibbling at cinnamon buns or pan-seared salmon. Pop into the theatre and you can see *Circle of Friends: An American Girl Musical*, before buying some outfits for you both.

There's a philosophical split among friends on the merits of choosing a doll with your own physical characteristics, then dressing like it, all at great cost. I am in the camp that finds the concept decidedly spooky – a bit like wearing the same clothes as your mother. But defenders point out that you don't have to get a look-a-like doll, that you can dress it in historical clothes and that even the public library stocks the popular American Girl books, which place fictional characters in different periods of history. Would a 'British Girl Place' take off? I can't quite see it.

There is a cheaper, trashier operation – Club Libby Lou – targeting tweens and under. Walking past a shop in the mall, I am transfixed by a baby-faced little girl staring out of the window. She has black eyeliner, green eye shadow, dark lipstick and gelled hair, a gothic version of a little girl pageant queen. But the experience is all meant to be good, clean fun, a 'sassy' party venue – get a makeover, become a 'VIP' (Very Important Princess), create a potion in Libby's Lab, be a rock star in the Style Studio. And you know the girls love it.

Is there any escape from all this? On a fine autumn afternoon in the park, girls and boys barely out of nappies and in oversized little league T-shirts chase the football. Later, when school is out, it is soccer as far as the eye can see. Today, the boys are doing soccer and T-ball (junior baseball), the girls single-sex soccer, the ages ranging from five right through to mid-teens. It is a sea of bobbing ponytails and parent-volunteer coaches licking their teams into shape.

This is just the practice. Games are at the weekend, when the serious 'soccer moms' come out to play. 'That is a good idea,' I concede to a parent who has brought a fold-up chair, with drink holder. Today, they have sunhat and sun cream (next week it might be an umbrella for light rain), mobile to make calls while watching and a book for when there's not much action. At the half time water break I spot one team which has a giant cool box filled with cold drink and snacks. The organisation of Amalie's team of six and seven-year-olds is a bit more haphazard but at least we have all remembered the girls' water bottles. One mom is clicking away with her knitting needles – the perfect occupation because you are still doing something but can watch the game at the same time. Reading the paper is fine, you just have to keep glancing up. 'I always bring my camera,' one old hand confides. 'You never know when that special shot is coming.'

'Has anyone remembered the team snacks?' Someone has. Luckily it is granola (cereal) bars which will make us look good next to the team with its own cool box.

'Look, they have their own bandanas,' one of the girls says. Sure enough, the players are wearing identical headscarves which match their kit.

Every so often, the local amateur sports league feels the need to remind the parents of their place. 'The Coach is responsible for the spirit of the game by being enthusiastic and patient, and by letting the children play their own game.' It is recommended that a volunteer parent be trained as Game Leader, to 'facilitate fun and the flow of the game'. And soccer moms and dads, watch your step: 'Spectators should support all of the children on the field with positive and enthusiastic comments, enjoy the company of other spectators, and leave the instruction to the coach.'

Friday, and the rain clouds are gathering. Better check the weather forecast. Looks like rain in the night. By morning it has nearly stopped but our 9am game for little girls is cancelled. Montgomery County Park and Permit Office, which runs the pitches, prohibits use of its sports fields 'in the cases of standing water, spongy grass conditions and possibility of lightning'. There's no chucking your kids out in the mud and rain here.

Tonight we head along to the local high school for an American football match with some neighbours whose son is a student there. This is the 'Homecoming Game', when former pupils traditionally join the crowd, the school band plays and students are crowned the homecoming king and queen. As we arrive, the dads are taking entrance money, the mothers are selling hot dogs and popcorn. The 'Pom' squad in their cheerleader outfits are working the crowd, selling homemade brownies, and more parents are manning the merchandise table, offering team T-shirts and teddies.

The excitement is mounting, families of players, band members and cheerleaders fill the stand and students, some with face paint and spray painted hair in team colours, pack the front rows. It's just like in the movies.

We are reminded that the All Sports Booster Club raises $10,000 a year, through plant sales, concessions and merchandise, contributing to athletic programmes and supplementing the county budget. The school has 16 teams, with more than 800 students taking part.

'A big thanks you to parents, teachers and staff for grillin' and chillin'!' says the compère. 'Get your popcorn-filled megaphone now – with free refills! Don't forget, tomorrow is the annual 'mums (chrysanthemums) and pansies sale, in front of the school from 9 until 2!'

Time to read the programme while *We Will Rock You* plays on the sound system. The senior American football team has a squad of more than 40 with seven coaching staff. They are listed by position, height (the tallest is 6ft 7in), weight (the heaviest, 290 lbs) and school grade. The junior team has even more members and a few tiddlers (115 lbs and 5ft 1in tall). The senior and junior cheerleaders also get a name check but no vital statistics. They are already in action, getting team chants going with a few dance moves and some gentle acrobatics. They are an encouragingly honest mix of teenage girls, all shapes, sizes and colours, not a slim blonde among them.

The school 'pep band', with members of the symphonic and concert groups, is on the pitch now to play the national anthem. Everyone stands and the dancers put their pom poms on their hearts. Each player's name and position is announced as they run onto the pitch through a line of cheerleaders, the crowd whooping and cheering. The announcer reminds everyone to promote good sportsmanship and fans are urged not to use bad language – 'be a positive fan and not a fanatic'.

I lose track of what is happening in the game but I do know that the home team is winning at half time. The band goes onto the field, playing popular classics. Then, effortlessly, they move into positions which form giant, human team initials before the pom dancers do their thing to a chart song.

Now the student government association presents the 'Homecoming Court'. On to the pitch walk four couples from each of the four years – seniors, juniors, sophomores and freshmen (aged 14 to 18). Each couple's biog is read out as they enter. 'Sharon is the leader of the Jewish committee and captain of the varsity cheerleaders,' says the announcer. 'John is a soccer player and does community work. He is the son of....' Looks do seem to count this time, the girls mostly have long glossy hair and short skirts, the boys all sporty.

When the results of their classmates' votes are announced, there are cheers and roses. The winning senior couple – he is in a corporate suit and she is from the Bible studies group – get to carry flowers and wear faux crowns for the rest of the night.

'She is such a cheerleader' is a phrase still used to describe a bitchy bimbo, the good looking airhead type, out to sleep with the quarterback. But is this stereotype of one of the symbols of American womanhood fair? I expect the worst when I speak to former cheerleaders of the Philadelphia Eagles American football team. The reason is an article about a peeping tom scandal. They claim evidence that for years, players and bosses have been spying on them in a state of undress, from peepholes in the next-door, away team, changing room. Their attorney Michael McKenna believes this legal action highlights the wider problem here of men in sport failing to respect the rights of women. 'The motivation for this case was anger and a desire not just to be the victim,' he says. 'What galvanized 120 women was that they were made a joke and the players laughed it off saying, "they are just cheerleaders". But they have more pride.' I am astonished to find that in the ranks of the former cheerleaders are lawyers, teachers, a neuro-psychologist, a vet and a US marine. Actress Renee Spei says she wanted to be a cheerleader to entertain fans and be involved in charity and community work. Pay was as little as $30 a game. Despite the dodgy stereotype, it turns out there are still more than three million cheerleaders in the US, from high school to professional sports, with a huge industry of competitions, camps and costumes. Defenders say that these days the successful ones who compete in the 'sport' are talented gymnasts.

It is my first professional American football game, at the Washington Redskins' home ground. Camper vans, pick-up trucks and SUVs fill the car park. Fans who have arrived hours before kick-off gather around open boots which are full of cold beer and food. The barbecues, tables and deck-chairs are out. This is tailgating. Team colours are everywhere and the music from different sound systems changes from country to rock as you walk towards the stadium.

From the stands, I am anxious to check out these cheerleaders. The men make a few fatuous comments about them having 'too many clothes on' (it is freezing so they have tight lycra instead of bare skin) but as soon as the game starts the crowd seem completely oblivious to their presence, even as they go through their routines on the touchline during breaks in play. Sorry girls, you may be pleasing dancers with long flowing locks, perfect figures and honey coloured skin but the red blooded American male wants to watch the game more than you.

If it wasn't for immigrants, no one round here would get a haircut. Did everyone wander around Capitol Hill with overgrown, sticking-out hair or were homegrown Americans in the trade before? First and second generations from the Philippines snip away in the budget joints along with co-workers from Vietnam, Europe and Latin America. The barbers' shop is dominated by male customers talking sports and kids smartening up for a special event. (The hairdressing salons allow men too but are controlled by women.)

The talk today, as usual, is about relationships. This is therapy with a blow dry. The perfectly manicured woman under the dryer, in her 30s, is blinking back the tears. She addresses us all. 'Last night I said to my boyfriend – we've been together a year, y'know – "listen, I need to know if this is for years or weeks". At first he says nothing and then he just looks at me and says, "weeks". I am devastated.' Her voice breaks and she takes a comforting sip from her grande Starbucks.

'What kind of guy would say something like that?' says her hairdresser.

'Quite a few, honey,' says an experienced 50-year-old, her head covered in tin foil for her highlights.

'Sounds like you are better off without him,' another hairdresser volunteers.

'But I want to marry him,' she wails. Oh dear.

Meanwhile a woman with bouffant hair and a business suit walks in, a man, also in a business suit, trailing behind her. He obediently sits in the chair while his partner and the hairdresser talk at length over his head. 'The last cut was really awful. We have to do something about these bangs,' she tugs at his fringe and the hairdresser nods vigorously in agreement. They continue to pull, poke and discuss. The man doesn't say a word, he has given up the fight. His hair is not his own.

The dinner party conversation tonight is of a male friend who has yet to find a life partner. 'The thing is, he's Jewish,' says one (also Jewish) guest. 'And he hates painted toenails. So that rules out all the Jewish women.' I look down at the toes of the women near me, who happen to be Jewish, and sure enough, all have glossy, immaculate paint. I spend the next week looking at other women's feet. I don't find any women who I know to be Jewish with naked toenails. But the Catholics and Baptists also seem to go for the painted look too. It is just the odd scruffy Brit who has no paint, or chipped, leftover varnish.

'I can't believe you haven't had a pedicure, since you have been living in America,' says Claire. 'It is so much fun. We must go.'

So here we are, bustled into big chairs with foot basins by beaming Filipino women in white coats. All around are women snatching a moment away from work or family to be washed, massaged, chiselled and painted. Hands free for mobile phone and Starbucks, 16 conversations seem to be going on at once.

'So when can we schedule this meeting?...'

'How is Dad?....I'll bring a side – how about a potato salad?'

Some are catching up on *People* magazine (gossip and celebs) and one woman appears to be fast asleep. We are whizzing along, flopping down the salon in supplied flip flops to the air dryers. 'It will last for weeks!' Claire assures me as she rushes off to pick up her daughter from Hebrew school. The experience is well worth the $20, plus tip, I decide, looking down at my feet, transformed to perfect softness and with dark red paint. Perhaps now I will get mistaken for an American.

'I went to a dinner party the other night and some of the other women said they were on anti-anxiety pills,' Sonya says in hushed tones. 'They pop them before big events for their kids like a sports game or when they are hosting a barbecue or going to a family reunion.' She had no idea this was going on.

I ask other mothers, who always seem to keep smiling through school volunteering, driving between endless activities and going to the gym, if they take anything. All say 'no!' and laugh it off, though a few add, 'but I know people who do'.

Sonya has a new baby and three other kids. She diets, runs on the home treadmill when the baby is asleep, ferries the others to their classes and is up at midnight doing her emails, all on four hours' sleep. It inevitably all gets too much. What makes a normal, grounded woman with a sense of humour push herself so hard to achieve perfection? The unspoken pressure for women in suburbia to conform?

When *Desperate Housewives* – billed as a darkly comic take on the secret lives of suburbia – starts on TV I watch carefully for real life parallels. I can certainly see echoes of Lynette, the harassed mother who gave up her career to be a stay-at-home-mom, and Bree, who strives for Martha Stewart-style perfection in every way. But I don't know anyone married to a crook or having an affair with the gardener. At least I don't think I do.

The thing about those 'perfect' American housewives is you never know what is going on behind closed doors. Take Mary Stalcup Markward, a mother and homemaker from Fairfax County just outside Washington DC. In 1951, a time of anti-Communist frenzy, she appeared before the House Committee on Un-American Activities and gave the names of 240 past and present Communist Party members. For seven years she posed as a loyal supporter. No one had a clue that she was really a spy.

Away from the city, a woman's lot is hard in different ways. In small town West Virginia, a state promoted as 'wild and wonderful', traditional wooden houses and trailer homes sit amidst the autumn trees. Artists have moved in, setting up shop to sell paintings, furniture and stained glass. But the second hand store remains, with 'lay away' options for those who can't afford to pay all at once. The church on the main street has a tombstone for those who have died from abortion. A roadside meeting house has a billboard, one side welcoming everyone in, the other saying 'all men and women are sinners'. It is tough out there.

On another weekend excursion, we head for Lancaster County, Pennsylvania. Our bed and breakfast hostess appears from the kitchen with homemade cookies and wearing a Mickey Mouse T-shirt. The old-fashioned drawing room is all antiques and lace. On the coffee table are family wedding photos and *The Daily Prayer Book*, a Labrador lying underneath. Nearby is a giant wide-screen TV.

At the local farmers' market, the Amish girls wearing blue dresses and overalls with pinned-up hair serve alongside neighbours dressed in jeans, with perms and make-up. Later, Keith, a local who shows visitors his home county, takes us on a horse and cart ride around the Amish farms. He has grown up with them and praises their hard work and quest for the simple life. A black, horse-drawn buggy goes by and we glimpse a family wearing straw hats and bonnets squeezed inside. Keith waves at his friends. 'I'd be Amish if I didn't like my beer so much,' he says with a hint of sadness.

Luke and Mary are an Amish couple who welcome visitors into their home to learn about their religion and culture. On the wall of the modern, self-built home is a family tree and birthday chart to help them remember dates for their ten children and more than 30 grandchildren. They still plough the land with mules, and Mary, who wears a white lace cap and whose dress is held together by pins, makes patchwork quilts by hand. The guests are a group of strangers from across America, who all just happened to turn up at the same B&B on the same night – a policeman, a school bus driver, government workers and us. We all sit round the long trestle table in the kitchen, sampling the simple farm cooking and asking questions about their way of life. Luke sits at the head of the table but Mary won't sit down. She bustles around the kitchen and passes the plates to her grand-daughter Rachel, who is washing up. In her mid teens, she tells us she is just about to cut her school days to one a week. The rest of the time she will work. The girls want to know how long her hair is. 'Real long, I never cut it,' she replies shyly. 'It takes forty minutes for me to pile it into a bun.'

Further north, in New York State, Joy Rose has broken away from all the traditional trappings of womanhood. I meet her at home in a blue clapboard house in a New York City commuter town, as part of an article on the 'mom rock' music movement. Family photos cover the walls and her kids' backpacks are on the floor. But she also leads a band, Housewives on Prozac, writing songs about shopping at the mall and cranky children (titles include *Eat Your Damn Spaghetti*). And she leads a movement of performing mothers across America, with entertainers coming together at the annual 'Mamapalooza' festival. Joy says, 'It is happening now because we are global, college-educated women who came out of the feminist movement. We have briefcases and business suits, but when we get into the arena of the home, it has not changed much. In America, once you have a baby it is like you cover your tracks. Forget make-up, deny your sexuality and make life clean, clean, clean. But women are still vital, sexual, passionate beings. Music and motherhood are not mutually exclusive.'

Chapter 11:
Power

A BIG SUMMER storm is on the way. The wind is up and the sky is black; it's only late afternoon but already dark. The lights suddenly go out, lightning or wind hitting the overhead power lines not too far away.

We are supposed to be on the Virginia side of DC by early evening and decide to give it a try – sometimes the storm just passes over. As we drive down our street, the rain comes down in sheets. A tree, taller than the houses, falls across the road, its roots quivering from the impact. The wind is whipping up and branches are flying everywhere. I turn into the next street, more branches flying in front of the car. Manage to turn onto the main road, wipers on high speed, barely able to see the other cars crawling along in the rush hour. The first junction is flooded and the traffic lights are out. All I can hear is the wind, the rain and some sirens in the distance. The normally calm and practical six-year-old in the back seat announces, 'We are all going to die.' It may be sunny in Virginia, but here we seem to be in the eye of the storm. We slowly crawl back, the wind getting higher, the sky as black as night.

Back home, we light some candles and look for torches. Seems like the appropriate moment to get out that packet of biscuits stashed away for the previously predicted bio terror attack.

The doorbell rings. It is Sally carrying a steaming kettle. 'Want some tea?' I fill my teapot. 'I got a gas stove when I moved South (she means to Washington) because of all the storm black outs,' she says cheerfully. 'I remember when it was off for days!' We sit on the steps with the girls, drinking tea and hot chocolate, watching the lightning.

It's 7am the next day and we are wandering around in the half light. The phone rings. 'It's me. You'll be wanting some tea.' Seconds later, Sally is at the door with her kettle. Wearing paint splattered corduroys and a homemade woolly jumper with patches on the sleeves, she is ready for an action-packed day clearing up the debris.

This year, Amalie goes to school on a yellow bus – just like in the movies – while there is rebuilding on the old site. The radio says school is open, the power is on, so we all line up at the bus stop. Parents and nannies compare notes.

'Does anyone have power?' No one does.

'Which roads onto Wisconsin have been cleared?' A few are OK.

'Where are they selling dry ice?' Someone thinks the liquor store has it.

'What do you need dry ice for?' I ask. They tell me it is a steaming block which you put in the refrigerator or freezer to try to prevent the food from going off. It is solid carbon dioxide.

As I wave goodbye to the school bus, Lena comes out to advise me to keep the fridge and freezer door shut for as long as possible.

I hear that central Bethesda has power, but queues at the cafés and restaurants are going to be a mile long. We could really do with a camping stove. I ring round the likely chain stores but everywhere is sold out. What I need is a small independent. Not many of those left in corporate America. Then I remember the little army surplus place and decide to give it a try. Only a five minute drive, past high rise condominiums, garages flying the US flag, coffee shops, steak houses, banks and hotels.

In the window it says 'Support Our Troops'. An old-fashioned showroom dummy models a T-shirt which reads, 'In God we trust. Everyone else gets searched'. There are army issue clothes, Vietnam vet hats, American flags and hunting knives. Everything is black, khaki or camouflage. The staff favour T-shirts that say 'sniper', tattoos and body piercing. 'We have several camping stoves,' says my charming assistant, explaining in detail the fuel needed and the best kind for different hiking situations.

'I can't believe you went in there!' a neighbour says afterwards, clearly amazed that I have come out alive. 'You didn't go in on your own did you?'

'Not exactly,' I reply. 'I took Josie (aged 4) but she was too short to see the weapons and they let her rearrange the camping mugs.'

A few days without hot water and we are all starting to feel grubby. Leah calls. 'Lets take the kids for a swim then we can all shower at the pool.' Great idea. We have a picnic afterwards, trying to use up all the fresh food which is about to go off.

'Do you think this is alright?' I ask, and she sniffs my ham. 'Should the cheese be that colour?'

'I think you should ditch it.'

The power company voicemail says we should be back on in a day or so but there is no guarantee. One neighbour can't stand it any longer and checks into the Hyatt. Still, at least we're not living in Kansas. There, a 6ft wall of water is reported to have picked up a car from a riverside motorway.

The next day, refrigerators whirr back into life and the air-conditioning units roar once more.

Scientists warn that North America is entering a new period of major hurricane activity. The last one to hit this part of the eastern coast was Hurricane Floyd four years ago, causing 56 deaths and $4.5 billion damage. And now Hurricane Isabel is on the way. Early predictions say the storm could reach the maximum category five, strong enough to take off roofs, pick up trees and destroy mobile homes.

People in its path in the Carolinas and Virginia are leaving home and booking into hotels. Ocracoke Island is evacuated, war ships are going out to sea. Isabel is expected to hit Cape Hatteras at the Outer Banks of North Carolina, smash into the mouth of the Chesapeake Bay and push flood water up the Potomac River to Washington DC.

Forecasters say it may slow down but still be potentially devastating. A state of emergency is declared in Maryland, Virginia and North Carolina and hundreds of thousands of people are ordered to evacuate. The power is bound to go again and there is a rush on batteries, torches and candles. Water and tinned food is also going fast. Sandbags are being given out to those near the river but they have run out already. Power workers are being drafted in from across the US – it won't look good to the rest of the world if the US capital is without electricity for too long.

Sally isn't worried. She recalls a hurricane in small town Connecticut where she lived with her family in a rented house on the beach.

'I remember the waves and the wind. The coastguard came by and said you have got to get out. We each packed a suitcase. We had to lean into the wind to walk.' Her advice is practical. 'Turn up your refrigerator before the power goes and make ice. Oh, and bring everything in from the yard that isn't tied down.' Then she adds, 'It's safer to sleep in the basement away from the windows, but the basement could get flooded. Bye.' And off she goes to check that her house is in good shape.

Today is the day. The forecasters say it won't hit until late afternoon at the earliest but no one is taking any chances. The Metro stops at 11am and schools and government offices are shut down. On the coast further south, 100 mph winds and an 8ft sea surge are reported. By 2pm, the rain pours down. The queue snakes round the video shop and back again. 'I'm getting in those classic movies I always wanted to watch,' says the woman next to me. We may not get through much before the power goes, I point out. 'That's true, but we're gonna have to hole up for a while before the worst hits.' We wait an hour to get to the front of the queue but there is nothing much else to do.

On the short drive back, the shops are boarding up their windows and putting down sandbags. People are still coming out of the Giant with trolleys full of food. The radio now says it will hit between 10pm and 2am. Then some advice on what to do. 'If you think your house is going to fall in, get in the bath and put a mattress over your head.' Hmm. Should I have a mattress handy in the bathroom? 'Keep away from windows and glass doors,' they continue. 'Don't go out, because trees will be falling and roads will be flooded.'

Football practice after school is officially cancelled. The kids play at friends' houses nearby, excited by the prospect of being in a hurricane. 'I'm going to stand out in it with my Dad!' (I think her mother might have other ideas). The rain keeps on coming and the wind picks up and then calms down again. The phone calls come from Britain after the story of the impending storm makes it on the ten o'clock news.

Around 9pm, the rain suddenly stops. The neighbourhood glistens under the streetlights and the cicadas are chirruping. There's just a light breeze. The dog walkers come out into the half light. 'The storm is going to kick in in an hour,' one shouts over to me. 'Don't be fooled. Don't drive.' It's getting later but the sky is getting lighter – a weird, pinkish colour. The trees and houses are bathed in the strange light as we wander down our street. Neighbours are parking their cars away from trees and taking painted wooden porch chairs inside.

So, here we go. Have decided against sleeping in the basement because of the likelihood of flooding but the beds are shoved away from the windows up against the walls. Head to bed after a last look at the weather channel.

I am woken up by the clock radio beeping as it loses power. It is 2am but it feels too light. I open the blinds and look out of the window. There's still a pinkish glow in the sky and huge trees are bending wildly in the wind. The usual quiet of the night is broken by the noise of the wind groaning and the sound of cicadas. It feels hot and tropical, strange.

We awake to a darkened house, with windows all still intact and no flooding. Soon, Sally is at the door with a kettle of boiling water for tea. 'Come and use my gas stove if you want to,' she calls as she picks her way over the fallen branches across the street. The dog walkers are already out, doing an early morning reckoning on storm damage. Someone has heard that a tree went into a roof nearby, another knows of cars written off.

We have got off lightly. Winds gusted up to 90 mph and, by the end, the BBC says at least 15 people were killed along the route of the hurricane, mainly by falling trees or car accidents. Nearly four million homes are without electricity along the east coast and damage is estimated at half a billion dollars. Flights were cancelled into the capital and government offices, public transport and schools have all shut down. Parts of Virginia and North Carolina have been declared disaster zones.

Leah is on the phone. She is cruising the debris-strewn streets in the car and reports that traffic lights are out and shops are in the dark. 'The Starbucks at Friendship Heights is shut,' she says breathlessly. 'I'm just going to check out Bethesda.' I hadn't realised just how important that coffee fix was. As I clear away branches with my travel mug by my side, several neighbours, who can barely disguise their desperation, ask a little too urgently, 'Where'd you get that coffee?'

'Oh, it's tea,' is my disappointing reply.

Leah is back on the phone, triumphant. 'The Barnes and Noble Starbucks is open! I'm in the line!' We arrange to meet there with the children. We have had enough of picking up branches and it is too dark and gloomy indoors.

Not many people have to be in work today so motorists are taking their time at the crossroads. The lights are out and the drivers calmly take it in turns to cross. The garage is shut as there is no power for the pumps.

As we walk into highrise Bethesda, with no trees and overhead power lines, the lights come on. The restaurants are all opening for business, the ovens are on in the bagel shop and the book shop is doing a roaring trade. On the top floor, which has the Starbucks franchise, the queue snakes round the bookshelves. Half the neighbourhood is here. Those, like Leah, who have taken their first sip of a grande latte are already looking relaxed, the ones still queueing, well, a little uptight. The kids have all got lucky with muffins and cookies today, a sign of parents' relief at getting through the hurricane intact. And getting their coffee.

Outside, the sky is brightening and people have already bagged an outdoor table for lunch. It's almost a party atmosphere with the dads off work and the kids out of school.

The radio says we could be without power for more than just a few days. The talk turns to dry ice. Lena hears that a liquor store nearby is getting a delivery. But the queues there are even longer than after the last blackout. The local power company has now stopped giving out dry ice, saying the firm that makes it has also lost electricity (you would think that kind of business might have a few generators). But the shopping mall is back open for business.

So you can get clothes, cosmetics and toys, just nothing to stop your food going off.

I start to notice teams of out-of-state power workers in trucks lined up along the roads, some sitting on the grass in the sun. Has no one told them where to go? Sally has an old generator in the basement that she thinks might still work. Dennis in the next street volunteers to have a go. Extension leads are rigged across the road so that when it starts, mine and Sally's fridge freezers will whirr into life simultaneously. Finally, everything is ready and we all wait for the great power surge. Nothing happens. Dennis goes off to check the leads and connections. The kids run backwards and forwards checking progress. In 15 minutes we try again. At first nothing, then the freezer roars into action. The cheers and whoops can be heard several streets way. But ten minutes later it is all over, the generator has conked out.

A neighbour's birthday party, planned before the power cuts, is going ahead anyway. So the babysitter, a cool teenage girl in sweatpants from a few streets away, has no TV, just board games and books by torchlight. We arrive at the party to find the guests sipping cocktails in a garden filled with candles. Generators power the sound system and the dakiri machine.

But as the days go on, anger mounts against the power companies. 'It is like being in the Third World. This is a suburb of the capital of America!' Most of the wealthy North West part of DC, just over the county line from us and within walking distance, has never even lost power. 'Why do we still have so many overhead cables? It's crazy with so many trees and all the summer storms.'

Then generator envy sets in.

'They don't know what it's like, they have a generator. The noise it makes is awful.'

'They aren't home, they've gone to stay with a relative with a generator.'

And generator guilt. 'I'm just bringing round some extra flashlights in case you need them. I feel bad about the guy on dialysis who had to check into a hotel.' Just as things could get nasty, the lights come back on.

I assume they are back in the whole neighbourhood and call

friends to share the jubilation. But their power is still out. With each call, I feel duty bound to invite more children over for a hot dinner and a bath. Everyone asks, 'How is the food in your freezer? Can you fit any more in?' Lacie is cooking all her defrosted minced beef to make Bolognese sauce. An hour later she arrives at the door laden with Tupperware and plastic bags filled with food to squeeze into our freezer. 'We had so much bacon to eat up before it went off,' she sighs. 'The kids will expect a cooked breakfast every day now.' She has just come back from the supermarket. 'I got the last pint of milk. Then I reached over for the yogurt and someone tried to swipe it from my trolley – I couldn't believe it!'

Power is back on at school and it reopens. But the supermarkets are still out of batteries and candles. Heavy rain has flooded many basements and, without power, it has been a job to get them pumped and dried out. Two weeks on, at ballet class, a weary mother-of-three says she is still without power. 'I have so had enough of this...'

Chapter 12:
Divided States of America

IT IS 9.30am in Starbucks in the suburbs. The staff work furiously, never forgetting a courtesy as they go, despite the queue to the door.

'You got it!'

'Anything else for you sir?'

'Have a nice day!'

Five people are already sitting at tables with laptops, another four are doing paperwork. 'Venti Americano (very large, espresso with hot water) please,' says a big man in a big suit. 'I need *all* my shots.' This is the going-to-work crowd. The woman next to me is in a sharp suit and wears an alarming amount of brightly coloured make-up. Everyone quick fires their orders – 'half decaf', 'extra shot', always 'grande' or 'vendi'. Here I come, on my way back from the farmers' market. 'A small, weak filter coffee please.'

The Republican Robert Ehrlich is governor of Maryland now and he has lifted the moratorium on state executions. In the next few months, the first death row inmate since 1998 is likely to be given a lethal injection. The Brady Campaign to Prevent Gun Violence says that last year (2002), 94 children and teenagers in Maryland died from gunfire. Sounds like an awful lot but it does include the mean streets of Baltimore.

I come out of Target, the American equivalent of Primark only bigger, laden with bargains. I'm at an out-of-town mall, 15 minutes drive from home, deeper into commutersville. Everything is more modest here. Lawns are still neatly mown, churches painted white but there is less money. I queue up at the coffee shop for some water. In front are two teenage Latino girls. We get talking about what high school is like. They think London sounds 'cool'. Both have hair like Jennifer Aniston from the TV comedy *Friends*, long and glossy with highlights. They wear the regulation teenage tight vest, baggy sweat pants and flip flops. Life seems good. 'I heard that parents are stricter in England,' says one. I reply that from what I have seen, that's generally true. 'My dad is real strict,' she continues.

Her friend laughs. 'Mine too!' Then, casually, adds, 'My dad has a shotgun in the basement.'

'Yeah,' joins her friend, 'mine has a handgun'.

They smile fondly at the thought of their dear old dads, armed with lethal weapons, as their pick up their grande skinny lattes. The boyfriends, in baggy jeans and bandanas, wait nearby, grinning, unconcerned. 'Good to meet you,' say the charming girls before climbing into a customised saloon car and roaring off.

Read today about a four-year-old boy who shot dead his five-year-old sister with a .45-calibre semiautomatic handgun. His seven-year-old brother was also seriously injured. The children, who lived in neighbouring Prince George's County, were being looked after by their 10-year-old sister. Police are investigating how the little boy got hold of the gun. 'He kept asking if everybody was okay,' said the police spokeswoman.

A neighbour tells the paper, 'This kind of stuff is just something that happens. Unfortunately it happened in our community.'

Meanwhile, recent crime reports for our part of Montgomery County include bicycles stolen from a shop, a flashlight stolen through an open garage door and cash taken from a dentist's office. We are living in a different world. Coming out of the bookshop early one evening, I see something astonishing. A huge, gleaming white stretch limo cruises by. But this is no ordinary one – it's a Hummer. I've never seen anything like this before, so enormous and flashy, and stop to stare. No one else even seems to notice.

The local NBC channel says all homecoming activities and classes have been cancelled at Anacostia Senior High School in South East Washington after 16-year-old student Devin Fowlkes was shot dead outside. DC School Superintendent Paul Vance says, 'I can think of no event as crushing or debilitating to the soul of the school system than for us to lose one of our youngest members, a promising athlete and student, in such a horrific way.'

If my daughters went to high school here, it wouldn't be in an economically deprived and crime-ridden neighbourhood. So, an incident like the Anacostia one would, statistically, be far less likely to happen. But there would be fellow students with guns in their home. And what's to stop an emotionally unbalanced teenager taking it to school and pulling the trigger?

It is Halloween and Captain Kirk from *Star Trek* is at the school bus stop. That night, following the packs of kids to the decorated houses, a piece of cheese and a waffle walk by. A gang of teenage girls stroll past in identical pastel coloured sweat pants and hoodies. They have words like 'sweet' written on their backs and I realise they are pretending to be a packet of Love Hearts. They all seem to be speaking on their mobiles at once, perhaps coordinating a meet with a group dressed as jelly beans down the street. Pass a house with dry ice being pumped out around fake coffins and sounds of screaming on loop.

As the British, consciously or unconsciously, name their children after monarchs (Victoria, Elizabeth, William), Americans do the same with presidents – Madison, Jackson, Lincoln, Cleveland, Reagan, Truman, Jefferson. We have yet to meet a 'Nixon' though.

Thanksgiving is an excuse for another American tradition – the parade. This weekend we are visiting Chicago for the holiday weekend and follow the crowds through the snow flurries for the big event. There are marching bands from high schools all over the Midwest, dressed in military-style uniforms with shiny buttons, the baton twirlers shivering in short skirts. They bang their drums and blow their trumpets, forgetting, for a moment, about their weight problems and teenage spots. These look like the kids who didn't make it into the sports team. Their coaches march, as if they are former military men, alongside. Here come the county sheriffs on horseback. Oh no! The giant balloon of cartoon character Spongebob Squarepants is going to get jammed under the railway bridge. We all crane our necks to see what happens. The team of helpers, whose job it is to hold on to the ropes to stop Spongebob flying to Canada, are pulling with all their strength, squeezing him under the bridge. The parade grinds to a halt, a stern row of policemen stopping the crowd spilling into the road. One last heave and Spongebob disappears under the bridge to loud cheers. It must happen every year.

Next, Chinese dancers swirl past. Then, an unforgettable sight: rows and rows of men and women in red waistcoats pushing lawnmowers in unison. Gleaming machines to keep that lawn pristine, big ones and even bigger ones. And here come the ride-ons, convoys of the best in mowing technology. Where else in the world would a lawnmower store take part in a parade? The crowd cheers and claps. Ernest policemen and army cadets usher us back onto the pavement. 'Keep your children on the sidewalk, Ma'am.' Here comes a giant, inflatable Frosty the Snowman and Rudolph. How on earth are they going to get a giant reindeer under the bridge?

Some cowboys on horseback trot past, behind them smiling walkers in Santa hats. 'Who are they supposed to be?' ask the girls. Then they spot their shovels and wheelie bins. 'They are picking up the poo!' Behind every group of horse riders they come, official shit collectors, so the marching bands don't have to skip over it and miss a step.

A last wave to Santa and it's all over. Now for some famous Chicago deep dish pizza. But where to go for the genuine article? Everyone claims that they, rather than their rivals, invented it. So we try three different restaurants over the weekend. All were delicious and authentic, we conclude as we waddle back to the airport, stuffed full of dough and melted cheese.

In the wealthier suburbs of DC, Christian residents don't do the plastic and gaudy outdoor 'holiday' decorations. Rather, a real tree, beautifully decorated, indoors. But head to the commuter towns at night and the fairy lights are out in abundance, twinkling deer and bells, giant inflatable Santas, snowmen and Disney characters. Whole house fronts are lit up, right through December. 'My neighbour doesn't go on summer vacation,' a resident tells me. 'He spends thousands of dollars on decorating his house for the holidays instead.'

It is the night of the White House holiday party for journalists and we line up outside in the bitter cold in our best frocks and wool coats. Other media, the Secret Service, staff, politicians, dignitaries and donors will be attending a succession of similar occasions. At the first guardhouse into the grounds we have to show our photo ID and get our names checked off the list. I half expect to be refused entry over some accidental state or federal misdemeanour. But no, I'm in, walking through the entrance like one of the cast of *The West Wing*. Past the next check and I start to take in my surroundings. It feels, well, small. We are not allowed into the private presidential quarters or into the West Wing, with the Oval Office and Cabinet Room. But we do stroll through the modest drawing rooms where dozens of presidents have greeted leaders and royalty from around the world. Past the giant nutcrackers, enormous baubles and tinsel everywhere, to the sounds of the Marine band, dressed in red. There's a gingerbread replica of The White House, six feet wide and three feet tall, made by the pastry chefs. Around it in the sugary snow flit characters from *The Three Little Pigs* and *James and the Giant Peach*. The theme this year, chosen by Laura Bush, is a literary one. Amid the ornaments are The Mad Hatter, the characters from *Little Women* and Harry Potter. Chocolate pours out onto the cake illustrating *Charlie and The Chocolate Factory*. The Green Room, an American journalist tells us, is where President James Madison signed the nation's first declaration of war in 1812. This led to British troops setting fire to The White House in 1814. The chattering classes sip eggnog (eggs mixed with sugar, milk or cream with spirits) and sample the fork supper of meats, salads and traditional deserts. 'This was Jackie Kennedy's favourite,' an older hack says wistfully as we wander into The Red Room. It was also, apparently, where the wife of

President Ulysses S. Grant hung a family portrait to show that life was back to normal after the Civil War. Men in uniform are everywhere. They look so clean cut it feels like they should squeak instead of talk. A long queue has casually formed, snaking its way through the party. It is for the ultimate holiday photo opportunity with The President and Mrs Bush. It's not everyday you get to meet a President so, rather sheepishly, we join the line. While making small talk to the ever friendly American press, I run through in my head all the things I want to say to George Bush. How the war in Iraq is a terrible mistake, it is unforgivable that 40 million people have no health insurance and no automatic right to health care, that a gun culture which results in the death of so many innocents cannot possibly be condoned. Just the usual, really. By now, we are getting near the room where the photo will be taken and there are even more soldiers. We are assigned our very own man in uniform to announce our names and to stick very, very close. Are we under even more scrutiny than everyone else because of our foreign accents? Or is it Roland's beard? One inappropriate word and I realise that I will be manhandled out of the room at gunpoint (or worse). My soldier tells me in a firm voice which of us will stand where (I'm beside George). Suddenly we are there, swiftly ushered next to a beaming George and Laura. 'Good evening, how are you?' they say, and snap!, we are off, led out of the room by the military. And what do I do? I grin like a fool. They must have slipped something in the eggnog.

Home for Christmas. We have been waiting around for a while to catch the evening flight from Washington Dulles to London. The staff in the boarding area don't know why we are delayed. Or are they just not saying? The other passengers are mainly British. We are stoical and chat about the American experience and what we are doing for Christmas. The children are too tired to sleep and have had enough of playing cards. Now there are more airline and security staff around than usual and there is noticeable tension in the air. Is this some kind of terrorist alert? More waiting. We have all had enough now. We just want to go home. Then airport police go through the boarding area. It looks like they are heading for the plane. More waiting. It is hours past the scheduled flight time.

Then a group of Virgin Airline staff appear and line up in front of us. Some are fighting back tears. They announce that the flight has been cancelled because the pilot has been taken away by police on suspicion of alcohol consumption. There is a moment's shocked silence from the hundreds of passengers before sighs and groans fill the air. Then, reverting to our national characteristics, we form an orderly line to find out what to do next. The answer is, more waiting. Waiting to reclaim our luggage, waiting in line for a hotel voucher or a cab home. Lucky we are so good at it.

We are back the next day to try all over again, joining endless lines and comparing notes on how long we have been waiting.

'Did you hear one woman missed her own wedding in India?'

'Someone else missed a school reunion they organised.'

'That lady missed her sister's wedding.'

'My husband has a pilot's licence, he could have flown it!' (He points out he has never flown a Boeing 747.)

The radio says security staff had noticed the pilot behaving erratically and smelt alcohol on this breath. Airport police later 'stormed' the cockpit to arrest him and he was expected to be charged with being drunk in charge of an aircraft. Everyone claps politely when we finally take off, 26 hours later.

Back home, there is the comforting round of visits to relatives and friends. The skies are still reassuringly grey, the traffic horrendous, the streets dirty and various politicians are in the doghouse. All the necessary ingredients for conversation in the pub. It feels good to be back.

The return flight is remarkably uneventful but there are changes at US immigration. As part of new security regulations, foreigners on work visas like us need photographs and fingerprints taken when we enter the country. Homeland Security Secretary Tom Ridge says the aim is for the US to be 'open to visitors but closed to terrorists'. The queue snakes round and round the barriers, while US citizens stroll through, the announcer apologising for any delays. The US now has more personal information about me than my home country.

The day after we arrive back, flights to the US are cancelled from Britain, France and Mexico. They think something is going to happen.

It is a week later and *The Washington Post* reports that nuclear scientists with radiation detection equipment have been working undercover in Washington, New York, Las Vegas, Los Angeles and Baltimore. From late December, they apparently scoured the cities for radiological or 'dirty' bombs, taking covert readings with disguised equipment. An Energy Department official is reported as saying, 'Our guys can fit in a sports stadium, a construction site or on Fifth Avenue. Their equipment is configured to look like anybody else's luggage or briefcase.' Goodness.

The crime statistics are out for last year (2003). Police figures say there were 248 killings in Washington DC – more per capita than any other city with a population of 500,000 or more. That makes it worse than Los Angeles or New York City. But at least better than ten years ago when 454 died, many from crack cocaine related violence.

The police chief says guns were used in 77 per cent of last year's deaths, despite the fact that the capital's gun safety laws are tougher than neighbouring districts. (The FBI's Crime in the United States study estimates that 67 per cent of the 16,503 murders in 2003 were committed with firearms.) Local politicians say that 97 percent of guns come from outside the city, 60 per cent from Maryland and Virginia. Just one DC police district, from the South East to Prince George's County, accounted for 66 of the killings. The wealthier, whiter suburbs, over the DC line, are predictably safer, with 21 homicides in Montgomery County.

Big news to cheer everyone up. Joe Gibbs, the coach who took the Washington Redskins to four Super Bowls, is back. Al at the Giant check-out is beside himself with excitement, deep in conversation with a little old lady.

'Remember those glory years? If anyone can bring them back it's Joe Gibbs.'

'I'm real excited too,' she says nodding as she hands over her Giant bonus card and Al packs her cans and vegetables.

'Have a nice day, Ma'am.' He turns to me. 'You know, it's the only thing that unites this city.'

Back at the diner for a teatime treat. A quarter each for the booth-side jukebox and soon *Hound Dog* and *Dancing in the Street* are playing. Order hot dogs and milkshakes and hunt for some more quarters to put in the musical clown machine. He wiggles about and out pop two plastic eggs. One has a martial arts ring inside, the other a plastic wrestler who fits on a finger. The television says the latest Code Orange alert might be going down to yellow. The diner's miniature train chugs over the cooks, who are flipping pancakes and eggs. Snow is on the way, according to the TV presenter. Then, over to the Democrat caucus in Iowa, a key popularity contest for the presidential candidates. It is all about winning over delegates who will vote for them at the nominating convention. There are shots of the front runners, John Kerry, John Edwards and Howard Dean, talking to party activists in school rooms and municipal halls. The hot dogs arrive and the TV is switched to college basketball.

My Big Fat Obnoxious Fiancé starts tonight on the Fox TV Network. Arizona schoolteacher Randi agrees to get engaged to fat geek 'Steve'. They are to be married in three days. If she can persuade her family to sit through the wedding they disapprove of, she gets half a million dollars. She doesn't know what the viewers know: that 'Steve' and his family are all actors – the joke is on her. This is so painful to watch. It is all going to end in a lot of tears.

It is bitterly cold and the comedy hats are coming out – hand knitted tea cosy styles, ones with huge bobbles or enormous earflaps. The kind of hats you wouldn't be seen dead wearing in Britain.

I sit in front of the TV, a log fire roaring, as George Bush gives his State of the Union address. He talks of the war on terror and why invading Iraq was right. He finishes with a letter sent by a child from Rhode Island. 'Dear George W. Bush. If there's anything you know I, Ashley Pearson, age 10, can do to help anyone, please send me a letter and tell me what I can do to save our country.' She adds a PS. 'If you can send a letter to the troops, please put, "Ashley Pearson believes in you".'

Now George says, 'Tonight, Ashley, your message to our troops has just been conveyed. And, yes, you have some duties yourself. Study hard in school, listen to your mom or dad, help someone in need, and when you and your friends see a man or woman in uniform, say "thank you". And, Ashley, while you do your part, all of us here in this great chamber will do our best to keep you and the rest of America safe and free.'

A few days later, off North Capitol Street, not far from the Capitol building where George Bush made his speech, Jahkema 'Princess' Hansen, aged 14, is gunned down by a killer who bursts into her neighbour's home. She had apparently witnessed another killing after starting to hang out in Sursum Corda, a notorious housing estate. The media and the authorities are split. Some say she was trouble, she asked for it, and blame the mother. Others refuse to say it was her fault. Despite everything, Princess was a child who was brutally murdered.

It is not yet the end of January and already in DC two babies have been beaten to death and two other teenagers have been shot dead.

Cruising the dizzying array of television channels on a Friday evening, I stop at Bill's outdoors fishing programme. Bill, who sits on a boat in white baseball cap, sneakers and jeans, has some useful tips about how to tell what is under the water. He is in no hurry and we get some camera shots into the murky depths. Looks like we are waiting for him to catch a fish, so decide to move on. I now appear to be watching a Montgomery County council meeting. Quite difficult to follow, but I think it might be about a planning application. Flick to a very old *Are You Being Served?* in which Mrs Slocombe has a particularly blue rinse. *Keeping Up Appearances* with Hyacinth Bucket is on later and something about the British royal family. On the plastic surgery programme, Elizabeth is having a tummy tuck. The shot moves to a freezing, windswept beach where she gleefully strips off to a bikini in front of her incredulous children. Nothing much seems to be happening in the motorcycle garage on *American Chopper* apart from tattoos and bumpy muscles. Back to Bill, who doesn't seem to have caught anything yet.

Pro-choice marchers crowd onto the National Mall today, defending the Supreme Court's 1973 Roe v Wade ruling which recognises the right to abortion. Driving onto Massachusetts Avenue, I stop behind a people carrier with the bumper sticker: 'Something inside dies after an abortion. Pro – woman, child, life.' It's not the first time I have seen this.

It is the day of the Super Bowl. This year's American football cup final is between the New England Patriots and the Carolinas Panthers. It is apparently the most unpopular day of the year to get married. The supermarkets are hard selling the traditional game food – chilli, corn bread, chips and salsa, hot dogs, ribs and chicken wings. It is a night for cold beer and sodas. The advertisers showcase their new adverts to 140 million primetime viewers – it is all about beer and cars.

But the game is overshadowed by the half time entertainers when Justin Timberlake 'accidentally' exposes Janet Jackson's nipple by ripping off more layers of clothing than planned. It is described as a 'wardrobe malfunction'. Puritanical America is in uproar, and it steals the thunder from the winning Patriots. Feels like double standards when a lingerie advert verging on soft porn or a scantily clad cheerleader is never far from the viewer. Not much left to the imagination there.

'Did you see it?' everyone asks.

'Na, I was flipping the steak on the barbecue.'

'No, I just went to fetch a beer.'

'I was cleaning up the kitchen and missed the whole thing.'

The next day, a star football player is killed at Ballou Senior High School in Southeast Washington. Gunshots could be heard in the cafeteria and hallways. Running back 'J-Rock' was 17. Another student has been arrested.

More people than usual seem to have *The Washingtonian* magazine in their trolleys today at the Giant. Wonder what's in it. At the check-out, I find the cover story is a guide to the top local divorce lawyers. Has it given some of these women ideas or will they be tucking in at the bottom of their jumper drawer, just in case? The other magazines on display indicate that an awful lot of American soap stars still have cellulite. An actress from a sitcom I haven't heard of is having a baby, a former child star is looking anorexic and a star's 'tragic' brother has a coke habit.

'Ma'am, Ma'am,' interrupts the check-out man. 'Can I help you?'

Here we go again. Prepare for snow, ice and school closures. A Washington paper for the homeless reports three deaths in the last month from hypothermia. 'Fathalle Salih, Fidel Cruz and Man Whose Name is Not Known.'

Head to a venue round the Washington Beltway for an article on the health benefits of belly dancing. I find the group of mainly African American women in the back room of a health food shop, near the Credit Union and the dollar bargain store, swaying to the music in sequins and brightly coloured skirts and veils. These are the have-nots, those with either basic or no health insurance, who have turned to dance and a raw food, whole grain diet as an alternative way of addressing fertility related problems and women's conditions like fibroids. The class is full of tales of the unaffordable cost of conventional medicine – $2,000 for a standard fertility valuation, $12,400 for IVF treatment. Elaine, a government worker with insurance, is still left with a percentage of the bill, $300, for a diagnostic scan. Ayanna, a social worker, finds that by taking a year's leave from work to have her baby, her health insurance ends after 60 days. She faces a bill of $618 a month for her and her daughter to be covered.

Last year, seven women in the class had babies, nearly all against the medical odds. Today Pamela proudly passes her seven-month-old daughter round the class. Amazingly, no one is bitter about the cost of healthcare, they just seem grateful they have found a committed advocate of alternative medicine and dance teacher with a $10 class.

Many workers receive health insurance coverage through their employers and most of the elderly are covered by the federal programme Medicare. Of more than 40 million under 65s that don't have health insurance, some low-income people, especially children, receive state administered Medicaid. But, according to independent researchers, even the poorest adults are generally ineligible if they don't have children. Over half of the growing number of uninsured adults have no regular source of healthcare and a fear of high medical bills.

Today I escape from the bitter cold at a 'hot yoga' class. It seems to be the latest thing – yoga in sauna-like conditions – with more people turning up to sweat and stretch every week. I will never be able to get my leg right over my head, I sigh to the woman next to me, immaculately turned out and I guess in her 50s. She looks surprised. Next time our mats are side by side again, I mention the cold weather. She looks surprised again. I assume she is having trouble with my accent.

Later I see Teresa Heinz Kerry, John Kerry's wife, on TV and notice she has a similar facial expression to the yoga lady. In a profile of Mrs Heinz Kerry I read she is a big fan of Botox. Suddenly it all becomes clear and I start seeing more and more women with a permanently surprised expression.

I notice that when some neighbours are sending community emails, they sign off proudly '(block captain)' after their name.

After the Madrid train bombing, I see that the bins are finally removed from the Metro platforms. The voice on the tannoy now says, 'Look out for suspicious packages.' The familiar message makes me homesick for the London Underground. I leave the Metro near the museums and law offices downtown, where the high flying graduates pass by, to find a place I never knew existed before. Through the swing doors of an unassuming building and down a corridor is a room packed with people, chopping, cooking and boxing. Trays are stacked and orders are barked, there is no time to lose. This is DC Central Kitchen, which gives out 4,000 meals a day to the hungry.

I turn up to talk to staff at a catering offshoot of the kitchen which offers rehabilitated drug users, alcoholics and ex-cons the chance to retrain for a career in the food industry. Darrell Jones can't quite believe how his life has changed. Working here is his first ever job, aged 49. Before? 'I lived the street life. I never had a home and stayed with friends or in shelters – whatever I could do to survive. I never had a job. I spent most of my life on the street or in jail for selling drugs or stealing cheques.' The turning point was going to rehab for alcohol and heroin addiction. His colleague Charles Mavins, 40, spent 15 years in jail for armed robbery, a crime committed while he was high on drugs. Everyone has similar stories, a spiral into drugs, alcohol and crime, homelessness, unemployment and poverty seemingly inevitable. After nearly three years in America, I am not surprised that everyone here is black.

Later, I watch them serve at a DC wedding, hired by a bride and groom with a conscience. It is another world and the staff can't quite believe they are in it. Most of the guests have no idea where the charming serving staff have come from. The bartender is a former heroin addict and the waiter serving the canapés has done time for armed robbery.

Channel hopping on TV again, and stop at *Extreme Makeover*. A couple host a party and announce to friends and relatives they are going on the programme. Everyone cries with happiness. Next, as is the tradition on reality TV, they get engaged. And the wedding is to be at the Fairytale Castle, Disney, Orlando, like the one you see at the beginning of films with the fireworks coming out of it. Now the lovebirds, who actually seem sweet people and look simply ordinary, are separated for seven weeks while they have extensive plastic surgery. It is awful to watch, all that pain and suffering and the tears to each other down the phone. The full transformation is kept from us until the big day. To gasps from the congregation, the groom turns and the bride walks up the aisle. They are both completely unrecognisable, turned into Ken and Barbie dolls. How do they know they are marrying the right person?

Go to a kids' film at the cinema and can't help but notice that the goodies are all beautiful, young Americans and the baddies all have English accents. So much for the special relationship.

It's career day at school and the message to our blessed children is that they can do anything. For example, they can be: an anaesthesiologist, an artist, an atomic physicist, an author, a dentist, a media star, an FBI agent, a government lawyer, a NASA aerospace engineer, a Pentagon commander, a pizza restaurant owner, a policeman/woman, a toy shop owner, in sports goods marketing, a TV network executive or a vet. And they are still only at elementary school.

But this does not feel like the land of opportunity for all children. The smiling face of eight-year-old Chelsea Cromartie looks out from the television screen. She was playing with her dolls at her aunt's home in Northeast Washington when a stray bullet came through the window and killed her. No one suggests this little girl is anything other than an innocent victim. She is the 13th child (under 18) to be murdered in DC this year and it is still only May 3rd.

Police storm a school in Prince William County, Virginia, today and arrest a 12-year-old boy dressed in full camouflage gear after an administrator found him with a loaded rifle and two other guns. They believe he wanted to scare or hurt students and take hostages. The guns belonged to his family.

Maryland death row prisoner Steven Oken was killed by lethal injection shortly after 9pm. He had raped and murdered 20-year-old Dawn Marie Garvin. The police got the right man and her family said they wanted him dead. But isn't it worrying that since 1973, more than 100 people have been released from death row in the US after being proved innocent? Former marine Kirk Bloodsworth, now in his forties and a crabber on the Maryland shore, was one of them. He was convicted of the terrible rape and murder of a nine-year-old girl. His fight for DNA testing, which proved his innocence, took nine years, two spent on death row. He still gets choked up when he talks about it. 'Being on death row is like having a terminal illness,' he says. 'You know it is going to kill you very soon. But when it is the Government that is going to kill you for something you did not do – for killing a little girl – that pain is magnified.'

Kirk, a quietly spoken man, describes himself as a patriotic American. But he believes the death penalty cannot continue if the innocent are to be protected. 'People are sitting there right now with a job and a life and suddenly their whole world will be destroyed by this thing we call justice.'

Chapter 13:
Strange Creatures

IT IS 88 degrees today and still only May. At the firehouse, the emergency crew are enjoying the sunshine in their regulation shorts and T-shirts, mowing the lawn, the sprinklers on to keep the grass green. The roadside noticeboard has a new safety message today – 'Don't use a grill on a balcony'.

WTOP radio ('Washington's News, Traffic and Weather') says a northern snakehead fish has been found at a local regional park. It is where we go to ride the miniature train and carousel, watch little league baseball and go ice skating. What is this predator, which eats fish, amphibians, reptiles and insects, and is illegally imported from Japan, doing at an all-American recreational park? Maryland Department of Natural Resources guesses it was an aquarium fish that was dumped after growing too large. With a voracious appetite and weighing up to 15 pounds, this scary fish can even wriggle short distances on land. Officials are draining the pond and blocking off a tributary to the river to search for more snakeheads. A regular at the lake, 70-year-old Sandy, tells WTOP he'll probably go target shooting now he can't fish.

The girls spot it first after weeks of media anticipation, a brown, papery skin stuck to the outside of the house, an exoskeleton so delicately formed it is the exact shape of the bug itself, only with nothing inside. Then another on the mosquito netting and another on a bush. A day later, and they are swarming everywhere. The much heralded Brood X cicada (pronounced si-KAY-da) has emerged, on time, after exactly 17 years.

Jars full of insects arrive at the school bus stop. The winged, red-eyed bugs sit conveniently docile on a child's palm.

'Have you got a girl or a boy? Hold it up to your ear to listen for singing. If it is making a noise it is a male.'

'Ew, you just trod on one!'

'This is George. Oh, he flew away.'

'My dad fried them and ate them.'

'Yuk, that is *so* gross.'

You can't help but like these harmless, bumbling, stupid creatures the size of a prawn, which fly into you by accident. The squeamish are carrying umbrellas for protection.

The more frantic the cicadas get to find a mate (they had been waiting 17 years after all) the louder the singing chorus grows until it becomes a wall of noise when you open the door. This sound, the schoolchildren tell me, is made 'by vibrating the membranes on their abdomen'. I hold the phone outside for callers from Britain to listen.

'What is *that*? It sounds like a plague of locusts!'

No, I am able to correct them, after reading up on the 'Cicada Mania' website. 'They are not locusts. And they are really quite sweet. They don't bite or sting and the only damage they cause is to the weaker branches of trees.' Then I remember to check on our new cicada pets Brian and Basil who are in a shoe box with some leaves in the porch.

'Watch out for them splattering your windscreen,' shouts Haley on her way to work.

'I thought I felt a drop of rain,' I say, surprised as there is not a cloud in sight.

'That,' says Haley gleefully, 'was not rain – it was cicada pee. It is called honeydew.'

The eggs look like a grain of rice. Most of their lives, they are underground, sucking tree roots. When it is time, the nymph crawls up anything they think is a tree and the emerging adult leaves the skin behind. Once their wings dry, they fly off to find a partner, mate and die. It all happens in about six weeks.

A week later, and an old lady waves at us excitedly from her front garden. 'Come over and look at this, kids, there are cicadas everywhere.' Sure enough, every bush, tree and plant pot is covered with red-eyed bugs, piled on top of each other and mating furiously in their very own suburban swingers sex club. Why do they wait 17 years for this much hyped orgy when their cousins do it every couple of years in smaller numbers? One theory is that it allows them to avoid the peak periods of their predators like squirrels, birds, raccoons and possums. Another is that it could be connected to climate.

'I woke up this morning and I could really smell rotting fish,' a neighbour, Carree, tells me in the street. 'Phil came home from a camping trip late last night and I figured he must have left his fishing gear out. But when I opened the back door the smell was real bad and then I saw piles of dead cicadas everywhere.' That will teach them to practise public fornication in God-fearing American suburbia, I mutter. Back home I check at the bottom of our basement steps and find the same rotting pile, with more heaped along the roadside gutter. The smell is disgusting.

Residents are now discussing in the community newsletter theories on the alarming number of dead birds around – it can be a sign of mosquito-born West Nile Virus – but conclude they have probably gorged on too many cicada carcasses. All the dogs are mad for them, the owners having to drag them away before they get sick.

And then, long after they have died, the delicate nymph skins still stick to the mosquito netting, a sad reminder of the funny little bug-eyed, Brood X cicada.

Pop some liquid lavender soap into the supermarket trolley and race to the milk section to get back before nursery school pick-up. A quick look at the soap ingredients as I unpack the shopping reveals more than a list of oils. There is a version of *God Our Eternal Father* by Rudyard Kipling, apparently adapted by the late patriarch of the family run company. Then it details the 'moral ABC'. I appear to have bought 'Made in the USA' religious soap.

'What church do you go to?' a parent asks another at a school meeting that night. They swap names and get talking about the church social scene, the potluck dinners and an upcoming spaghetti and meatballs night. I am hoping no one asks me, as an awkward silence will follow when I reply, 'I don't'. Luckily no one does. They either think I am Jewish or a godless Englishwoman.

Meanwhile, there is a gardening mutiny happening down the street. 'I am not growing vegetables anymore,' Sally announces crossly. 'The opossums and the squirrels just eat them.' She recounts a recent opossum encounter. 'I threw an apple at it to scare it away and it went completely motionless. I was terrified I had killed it. Then I realised it was *playing possum*!'

The opossum, we discover at the library, is a curious creature. It is one of the world's oldest surviving mammals and has the ability to go completely limp and appear dead when attacked. It can keep up this charade for six hours. It has a pointed snout and a long tail and is cousins with the koala. This means it can easily be mistaken for a big furry rat. Neighbours don't like to shout about rat discoveries, and 'I think it was a possum' is sometimes a euphemism. But every so often, the exterminator van appears outside someone's house and you had better be on your guard. I once met a woman who heard scratching in the night and found an enormous rat on her pillow.

Raccoons are another public enemy in the suburbs. There are tales of neighbours watching bushy tailed troops of them heading through their garden at night, on the way to a favourite haunt, and of the critters unlatching house doors and breaking into dustbins in search of human leftovers.

In the hills of West Virginia they shoot raccoons, but in Chevy Chase they have it easy. We just make sure our dustbins are secure.

When it is autumn, suburbanites and urbanites head out to the countryside to appreciate the fall foliage. It is a time for an idyllic walk through the woods with the sun filtering through the burnt orange leaves. But before long, notices start appearing, warning it is 'coon hunting' season. Visitors with small children are advised to stay away from hunting areas. Watching a small friend skipping through the woods in a grey fleece coat, I can see the problem.

The magazine at our cottage rental fills me in on the details. The hunt starts at dusk when raccoons, with their distinctive black faces, come out of their dens to feed and play. According to one fan, 'it has all the drama and music of an opera'. At CoonDawgs.com! you can enter your dog for Coonhound of the Month (ideally submit a photo of snarling dog chasing prey up a tree).

Back in suburbia, a bucket of water is recommended to scare a raccoon away. If they persist in working out how to get into your dustbin, put ammonia soaked rags at the bottom and sprinkle cayenne pepper on the rubbish. They can't stand the smell.

Legend has it that one Chevy Chase neighbour illegally kept a pet lion (nice story but I fail to find evidence this actually happened).

I always thought you had to head to Montana to find serious wildlife but, amazingly, there are between 300 and 400 black bears in Maryland. They don't often make it as far south east as Montgomery County. But if one does, I am reassured to know that a black bear response team is on call 24 hours a day, seven days a week, ready to deal with any emergency.

If one lumbers into the back garden, usually attracted by dustbins or bird feeders, here is what the Maryland Department of Natural Resources advises:

Don't panic Don't shoot! Don't approach it!

*Back away slowly.

*Go inside and wait for the bear to leave.

*Most bears fear people and will leave when they see you. If a bear woofs, snaps its jaws, slaps the ground or brush, or bluff charges: *You are too close!*

*Learn to tolerate bears. Many bears are killed or injured when not causing problems.

We are driving round the National Parks of Wyoming and Montana, a breathtaking landscape of snow-capped mountains, lush forests and crystal clear lakes. Our mode of transport is a camper van ('all the British do that!' laughs an American mother at the school gates before we leave). We think it is pretty cool, shaped like a U-Haul van with beds over the cab and at the back, a mini loo and shower, kitchen, table with seats and a DVD player. The volume is cranked up on *Born to be Wild* as we cruise along the highway, contents of the overhead cupboards rattling furiously.

Here in the mountains, the possibility of coming face to face with a bear is real. Rangers routinely warn campers of recent sightings and patrol the area, checking visitors for bad bear etiquette. 'You know the rules?' asks one, standing before us in an immaculate brown uniform and wide-brimmed hat. Yes, we nod meekly but he solemnly tells us again anyway. The general message is never to keep food in your tent and to store it instead in a building, vehicle or bear proof container. And sloppy campers beware – if you don't clear up the rubbish before bedding down for the night, you are increasing your chances of an unwelcome visitor.

As the sun is sinking behind the mountains at Holland Lake in northwestern Montana, talk among fellow campers turns to the legendary grizzly bear who hangs out in the nearby mountains and comes down to drink. Today is a hot one, 90 degrees, and it is about time he woke up from his nap. We all look through the trees, wondering if he is on his way. Patti, a mother-of-four from Montana, tells her bear story. 'We were at another campsite and a grizzly strayed in and started crashing around outside. I was terrified. I stayed up all night banging a pan to scare it away. No one got any sleep but at least it didn't come in the tent.'

After a cold beer by the lake, watching the sun go down over the mountains, we head back to the campsite. 'Goodnight, see you at the lake in the morning,' everyone says.

Patti starts walking off then runs back for a last, hushed word. 'If the grizzly comes, can we come in your van?'

Over in Montana's Glacier National Park, members of the Blackfeet Nation tell visitors about their culture, politely tolerating the invasion that at least brings some extra money into their otherwise visibly poor economy. Other Indian reservations we have passed through around the country have been similar – trailer homes and shacks with a few roadside stalls selling crafts. There is the occasional sign of grant money in the form of a sparkling new community hall or playground, the odd injection of wealth from the casino business.

Tonight the Blackfeet leader stands on stage, resplendent in feathered headdress, and can hardly stop himself laughing as he talks about how the tourists cope with bears. The young drummers, waiting to perform, are all grinning too. 'One visitor,' says the leader, 'bought some bear repellent and sprayed it on his whole family, then wondered why it made them sick and ruined their clothes. It's supposed to be sprayed at the bear!' (The drummers fall about at the thought of a family of screaming tourists ripping their clothes off.) Then he has a more serious message. 'It isn't hard to live in harmony with them. When we are sleeping outdoors, we string our food up a tree. If we see one, we make a constant noise, like singing, so they know we are there.'

We have our own personal bear encounter at Yellowstone in Wyoming when we spot a little black bear cub frolicking through a wildflower meadow. It doesn't see us watching from the bank above, too busy searching for food, but mom is almost certainly somewhere near. Soon we are joined by other wildlife watchers, who pull up in their vans and cars, wondering what we are looking at. Then a park ranger appears – news of a sighting spreads quickly – to make sure no one gets too close. We don't even need to sing.

School is shut for Memorial Day, and we catch the Metro downtown to go to one of the free museums, spoilt for choice between displays of fine art, science, nature and history. (The Smithsonian Institution is the world's largest museum complex and was born at the request of a wealthy, philanthropic British chemist who died in 1829.)

There's a parade to mark the day and we wander over to have a look. It is the same kind of marching bands, from Wisconsin and Illinois, which were performing in Chicago at Thanksgiving. We weren't planning on staying, but a grandma in the crowd has already found the girls a spot at the front and Vietnam vets give them a handful of American flags to pass around. Today is about remembering veterans from the American Revolution to today. Banners and soldiers represent World War I, World War II, Korea, Vietnam, Iraq and Afghanistan. Mothers' support groups go by, elderly women in their Sunday best, the ones that got left to cope alone.

'Wave at the grandpas!' the kids yell as old boys in blazers and medals pass on trucks. A surprising number of young people are in the crowd, many seem to be students. The ones next to me say they are on a study trip to DC and have stopped off to cheer. War has changed the lives of all the marchers in some way but I wonder how many of them believed in the cause and wanted to fight when they first put on their uniform. There is no counter-demonstration against the Iraq war even though thousands turned out to march at official protests. As the last band goes by, we head off to the Air and Space Museum. 'Why were so many of the grandpas crying?' Amalie asks.

The next morning the gym is full of women, straight from the school run or the doctors' surgery. I notice that an elderly lady who uses a zimmer frame is lifting considerably heavier weights than me. They wear the usual T-shirts, telling where they work, what run they have done or where they went on holiday. A plump, middle aged woman is sweating profusely and is really red in the face. I ask if she is OK. 'Sure,' she says, 'I am sweating to lose weight. My doctor says I have to. My kids are so worried about me.'

A Lycra-clad woman puffs encouragement from an exercise bike. 'You look like you are doing great!' The lady on the leg press puts down her copy of *Newsweek* to add her encouragement.

'I put on weight when I went through a bad divorce,' the red-faced woman continues (now everyone is listening). 'I did it natural – no drugs.' There is a chorus of approval at this great achievement.

'A divorce with no drugs – that's something,' says the bike woman who sounds like she has had first hand experience.

'But you know what happened?' continues our drug-free sister, clutching my arm. 'I ate lots of fruit and put on weight with all that sugar.' The superfit woman on the leg press says she only got slim by cutting out fat and carbs. I say my goodbyes and leave the premises before someone has a heart attack or faints from over-exertion or starvation.

The sunshine brings the joys of a weekend on the Delaware coast. Trolleys are piled high with deckchairs, sun umbrellas, giant cool boxes, toys and sports equipment, and dragged from car to beach.

Small villages of brightly coloured plastic are springing up on the sand. The lifeguards look the same as last year. The guys do their press-ups and sit-ups in the sand before going on shift and the girls keep their hoodies on until the sun gets hot. I worry that they don't wear a sunhat. I fret that there is no sign of sun lotion. An enormous tattooed man is plunging into the surf, oblivious to the dolphin dipping in and out of the water 100 yards away. Go out in a boat and you can be surrounded by them leaping through the waves alongside.

Sharks are out there in the warmer months but they stay in deeper waters. The highest numbers of attacks on humans are in Florida, followed by Hawaii and California. But a few weeks after we leave Cape Cod in Massachusetts, further north up the coast, a 15-foot great white is spotted in shallow water off its shores, unusually close to land.

It's summer camp time again and today there was a kids' talent show. My children came over all British and politely declined to do anything. Acts from the enthusiastic participants include singing the American national anthem and *Oh Susanna*. One keeps a stack of hula hoops swinging round her waist for over a minute. Another kid does a one-handed cartwheel. Everyone thought that was really cool.

Driving up to an outdoor concert in Virginia, there are stewards in fluorescent tabards and cops in mirror shades everywhere. We are ordered to park in exact spots in straight lines. Bottles of water are confiscated at the gate – 'You could have vodka in there, Sir.' But beer and margaritas are on sale on the other side. The uniform tonight is chino shorts and T-shirts or, Hawaiian shirts. After half an hour of sitting obediently in my seat, I come to the conclusion that the only women here with short hair are me, a couple of lesbians and Annie Lennox.

Claire is on the line. She has just moved to Colorado and there is big news. 'I am calling from a *drive thru* Starbucks!' she tells me with undisguised excitement. I can hear traffic and someone saying 'decaf, half-fat, grande, latte' in the background.

Hear that house prices in London are getting crazier but it doesn't feel great here either. Almost one in every five Washington DC households has what the government calls 'severe housing cost burdens'. This means they spend at least 50 per cent of their (usually low) income on housing. The gap between availability and demand for affordable housing has jumped from less than 4,000 to nearly 24,000 in less than a decade, according to the DC Fiscal Policy Institute.

It's too hot out and we are loitering in the children's section of the book shop. They have just had a storytelling and books are everywhere. The place is trashed – there's a huge spill of Cheerios next to the Dr Seuss shelf. The toddler in a pink dress next to us doesn't want to leave. You can feel a tantrum coming on as she stamps her foot and shouts 'no!'. We carry on reading and I assume the mother will pick her up and run out, but no. Her mom is explaining in a gentle voice, 'It is time to go now, sweetie.' Then mom starts singing, 'Bye, bye bookstore, bye, bye bookstore, bye, bye bookstore, bye, bye bookstore.' Now Grandma joins in (the little girl is really yelling now and throws a book) and before long so is Grandpa. Dad appears from the direction of the sports section to add his voice to the 'bye, bye bookstore' song. Finally, he picks her up, kicking and screaming as the whole procession moves off, still calmly singing.

I keep seeing 'VeggieTales' on kids' T-shirts and I'm sure I saw it somewhere in the children's section of the video shop. A cartoon to spread the word about vegetarianism, I wonder? Seems unlikely. The videos are everywhere – must be popular. The blurb says the show stars Bob the Tomato and Larry the Cucumber. I find out it all began in Tennessee with 'the goal of creating values-based family media products'. The first computer animated episode was titled 'Where's God When I'm S-Scared?' By 1998 it was apparently one of the most popular children's video series in the world, moving from Christian retail shops to Wal-Mart. Then out came *Jonah – a VeggieTales Movie!*. The creators say, 'Fans all over the country packed out their local theatres for the biggest fish story ever told by singing vegetables and made Jonah one of the most successful family films of the year.'

Could it be a big seller in the UK? I can't quite see it flying off the shelves in Woolworths.

Chapter 14:
Road Trips

SATURDAY MORNING, and I flick through the radio channels while clearing up the oatmeal and bagel remains. WTOP radio says there's a wreck on the outer loop of the Beltway but vehicles are moving. It's going to be hot. Now onto news of today's game. I move on to NPR and hear raucous laughter and shouting. It can only mean one thing – Click and Clack the Tappet Brothers, hosts of *Car Talk*. Otherwise known as Tom and Ray Magliozzi, the brothers got their nickname from the sound that old cars make. Right now they are giving out maintenance advice – you can almost hear the enthusiastic callers getting the tool box out in the background – reminiscing, telling anecdotes, having a laugh, like we are hanging out at the diner.

It turns out that these guys, who started out as mechanics in Cambridge, Massachusetts, are a national phenomenon. It all began when they went on local radio to discuss car repairs. Their own show followed, then they got picked up by NPR and asked to present a national programme. They are a couple of old timers who now have four million weekly listeners on 588 public radio stations, reflecting a need for nostalgia while nurturing the national love affair with the automobile.

And then there is Dr Gridlock. Twice a week, I skim through the local news sections of *The Washington Post* to find him and his fans, the disgruntled motorists and transport users who want to air their grievances and pass on tips.

'Dear Dr. Gridlock: When tailgated, I keep my right foot on the accelerator to maintain my speed while depressing the brake pedal with my left foot just enough to light my brake lights,' recounts Jan from Olney.

Dr Gridlock himself, Ron Shaffer, strikes a note of caution. 'I don't recommend gimmickry, as it could escalate into road rage. Rather, I'd immediately put on my right turn signal and change lanes as soon as I could.'

Chhaya from Washington complains, 'Despite posted signs indicating that it is unlawful to eat or drink on buses, I see violations of that rule all the time. What concerns me most are the safety issues surrounding the consumption of beverages on moving vehicles.'

Gae of Manassas is after suggestions for a vehicle suitable to transport a double bass. Andrea of Montgomery Village suggests, 'Try a station wagon! I have a 1997 Saturn SW2, and I adore it. It gets excellent gas mileage for a large car, and I can transport an entire troop of Girl Scouts (everyone seat-belted, of course) or a drum kit with no problems.'

Readers want to know where you can buy 'Support Our Troops' yellow ribbon magnets. Joan from Rockville says to try Mid-Pike Plaza while Sandy from Silver Spring suggests Westfield Shoppingtown.

In defence of the big car, Cathy from Oakton writes, 'Safety laws force parents to use minivans, especially if they want to carpool or take the gang to the pool or the movies. That doesn't explain why so many people use big gas guzzlers, but the days of piling lots of kids into the old station wagon are over.'

I've known Elaine quite a while before she makes her confession. We've cruised the thrift stores, laughing at kitsch salsa dishes crafted to look like swimming pools, and tried on silly hats. We've watered each others' plants and fed the fish. She's a New Yorker, made of stern stuff, but there is something she has to tell me.

'I've never driven on the Beltway,' she announces. 'I know others who are the same. I'm terrified of getting on it by mistake. I don't like the entrances and exits and the way some wiggle into each other.' (She is getting into her stride now.) 'The speed everyone drives at is crazy and I hate people who tailgate. Why can't they space themselves out? Nobody signals. And the idea of being broken down...everybody gets killed when they break down!'

I put the kettle on – we both need a cup of tea. I drive on the Beltway out of necessity but I agree with everything she says.

We sit down. 'All the hype on the radio doesn't help,' Elaine says. 'All that talk about wrecks, which seems to be a southern thing for fender bender. And then there is the inner loop, the outer loop and the mixing bowl!' (This is where highways 95, 395 and 495 come together, a mass of criss-crossing, high-speed local and long distance traffic, combined with constant road works. It makes Spaghetti Junction look like a mini roundabout.)

I share my concern about the standard of driving. 'Why do so many people just look straight ahead? Why don't they check their mirrors to see what's going on around them?'

Elaine nods, adding by way of explanation, 'They are worried they could be shot if they risk eye contact.'

And has the increasing popularity of tinted windows changed the tone of the open road? 'You used to have tinted windows on cars if you had something to hide,' she says. 'Then it was for security so the criminals couldn't see in. Now lots of new cars come with them automatically. It looks so sinister.'

Haamid the cabbie is a veteran of driving inside, outside and on the Beltway but I can't get his opinion on road etiquette until we have discussed the day's news. 'Did you hear OBJ on the BBC?' he asks as we pile in, closely followed by, 'What is going on with Tony Blair?'

Political discussion over, we get onto road behaviour. Haamid is usually generous about Americans, but the standard of driving? He shakes his head. 'It's not good,' he says. 'They drive too fast and they don't look.'

Haamid says he never broke the speed limit until one day a passenger was desperate not to miss her plane. She pleaded and he gave in. The Virginia traffic cops were onto him like a shot and soon he was in court, his livelihood and dreams on the line. But the judge was surprisingly lenient, impressed by his previous clean record, his education and his attitude. He let Haamid go with a minor punishment. 'I was so pleased. I stood up and shouted, God bless America!' He still laughs about it, his huge shoulders shaking at the memory. 'God bless America! I said to the judge!'

Around DC, drivers have to contend with huge minivans, whose drivers have no idea you are there, and cross workmen in pick-ups in a big hurry. But as you get further out of town, onto the motorways that cut across the length and breadth of America, there is a worse terror. When you are happily cruising along admiring the scenery, they roar up behind you, their front grills a snarl, just like in the Steven Spielberg film *Duel*. The trucks of America are the biggest and the scariest. The 1971 film is about a travelling salesman who is terrorised by a psychotic lorry driver after making the fatal mistake of overtaking. The trucker is out for revenge and tries to force the car off the road and into the path of an oncoming train. So, I'm not going to risk overtaking, just in case.

Soon I will be driving solo, with the children in the back, from Washington to Boston, to meet Roland from the Democrat convention and head off for an east coast holiday. My friends are concerned.

'Anne, have you ever been across GW Bridge before?' asks Kathleen, referring to the crossing between Manhattan and New Jersey.

'No,' I reply. 'I looked on the map though and doesn't the I-95 take me straight over it?'

She pauses. 'Kind of. It's fine as long as you know your exit. You know what? I'll give you my brother's number. He's a firefighter there and you can just call him if you get into trouble.'

This is worrying. The bridge is so scary that I might need to be rescued by one of New York's finest. I find out more. The Port Authority of New York and New Jersey says the George Washington, crossing the Hudson River, is the world's only 14-lane suspension bridge and one of the world's busiest bridges. By way of explanation, the Port Authority says, 'Two four-lane approach and departure roadways connect to the upper level, with connections to and from the lower level via two three-lane tunnels through the Palisades. The New Jersey approach system provides connections between both levels of the bridge and highways US-1, US-9W, US-46, NJ-4, I-80, I-95 and the Palisades Interstate Parkway.' Blimey.

'Anne, how about you hire one of those automatic navigators so you know where you are going?' Kathleen says the next day. 'I could give you my sisters' numbers too. They would come and get you if you get lost.'

Sonya can tell I'm anxious. 'You could go on the Garden State Parkway. That way you would miss the GW Bridge and you wouldn't hit the city traffic,' she suggests. Garden State Parkway, I like the sound of that.

A few weeks later and I am cruising along the GSP. Hit a bit of traffic near New York but otherwise it is all going swimmingly. I haven't got lost once and I'll soon be back on the I-95. But there are more trucks as I get further north and, hitting Connecticut, they are everywhere. Most are flying the American flag and the truckers sport bandanas, mirror shades and sleeveless T-shirts (all the better to show off drivers' muscles and 'love and death' tattoos). These days they have their own online chat rooms with login names like Hellcat, Captain Chaos and King Chicken. An enormous black truck roars up right behind me, flashing his lights. Does he want me to change lanes? The trouble is, I can't. To my left and right are other enormous trucks going at the same speed. Straight in front, yet another. I can barely see daylight. If the driver behind, who I strongly suspect is called Black Max, gets any closer he will be sitting in the back seat. With my knuckles white on the steering wheel, I resist a strong urge to shut my eyes. There's nothing I can do but drive like an American and look straight ahead, studiously avoiding the eye of the trucker to my left, who I'm convinced is Captain Chaos. After more intensive light flashing and honking, which I know is directed at me, they overtake or pull off.

Exhaustion is setting in and we need to find somewhere to stop for the night. But outside all the cheaper motel chains there are trucks lined up. Perhaps not. I hear Sonya's voice in my head – 'You're on your own, just check into a Courtyard Marriott.'

Suddenly there's a sign to one. We pull up into safe, bland, corporate America. Marlene at reception is plump and beaming. 'You all look tired, ladies. Help yourselves to a cookie. I made them myself.'

The next day and we are nearly at Boston. The hotel receptionist on the phone says the directions are easy, I just have to get the right exit. Then to my horror I realise that the exit number doesn't exist. They must have thought I was coming in on a different road. I remember Kathleen saying, 'You'll be fine, as long as you don't end up in The Big Dig.' As signs start appearing describing road closures, new routes and road works, I fear the worst. I am stuck in the most complex tunnel and road construction project in American history. The traffic is speeding up as we go through a tunnel and none of the signs resemble anything on the map. By now we must have gone under most of Boston and be about to come out the other side. Suddenly, amidst the road works, I see an exit to a car park and swing in hoping I can turn around. After driving round in circles I find the exit. I explain apologetically to the woman at the barrier kiosk and ask if she can give me directions. Without flinching, she says, 'That will be twenty-five dollars, Ma'am.'

'But I've only been here a few minutes, I haven't even parked,' I protest.

'You have no ticket. It is twenty-five dollars.'

By now the cars behind are honking and I pull over. The girls are crying and I am trying hard not to, but failing. Then I remember the advice I got from the queue in the post office. 'Always ask to see the manager.' The garage attendant glares harder but calls him. He appears wearily, another problem customer to cloud his day. A man of few words, he listens. I sense he doesn't understand my accent, but he glances at the crying children and the piles of luggage. 'Show me your map and I will help you,' he says. 'It is OK, be calm. You do not have to pay twenty-five dollars.' The attendant looks like she wants to shoot me. I am hoping she isn't armed.

Almost there, but the map doesn't show one-way streets. We stop a fourth passer-by and they enthusiastically try to help. The locals must have their work cut out with The Big Dig. Finally make it to the hotel and drive into the car park. The parking attendant strolls up. 'Did you have a good drive, ladies?' he asks, before noting our tear-stained faces. 'Where you from?'. He comes from Mexico but has a cousin in London who he hopes to visit one day. 'We're both from somewhere else, right? We know what it's like,' he says kindly. 'I'll take care of the vehicle, you ladies just relax.'

A few hours later, we're wandering around the leafy streets of Boston. It could almost be Britain – the old buildings, the Irish influences, a bandstand in the park. It's a few months before the US presidential election and I am a shameless voyeur, wandering up Beacon Hill to see the house where John Kerry lives. The red brick streets, with their perfectly maintained town houses and quiet elegance, get increasingly smart as we approach.

There is hardly anyone about. I know when I'm there because a trademark muscle man in shades (on a cloudy day) is outside talking to some dog walkers. The cop, thinly disguised in a Hawaiian shirt, darts a look in my direction. Another policeman, in the same faux civilian dress, appears from the door. Assume Kerry isn't at home as there is not even a photographer around.

Cape Cod has the flower-filled gardens and quaint houses of an English country village. It is full of people yearning for how life used to be, riding bikes to the old-fashioned general store, watching the sunset over a rocky cove, fish and chips and ice cream. There's an old drive-in movie screen where families turn up in pyjamas with blankets and eat popcorn under the stars.

Chatham, 'the patriarch of Cape Cod towns', is so picture perfect, so refined, it doesn't feel real. It is nearly dusk at the Chatham Light, built in 1878 to guide ships to safety, and before us is a classic American scene. On an immaculate green lawn, under the US flag, young uniformed coastguards are playing baseball. And walking by are the perfect Ralph Lauren family, four kids with mom and dad, all beautiful, blonde, tanned and fit with gleaming teeth, everyone wearing bright, white polo shirts and beige chino shorts. Not a stain in sight.

In Cape Cod, the clientele changes with the landscape. As you drive around Cape Cod Bay, along the strip of land that stretches into the Atlantic Ocean, dunes and windswept beaches take over, with weather-beaten wooden houses. Provincetown is the equivalent of Key West in Florida, the last tip of land before the mighty ocean takes over, a magnet for writers, artists and the gay community. When you can't take that squeaky clean whiteness any more, here is a place where you can roller skate down the street in a leather cat suit without getting a second glance.

On the road again. We miss the weekend traffic bottleneck off the Cape by starting early and head up the I-95 towards Maine. Turn off to Kennebunkport for an ice cream stop and to take a peak at the Bush family holiday home. George Bush Senior's summer pad is on a spit of land called Walkers Point. It is no McMansion, but low rise and low key, and you would never know its significance if it wasn't for the black Secret Service vehicles parked nearby.

In town, a man in a black suit and shades directs traffic into the car park. It's usually a task performed by someone in a fluorescent waistcoat, but here more men in black suits with ear pieces are standing at the side entrance to a hotel. A uniformed policewoman is coming out from behind some bushes in a nearby back garden. A police patrol car is parked up over the road. What is going on? The lady at the ice cream shack has the answer. 'The president is attending a family wedding,' she says in slightly bored tones. 'What can I get you?'

A tanned teenage girl sips on an electric blue crushed ice drink, dangling her flip flop from her toe and telling her mom who else is at the wedding. Locals stop by to pick up some fried seafood. Then three young men in dark shades and patterned shirts stroll up and order wild blueberry ice cream, looking around them, just a bit too casually – definitely Secret Service.

Head for the mountains of Maine in torrential rain with lightning on the horizon. The Wal-Mart seems even cheaper here and the traditional lobster is cooked at roadside shacks by Russians. On the trails of Arcadia National Park, we meet well off city people in hiking gear, getting their nature fix, stopping to chat about the walk and their dogs. The trailer park crowd hang out at the pirate-themed crazy golf course with its showroom dummy Black Beard and fake cannon explosions. The smiling girls ahead of us, who say they are 11 and 12, are so fat they can hardly bend down to pick up their balls. Their mother is the same. Dad is a skinny, tired-looking man in a baseball cap with a weather beaten face, bending down to fetch the balls for his puffing womenfolk.

We start the long drive home on the back roads, through one horse towns, past petrol stations, churches and diners. Arriving late at a lakeside town in New Hampshire, we pass amusement arcades and groups of bikers. Everywhere seems to say 'no vacancy'. 'What? Are you crazy, lady?' says one cross hotel boss. 'This is a holiday weekend.'

On the road out of town, we pull up next to some wooden huts beside a B&B with a broken neon sign. In the office-cum-living-room is the landlady, all black eyeliner and bleached hair, sitting in a haze of smoke amid faux leopard skin furniture. It feels like she should tell my fortune. 'Sure I got a room, hon. Just had a cancellation. It's cash only, in advance. You missed the biker convention but there's fireworks tonight.' We get a hut complete with beds, kitchenette and bathroom.

Eat some pizza as the last jet skiiers roar across the lake. A local blues band is playing to a white, blue collar crowd, kids and grannies showing the most interest. In the amusement arcade, everything is cheap and the plastic prizes plentiful. At the shooting range, a dad is showing his toddler son how to shoot a rifle.

'You're gonna hit that target son and win us a prize!' he says.

'Aw, ain't he cute,' says mom.

A man in combats is shouting at the little old lady in charge of prizes. She's tougher than she looks – 'Get outta here or I'll call security,' she says firmly. The girls have won bouncy balls on a game which involves bashing a groundhog with a mallet. She gives them extras and says, 'The fireworks will be on soon by the lake. Don't miss 'em!' Outside, there is an enormous bang. 'Don't worry, that's just the veterans,' she says. 'Have a good night.' It turns out the vets, who keep a house on the lakefront, are proud owners of a civil war cannon that they like to fire of an evening.

Back at the motel, the landlady and the other residents are sitting outside in front of a campfire, waiting for the firework display to begin. 'You must be the guests from Ireland,' says a middle-aged woman. 'Pull up a chair and have a beer.' I explain we are actually English. 'Oh really, I speak to someone at work who is English,' she replies. 'His name is Colin, you probably know him.'

'So what is Dublin like?' asks another.

'Oh, it is lovely,' I reply.

A teenage girl in sweatpants and flip flops bounces up and gives her mother a hug. 'Are those your little girls?' she asks. 'Is it Ok if I give them some fireworks? I saw them earlier on the swing and thought they might like them.' She produces a brown paper bag and hands out multi-coloured sparklers, giving careful instructions on how to hold them safely. Then, as if it couldn't get any better, she demonstrates how to walk on your hands, do a perfect cartwheel and a backflip.

We move on to the Berkshires of Massachusetts, idyllic countryside and culture. We stay in a chintzy bed and breakfast where Thomas Edison is said to have worked on his inventions. It is run by a Dutch couple. 'We travelled all over the world for work but we liked the US best.' When it was time to stop moving their kids around, they decided to stay here and live the dream.

You notice it wherever you go. Unless you can keep to the back streets and trails, it is hard being a pedestrian in the USA. This is car country. 'Take the Metro downtown – the kids will love it!' I suggest in DC, but not many do. 'Going to New York is so much better by train or bus,' I argue, but most simply smile and drive anyway. It is what they are used to. (Meanwhile, Elaine and I join an old folks coach trip to New York rather than risk the car.) And trying to cross a six-lane road as a pedestrian, even if district law dictates vehicles must stop, is never easy.

I pull up on Connecticut Avenue, on the DC side of Chevy Chase, to let an old lady with a stick go over the crossing. A van in the next lane screeches to a halt just in time, but the truck in the outside lane speeds on, narrowly missing the woman. The driver didn't even notice. The frightened lady hobbles back to where she came from. It could take all day.

The next time I try to cross the same road on foot, from Magruder's grocery store ('always fresh for less') to Safeway, the pedestrians are fighting back. In holders at either side of the road are fluorescent orange crossing flags. Some students try them out, holding the flags out in front as they purposefully stride over the crossing. Vehicles (supposed to be going at 25mph) are slamming to emergency stops and the pedestrians all make it, just. OK, here goes. I hold out my flag, empowered by my pedestrian's rights, and keep walking and waving, not daring to look as the traffic thunders closer.

Today the notice outside the fire station asks, 'Have you got an emergency plan?' Back at school, it is suggested to kids that they have a family code word.

'What is ours?' asks my eldest daughter.

'How about "crikey",' I say, and she gives me a stern look. I am not taking this nearly seriously enough.

Chapter 15:
War, Guns and Votes

MICHAEL MOORE is a local hero. His anti-Bush, anti-Iraq war film *Fahrenheit 9/11* is playing to sell out cinema audiences here. Everyone stands up and claps at the end of the screening I go to. I can't remember ever witnessing that before. Moore may sometimes be prone to exaggeration but, by daring to criticise the President and show the human cost of the war, he has initiated something sorely needed in America since 9/11 – a debate.

The dissidents have always been out there. After 9/11, publishers pulled the plug on Moore's book *Stupid White Men* when he refused to tone down his criticisms of Bush and the American establishment. They relented following a mass anti-censorship campaign by angry librarians. But the pressure to keep quiet, to be patriotic, has been immense since September 2001.

'I saw your Tony Blair at Prime Minister's Question Time,' says Elaine. 'I wish we could do that here.' People are both shocked at how the British media and opposition politicians attack the country's leader so mercilessly, and envious at the very public freedom of speech. Here it is left largely to the angry funny men like Michael Moore and Jon Stewart on *The Daily Show* to ask the awkward questions.

Two months to go before the presidential election, and lawns everywhere are covered in golden leaves and 'Kerry/Edwards' placards. A few brave souls, and Republican party workers, dare to put out 'Bush/Cheney' signs. If the feeling in this neighbourhood is reflected in the rest of the USA, John Kerry will walk it to The White House. The politically savvy fifth graders on the school bus sport Kerry badges and soon have the younger kids on message, chanting for their man as if he were a baseball star.

The kindergarteners are learning The Pledge of Allegiance, standing before the Stars and Stripes every day, and a morale-boosting school tune about 'the best school in the land'. They practise the Star-Spangled Banner in music class. Josie says the pledge in her best American accent, 'one nation under Gaard', complete with her new last line (to be delivered with utmost solemnity), 'please be seated'.

Here are the jobs I can volunteer for this year: room parent (that's the party planner and PTA recruiter), member of the learning committee, member of the staff appreciation committee, diversity night helper, field trip chaperone, writer's workshop editor, computer lab assistant, tutoring, science kit inventory person, Scholastic book orders organiser, member of the 5th grade graduation committee and last, but by no means least, lice checker.

Money pours in on back-to-school night, $20 suggested for the class fund (to cover parties and teacher's gift) and $50 for the PTA. The pressure is on to buy fancy, fundraising gift wrap but it's not for me. I will be reusing, recycling and supporting the homeless instead – my own (very quiet) rebellion.

The imminent chemical attack which the authorities have been warning us about for ages finally happened yesterday. At least, that's what everyone thought. Fire officials treated it as a potential 'mass casualty situation', the stock market plunged and 1,500 people were evacuated from a building near the World Bank and International Monetary Fund in downtown DC – both seen as potential terrorist targets. A decontamination area was set up as victims complained of breathing difficulties and burning eyes. Turns out a teenage boy from a nearby school had grabbed a girl's neck chain, setting off its mini canister of pepper spray near a café's air vent.

Aah, fall is here, the season of roaring blower machines and leaf peepers out in search of the best oranges and reds. I sit on the step and check out the colours in the street: not bad at all. The 'Smooches 4 Pooches' van drives by, advertising dog training, walking and pet sitting. Then a pick-up truck loaded with wood pulls up and out jump two men in lumberjack shirts and with goatee beards. 'Need some logs, Ma'am?' asks the older one. They have driven over to the suburbs from Virginia. 'I lurve your accent, Ma'am,' says the boss. 'French, right?' They have some iced water while they are stacking the wood. 'Make sure you keep it dry under some tarp,' he says, 'and it will be good for the winter. Gonna be a cold one they say.'

Former US politicians have joined with doctors and bishops to put pressure on the Supreme Court over the legal execution of juveniles. They say it is unconstitutional to execute those who committed crimes before the age of 18. Right now, the US is one of only five countries known still to be doing this. The others are China, Pakistan, Democratic Republic of Congo and Iran. Since 2000, there have been nine recorded executions of child offenders in the US, carried out by three states – Texas, Oklahoma and neighbouring Virginia, just across the river from the self-proclaimed capital of the free world.

In Wholefoods, the mothers are racing round the aisles to get their dinner party ingredients and organic kids' snacks before it's time to meet the school bus. The distinctive sound of Cat Stevens comes over the speakers – 'Oh baby, baby it's a wild world.' Later, I hear on the news that a flight from London to Washington was diverted after US security discovered that Yusuf Islam, formerly Cat Stevens, was on board. He is apparently on the US government's 'no-fly list' and was detained on 'national security grounds' before being deported. This is the man who expressed 'heartfelt horror' at 9/11, promised a portion of CD profits to victims' families, and is famous around the world for singing *Peace Train*. Sounds absurd to me. But not everyone around here agrees.

'Didn't he support the death sentence on Salman Rushdie?'

'What about all that money he gave to Hamas?'

Fair points, I reply, but the first he claims to have been misquoted on and the second that he had no idea donations made to help Palestinians were going to the militant Islamic organisation.

'I don't buy that – how can he not have known?' is the response.

'I might be being naïve, but it's possible,' I say. 'After all, how much money that well-intentioned Americans donated to the Irish Republican cause ended up financing a terrorist bombing campaign? I don't remember US citizens getting stopped at Heathrow and sent home because of that.' Three years in America, and I'm coming over all Michael Moore. I'll be blacklisted from all the barbecues at this rate.

An acquaintance in the street isn't her usual smiling self.

'How are you?' I ask.

'I'm pretty depressed right now,' she says. Her brother, a Mid West construction worker in the National Guard, has just been called up for duty in Iraq. He goes tomorrow and she is already counting the days until his return. 'I am really frightened. It is so bad out there.'

I head on to ballet class and a minivan parks up with a sticker which proudly proclaims, 'My son is serving in the US air force'. Yellow ribbon 'Support Our Troops' car magnets are everywhere. Every journey you see them, even more the further you go out of the city. Solidarity is displayed on the billboards at the front of roadside diners, 'Support Our Troops' next to 'burger for 99c'.

A story in the local news round-up tells of a sheriff's investigator who shot his wife while he was cleaning his small-calibre handgun. Authorities say the incident, in Lovettsville, Virginia, appeared to be an accident. The woman was airlifted to hospital and should be OK. You can't be too careful with these killing machines. I wonder what she was doing at the time. Clearing the dishes, reading her book, watching TV?

We escape from the suburbs to a party on Capitol Hill. It's a balmy night and still warm enough to go outside. The champagne is flowing and the candles are lit. Journalists mingle with lobbyists and Democratic Party workers. A man from its National Committee is trying hard to be upbeat but can't hide the underlying feeling of doom. 'I wish Edwards had beaten Kerry,' he admits, talking about the runner-up in the Democrat primaries. 'He would be so much easier to sell.'

Nearby, a fresh faced activist, in silk shirt and tailored trousers, is refusing to be downhearted. Her job is to cold call single mothers in swing states to try to persuade them to vote for Kerry. I wonder what a young mother on a trailer park in Ohio would make of this well-groomed college graduate calling from Washington. Would they speak the same language?

A New Yorker on the lookout for a media job is working the party. He looks like a young Woody Allen but seems to have twice the confidence, snaking round the room in a baggy suit and black-rimmed glasses, talking non-stop about politics. He swiftly wants to know everyone's job title, what company they are with. I am instantly dismissed (what use is some part-time freelance who looks after the kids?) and he strikes up a conversation with a bureau chief directly over my head.

A friend who has attended parties on both sides of the political divide confides the next day, 'Republican parties are better. At the Democrat ones there is a lot of serious conversation. At the Republican ones everyone is just having a good time.'

While waiting at the carwash, I snatch a moment to read the paper, but it's hard to concentrate. The young woman next to me, in long wool coat and baseball cap, is talking loudly and completely unselfconsciously into her mobile phone. 'You should have been there last night, it was a blast! One guy was really cute, yeah, I got his number. And I spoke to a guy who said he could get you a job on the Hill. I have his card!'

The Washington Post has a leader today headlined *21 not making it to 21*. Michael Swan, aged 13, was shot dead yesterday and 20 others have been murdered before making it to their 18th birthday so far this year (2004) in the capital (there are still three months left). Politicians in the House of Representatives could make things even worse. *The Post* says, *That the blood of DC youth may be on their hands does little to dissuade congressional gun lovers, who are out to repeal the city's gun control laws and to win political points with the national gun lobby.*

A 'Dear Neighbour' letter arrives today from the local fire brigade asking for financial help. They need new apparatus, to modernise fire stations and to recruit and train a volunteer reserve corps of 'second responders' to back up the 'first responders'. Our area, we are reminded, 'contains tempting targets for explosive and biochemical incidents'. I also get a copy of *The Firefighter* newsletter from the Community Relations Committee, which includes a prayer for the armed forces – *May it be Your will that the dominion of tyranny and cruelty speedily be brought to an end and those who gallantly serve our nation return safely home.*

Virginia police say that an elementary school teacher found a loaded, semiautomatic handgun in a child's backpack. The father, who keeps it for self-defence and has a permit to carry a concealed weapon, says he had put it in the bag at soccer practice and forgot to take it out. He is charged with allowing children access to firearms.

At the weekend, whole families turn up to take part in the local fun run, many enthusiastic entrants sporting previous years' T-shirts. Volunteer stewards stand in their usual place and helpers prepare a feast of bagels. Not a fat American in sight.

My favourite talk programme, *The Diane Rehm Show* on WAMU American University Radio, has on a doctor from the NIH (National Institutes of Health) speaking about the shortage of flu vaccine. Supply is halved this year because of production problems in Britain, and the mood is frankly getting a little hysterical. The very young and old, those with specific medical conditions and health workers, get priority. These elderly Americans are no push-overs. Noisy lines of stick waving oldies spring up anywhere where it is rumoured to be available. With all that excitement, heart failure will get them before flu does.

The presidential election is weeks away now and the formidable National Rifle Association is out for John Kerry's blood. In adverts in swing states, he is portrayed as a French poodle with the words, 'That dog don't hunt'. Key states are said to be won and lost on hunters' votes, and the gun question inevitably comes up in the televised candidates' debate. Bush says, 'I believe law-abiding citizens ought to be able to own a gun.' And he adds, '....the best way to protect our citizens from guns is to prosecute those who commit crimes with guns.'

Kerry is anxious not to lose those votes. 'I am a hunter. I'm a gun owner. I've been a hunter since I was a kid – 12, 13 years old. And I respect the Second Amendment, and I will not tamper with the Second Amendment.' (The right of the people to keep and bear arms.)

But he does dare to criticise politicians who didn't fight to extend the Clinton-era ban on assault weapons, saying, 'Terrorists can now come into America and go to a gun show and without even a background check buy an assault weapon today.'

The mood in the neighbourhood is upbeat the next day. 'I think Kerry did good last night. It should have got him some votes.' But what about the other America? Twenty miles from The White House in Fairfax, Virginia, anti-Kerry sentiments are being pumped out from the NRA headquarters. An article billed as, 'The truth behind John Kerry's record on your firearms rights', accuses him of merely posing as a hunter, of being a 'faux good old boy', a 'silver-spoon Boston Brahmin' and 'an unthinking zealot who has never missed an opportunity to work to diminish our rights'.

At my nearest out-of-town K-Mart, you have to go past the cheap clothes, toys and bedding, through electricals and gardening, before finding them near the cool boxes and fishing tackle. Shut into a glass case, there are around 18 different kinds of rifles, for $150 or $250. The notice says you have to be 21 and meet Maryland regulations to buy.

Dealers have to conduct a background check under Federal law and are not supposed to sell to ex-cons, fugitives, drug users, the 'mentally defective', illegal aliens, dishonourably discharged ex-forces, those who have renounced their citizenship, stalkers, people convicted of domestic violence or under 21s (unless it is a shotgun or a rifle in some states). An instant check is available through the FBI.

Maryland has added some extras, including that dealers should not sell to a habitual drunkard. A person may not buy more than one handgun or assault weapon in a 30-day period.

Government statistics say there were 1,482 federally licensed firearms dealers in Maryland in 2001 and that in the same year 607 people died from firearm-related injuries in the state. In 2000, 8,346 machine guns were registered in Maryland.

So what's the problem if states have strict laws to make sure weapons aren't sold to the wrong people? The trouble is, not all states do. According to anti-gun violence campaigners, police acknowledge there is an 'iron pipeline' of guns illegally trafficked up and down the east coast, with gunrunners travelling to states with more relaxed laws like Georgia, Ohio and, predictably, Texas.

Texas is a constant thorn in the side of liberal America, the black sheep relative who still has to be invited for Thanksgiving dinner because he is part of the family.

'We call it the Independent Republic of Texas,' says Leah.

'I couldn't believe it when I arrived at the airport there,' Claire remembers. 'They really do all wear those hats!'

A paragraph in the paper today says that the father of a four-year-old boy, killed when he found his dad's loaded handgun during a game of hide-and-seek, will appear in a gun safety video. The man, from Catonsville, Maryland, escaped a fine for leaving a firearm within a child's reach.

A car goes by with the sticker, 'no one died when Clinton lied'. That's the first anti-war one I have seen.

Today's news says a Minnesota senator has shut down his DC offices, sent his staff home and advised people not to visit Capitol Hill. It seems to be in response to a worst-case scenario painted by intelligence analysts of mass, simultaneous attacks across the states. Comfortingly, every other politician is staying put and they have branded Mark Dayton 'ill-informed', 'reckless' and 'paranoid'.

Then there's a piece saying US students are being advised to change their attitude when travelling abroad. The main message, similar to the one reportedly given to US athletes in the Olympics, is 'Try to be humble and don't talk about God'.

The book shop is part merchandising outlet, part community centre. There is Starbucks, toilets, a children's area and tables and chairs for laptop users. Some people stay all day without buying anything. It is open from 9am to 11pm every day. On a weekday morning there are moms with toddlers and the elderly, then come the office lunch crowd, students after school or college, then evening diners and moviegoers. Today, parked neatly outside, is a supermarket trolley full of carrier bags. A homeless person who has accidentally strayed into the suburbs? Sure enough, there she is, wandering around, happily talking to herself, resplendent in woolly hat and felt slippers, the first bag lady I have ever seen around here. She seems to have a purpose, as if she is looking for something specific. Later, I see she has stopped in science fiction and fantasy. A young man in sports gear is fast asleep, his head on the table, beneath a poster for *Of Mice and Men* by John Steinbeck.

School is encouraging kids to choose positive characters for this year's Halloween parades and parties. 'Any costume accessories with dangerous or sharp edges or simulated weapons will not be allowed in school. These include such items as toy swords, pitchforks, guns, knives etc.' Scary masks must be left at home so the younger pupils don't get frightened.

A vacant supermarket has been turned into a Halloween shop. One man has the job of marching up and down the road outside with an advertising placard. Yesterday he was dressed as cartoon character Spongebob Squarepants. Today he walks miserably up and down in the pouring rain as a giant M&M chocolate sweet, the trucks honking their horns. Inside are hundreds of costumes for children and adults. Tiny pumpkins and devils for babies, cute, cuddly animals, skeletons and witches. Small boys are jumping out from behind the racks in scary masks. Josie is already caught up in a fake cobweb, and a teenage girl is having a stand-up row with her mother who is refusing to buy her a French maid's outfit. A middle aged woman can't decide which long flowing dress to buy. 'It depends if you want to look like a princess or a pilgrim,' I volunteer. A pale teenage boy stands at the check-out with an enormous scythe. We settle on vampire and Pocahontas costumes and join the line. In front is a big man in his 20s, nerdy looking with glasses and earring, wearing a cult band T-shirt. He is buying a giant furry chicken outfit.

The check-out girl, unselfconsciously modelling devil horns, confides after he has gone, 'I *never* thought we would sell that. It's a $100-worth of chicken.'

Driving through the neighbourhood behind a car with a 'Give me a coffee and nobody gets hurt' sticker, I notice even more Kerry/Edwards signs, with extra placards on local voting issues. These people know their politics. 'We were going to have a party to celebrate a Democrat win,' Elaine says. 'But you know, it may not happen. So we are having one anyway before the vote.' Then she announces with a twinkle in her eye, 'It's a "Let the Cat back" party!'

We arrive to the sound of Cat Stevens singing *Peace Train*. A room full of people drinking beer, eating Mexican wraps, and talking about how different things would have been if Al Gore was president. The Rolling Stones and Bowie are on the turntable and the strobe lights flash through the window into the suburban street. No one mentions the unmentionable – four more years of George W. Bush.

There are some scary people out there. Tattoo parlour owners in Virginia are being held in jail for possessing firearms, according to the local paper. They are already convicted felons. In a raid on their home, police found 26 high-calibre weapons including an AK-47 and a grenade launcher. There were also 60 Rottweilers.

The boys on the school bus are euphoric this morning after watching the Boston Red Sox win the baseball World Series last night. 'No more Curse of the Bambino!' one shouts. (The Red Sox had not won the competition since 1918 when Babe Ruth, 'the Bambino', was on the team. He was sold to the New York Yankees, who went on to win a succession of titles.) No one admits to supporting the St Louis Cardinals now they've lost.

A columnist and author is speaking to the school PTA tonight on the subject of 'Over-focused parents/overscheduled kids'. I wonder if those that need to go will find the time in between ferrying their offspring to classes. It might be interesting, but I haven't been focused enough to book a babysitter.

It's so convenient – a ten minute drive during school hours and you can tick off those household things lingering on the shopping list as well as stock up on kids' presents. Linens 'n Things is always useful, then there is Bed Bath and Beyond just up the road, and it's hard to beat Toys R Us for prices. Not at all the kind of suburban shopping strip where you would expect a shooting. But an off-duty policeman shot dead another motorist yesterday evening, right there in the car park of Toys R Us and Linens 'n Things. The area was busy with families doing Halloween shopping. The deputy US marshal, a federal law enforcer, opened fire following a traffic dispute.

I pick up some prints from the photo shop and read a new sign behind the counter. 'Lose 150-200lb of ugly fat – better than low carb or Atkins!' What's that all about? It goes on to explain how your ex-husband can be edited out of a favourite group photograph.

It is the weekend before the presidential vote, and Sherri is walking her dog before heading off to Pennsylvania to get the vote out for the Democrats. The mood on election day itself is sombre but not defeated. Until all the votes have been counted there is still hope. But not for long. The next morning it is clear that Kerry has lost.

A mother at the school bus stop fights back tears. 'Bet you are glad you are British. It's alright for you, you can go home.'

Leah is distraught. 'I feel like an alien in my own country.'

Others are simply frightened for the future. 'It's going to be World War Three,' Haley wails. In the book shop, a customer says she wants to find out about emigrating to Canada. Can they recommend anything?

Across the country, Bush got 51 per cent of the vote and Kerry 48 per cent. In DC, Kerry won 90 per cent, and in Maryland 56 per cent. Nationwide, Bush got more votes than Kerry from men, white people, protestants, Catholics and evangelicals, those who cared about moral values, terrorism and who supported the war in Iraq. More Democrat voters were concerned about the economy, jobs, health and education. They mainly disapproved of the war. Later, internet cruisers see the front page of the *Daily Mirror* which has a picture of George Bush and the words, 'How can 59,054,087 people be so DUMB?' One voter miserably sums up a now familiar sentiment. 'The rest of the world must hate us'.

In his victory speech, George Bush singles out the people of Texas for a special mention. 'We have known each other the longest, and you started me on this journey. On the open plains of Texas I first learned the character of our country: sturdy and honest and hopeful as the break of day.'

There's not much hope left around here.

A DC mother is calling for police and the public to do more to stop murders in the city after losing her second son to gun violence. Valencia Mohammed, a former community activist, wants to encourage people to come forward with information on crimes and for the police to do more to protect them. Her sons were aged 14 and 23. Their killers have not yet been caught.

While flicking through the TV channels on Saturday morning, I come to an aerobics class. I could do with some exercise and decide to join in. The session is led by Regie, who directs us to pump, stretch and bend. A small group of friends do the movements with him and he passes on tips and encouragement. Everyone is very jolly. Then it starts to dawn on me that this is no ordinary class. In between exercise directions and talk about the importance of keeping fit, Regie now calls out, 'Good job! Hallelujah!'. This is part exercise class, part religious meeting, a body, mind and spirit experience. It is *Gospelrobics*. We are working out to high energy gospel music with a teacher who is both fitness guru and minister. As Regie puts it, 'Are you pumped for purpose and fit for the call?' I wonder if other viewers are Republican voters. (George Bush is very strong amongst white evangelicals and born-again Christians.) But Regie is black and statistically likely to be a Democrat, so maybe not. Back on the TV, the exercise part is over and Jenine comes on with a quick word about healthy eating. Then a plug for a beaming entrepreneur who has set up a gospel clothing company. 'I made a gospel sweatshirt for one of my family and they liked it so much I thought, God must be talking to me!' The rest is history and you can buy his T-shirts to wear at home while you are doing Regie's class, so you can feel part of the gang.

Another week, after *Priscilla's Yoga* has finished, the announcer cannot conceal his excitement. 'NOW herrrrrrre's Regie!' Today Paula is joining him to lead an Afro-Brazilian workout. The team, sporting programme T-shirts and permanent smiles, are really getting into it. It is quite uptempo and I keep getting left behind. But Regie is on fire. He starts singing 'livin' in the glory, huh, huh, praise him,' while grooving to the beat. 'Pump it! Give the Lord to me, oh yeah, uh huh.' The team are still going strong but time is nearly up and 'fit facts' come up on screen before the credits. A few hours later, driving up Massachusetts Avenue to the library, a church billboard reads, 'The bread of life never gets stale'.

Drive up to a farm in Virginia for the afternoon to watch the horse show and see the animals. The leaves have all turned and a blaze of orange surrounds the old Dutch barn. Near the country store, selling gifts, Christmas decorations and toys, musicians are starting to congregate. More appear with banjos, guitars and a double bass, and a country music jam session begins. They peel off into little knots, plucking and singing, greeting new arrivals, old-timers in denim and check shirts, long haired folky women and keen young men. Players move from group to group, choosing different parts, suggesting songs.

They don't care if anyone stops to listen or not, more than 20 now, unselfconsciously playing away. It feels like it could be 1930.

The fire station notice board this week advises, 'Never Cook in Loose Clothing'. Their colleagues on Connecticut Avenue ask, 'Is your furnace ready for winter?'

It is Thanksgiving, and that means travel hell, fares at twice the price and journeys that take twice as long. The wise stay at home. Now that I'm a pro, practically a native, I know that pumpkin pulp for the pie is best from a tin and that cranberry is also traditionally from a tin in some households (looking like dog food minus the meat). Marshmallows are cooked on top of the sweet potato.

The secretary of health and human services, Tommy Thompson, has announced he is resigning. 'For the life of me, I cannot understand why the terrorists have not attacked our food supply because it is so easy to do,' he says. Thanks for telling them, Tommy.

The roadside Christmas tree plots have opened up and Wholefoods is selling mini, tabletop versions. I am drawn to a more natural-looking type, not manicured like the rest, and find it is labelled a 'rustic, sinewy Euro tree'. Starbucks is selling gingerbread and eggnog lattes, the Chanukah Menorah has been lit and the lavishly decorated trees are up in the mall.

'Did you hear there was an armed robbery in Chevy Chase?' Haamid says as he picks us up in his cab. 'I think it was that house down there.' Two of the robbers had handguns. In another part of town, it would probably not even have been reported.

Chapter 16:
Them and Us

WHERE DID they come from? Huge wheelie bins have been left outside every house, like a blue army marching through suburbia. It turns out the council has left them for recycling after hearing the plastic boxes we currently use weren't large enough for some residents. There is uproar. The community is split between those who think 'great idea – thanks Montgomery County!' and those who think it is 'a monstrosity, a huge waste of our money!' Lena and Sally call the council and demand they take them away. I agree, they are too big – large enough to fit an adult or several small children, depending on your needs – but decide to keep it anyway. The middle school kids take turns to push each other down the street in one but later abandon it (too slow and heavy).

Americans aren't bad at recycling – their rate was around 31 per cent last year compared with 22 per cent in Britain – but then so they should be. They generate over 4 pounds of waste per person, per day, more than any other country in the industrialised world. Just one trip to a big chain supermarket tells you why, with the excessive packaging and an aisle full of paper or plastic cups and plates. It once took three days and the combined efforts of four adults to open a heavily wrapped honeycomb at our house.

The crime statistics for 2004 are out and the murder rate in Washington DC is down to 198 from 248 the previous year. (In Montgomery County the figure is 17.) 'It's much better than it used to be,' says a neighbour. They are sceptical when I point out DC is still, statistically, one of the deadliest cities in the country. When population is taken into account, it has a homicide rate of 35 per 100,000 residents. New York's is 6.9 per 100,000 and London 2.4. The DC death toll includes 24 under 18s, all black. An FBI study estimates that 66 per cent of the murders in the US last year were committed with firearms.

All sounds a bit grim to me, so I am heartened when the Brady Campaign to Prevent Gun Violence announces it has awarded Maryland an 'A minus' for its above average laws to protect children and a 'Sensible Safety Star' for tightening up the law to disarm 'domestic violence abusers'. But the campaign fears gun violence could increase after Congress failed to renew the national ban on assault weapons. Maryland law doesn't limit the sale of assault rifles like the AK47.

The indoor ice rink is closed to the public when we turn up for a spin. An ice hockey game is in progress and we watch while we wait. It's a clash between teenage boys from different parts of Maryland. The dads line the side of the rink in LL Bean windcheaters, baseball caps and jeans. There are a handful of moms and some girlfriends in tight jeans with matching pale pink hoodies and Timberland boots.

The parents shout comments to the referee – 'Too right, ref, that's my kid he cut up!' – and encouragement to the boys – 'Way to go!', 'Good job!', 'Play clean boys'. Then the drama begins. Two opposing players crash into each other and one careers into the side wall. He hits the ice with a crack, writhing in pain. A squat, muscle-bound man with 'coach' written on the back of his bomber jacket angrily calls for a foul to be given but the referee shakes his head, stopping play only for the injured teenager to hobble off. But the coach doesn't let up, his face looks taut with anger from under his baseball cap. He stays standing, still protesting. As the ref goes over to talk to him, he screams, 'Fuck you!' Parents on the opposing team are in uproar and shout, 'Shame on you,' and, 'Great example coach.' Amid boos from the crowd, he gets sent off, sullenly walking across the ice to the naughty corner.

The mood is ugly now, tempers are high and tackles are vicious. I think we should leave before it's a bloodbath but the children haven't noticed that it's turned nasty. They are too busy smiling at the girlfriends who are now feeding them sweets. The parents are worried for their boys – 'Hey, watch my kid!' 'Did you see that?' 'These kids are animals!' There's a scuffle over a foul and suddenly a player swings a punch into his opponent's face. The parents cheer as he gets sent off, joining his coach in the naughty corner. The final whistle blows and the players glide off. 'Whew, that was a dirty one!' the dad next to me chuckles.

I tell a neighbour about the experience. 'Sport can get tough here,' he acknowledges. 'Winning really matters in America, no one cares about second place. We don't champion the loser like you Brits did with that skiing guy... what was his name?'

'Eddie the Eagle Edwards,' I say as he laughs and shakes his head at the memory of the hapless ski jumper.

It's inauguration day, when George Bush is sworn-in to a second term in office. Those who work downtown try to take the day off to avoid the tight security and there is a general feeling of apathy and gloom. (Here in Montgomery County, Kerry got 66 per cent of the vote to Bush's 33 per cent, a bigger majority for the Democrats than in the Bush/Gore race.) May as well watch the speech. Talking in front of the US Capitol, George Bush says, 'We have seen our vulnerability – and we have seen its deepest source. For as long as whole regions of the world simmer in resentment and tyranny – prone to ideologies that feed hatred and excuse murder – violence will gather, and multiply in destructive power, and cross the most defended borders, and raise a mortal threat. There is only one force of history that can break the reign of hatred and resentment, and expose the pretensions of tyrants, and reward the hopes of the decent and tolerant, and that is the force of human freedom.' He ends with, 'May God bless you, and may He watch over the United States of America.'

It is not just the great and good in Europe who are worried about a second Bush term. Former US diplomats, government and military officials, university and religious leaders have formed the National Committee to Unite a Divided America. Their aim is to promote inclusive leadership, forging national unity from a polarised nation.

Those who don't have the clout of former office or organisation make their point in whatever way they can. On Wisconsin Avenue, anonymous homemade posters have been taped to roadside poles. They read 'Impeach Bush... remember Nixon'.

I am in the print shop, doing some photocopying, when my mobile rings. It is a company which was supposed to do work on the house months ago and has continually failed to show up when arranged. I launch into a speech I have been rehearsing in my head about how their service is simply unacceptable and their timekeeping, frankly, abysmal. The receptionist, who I have previously tried to keep on friendly terms with, doesn't like it one bit and eventually hangs up. About six other customers have been forced to listen to my tirade and I feel awful, going round the shop to apologise for my loud, obnoxious behaviour. They seem surprised, as if they hadn't noticed anyway. The last, a woman in her 30s in a business suit, replies, 'Don't be sorry. I thought you sounded very organised and efficient. In fact, you are just the kind of person I am looking for. I need someone like you for my new company.' She says it involves selling shop outlets in malls and is paid by commission. 'You could make a lot of money, think about it and call me,' she says as she hands me her business card and rushes off to a meeting. Well, how about that? Shout down the phone here and I get offered a job. I'm sure equivalent behaviour in London would have provoked a chorus of 'shoosh!'.

You can ski in Pennsylvania, Virginia or West Virginia on a weekend or even a day trip from Washington. We go to shake off the post election malaise. The resorts are filled with white-collar city families in pristine sports outfits and blue-collar country types in the khaki gear they also use for hunting and fishing. My instructor is one of the latter, a local grandfather, cheerfully trying to knock a bunch of women from the suburbs into shape. As we stop for a rest, a class of five-year-olds glide past, skis in pizza shape, arms outstretched, in single file like little ducklings. 'How do you keep those babies safe with all these snow boarders going by?' one woman asks the instructor.

'The Good Lord watches over them,' he says. 'They all have their own guardian angel. If you look close enough, you can almost see it hovering above them.' The others nod in agreement.

'And they have a crash helmet,' I volunteer.

A 14-year-old boy shot a 16-year-old in the face at a school bus stop near Manassas, Virginia, it says in the paper. Police think they had been fighting over CDs or DVDs. The victim is recovering in hospital. The police investigator said he must have had 'an angel on his shoulder'.

It is now two years since the government warned of a biological or radiological attack and nothing has happened. But the leaders of the acclaimed 9/11 Commission are worried. They have joined forces with the non-partisan America Prepared Campaign to publish a letter to fellow Americans in *The New York Times* magazine. They say we have moved on from the mostly cosmetic Cold War civil defence drills from the Sixties. *When it comes to terrorism, taking simple steps to prepare and be informed about how to protect yourself and your family will often save lives and mitigate psychological and economic damage.* They want Americans to make a family communications plan, to have an emergency supplies kit and to learn about dealing with different kinds of attacks.

There has been some snow overnight but the highway crews have already cleared it. As the announcer on the local radio traffic report puts it, 'The roads are like a well-groomed poodle.'

I take the Metro to an art gallery but barely get in the door before an officious attendant confronts me. 'Do your children know the rules?' I reply that of course they know not to touch the paintings or go too close. We start going round, choosing which pictures we like best. The same attendant keeps popping up in different rooms, watching us intently. The youngest gets tired and I put her on my shoulders. The attendant pounces. 'Children cannot be carried on shoulders, Ma'am, they might touch an exhibit.' On we go and there she is again, 'Ma'am, your child must stay two feet away from the exhibit.' I protest that she is and wish I had a tape measure in my pocket. 'That is not two feet, Ma'am,' says the attendant.

I'm getting a bit fed up with the rules at the theatre too. I'm all for switching your phone off and carrying out screaming babies, but must the front-of-house staff go on about it so much? Every performance is preceded by a long speech about violations. One venue puts a list of rules in its programme. They include: *Take it easy with the atomizer: many people are highly allergic to perfume and cologne. Unwrap all candies and cough drops before the curtain goes up or the concert begins. Note to lovebirds: When you lean your heads together, you block the view of the person behind you. Leaning forward also blocks the view.*

Neither should you beat time with a 'body part' or 'jangle the bangles'.

'She is giving us a bad name,' Gail says crossly after reading about Judith Warner's book *Perfect Madness: Motherhood in the Age of Anxiety*. The author has made the cover of *Newsweek* and the *Today* show with Katie Couric, hitting the jackpot with her take on the 'mommy mystique' and criticising the oppressive culture of motherhood in America. The pressure to perform and to be selfless hit Warner after moving back to the US from France.

'What do you think about it?' asks Sonya. 'You have the perspective of someone from another country.'

'Well, taking the role of motherhood too seriously certainly exists,' I reply, 'but I don't think the book is about people like you.' Her kids go to state school where the early years are still all about learning through play. Yes, she ferries them to a few after school activities but only things that the children themselves want to do, and they are often chaotic, volunteer-run affairs. Judith Warner's own experience is mainly with the private school moms of the wealthiest part of Washington DC. Her kids go to a $20,000 a year private place with a longer day, where your five-year-old has to take an intelligence test before being admitted.

But Warner has identified a type of woman I have met around here. Hanging out outside the yoga class or at ballet school, they are always immaculately groomed and gravitate to one of their own. The 'perfect' moms speak incessantly about their child's academic level, piano grade and sporting prowess (and it turns out they are still only four). I tried unsuccessfully to get chatting to them a few times, later wondering if, in my jeans and trainers and with a foreign accent, they thought I was a mere nanny. Turned out the nannies are much more fun anyway, a jolly international band, trying to stifle giggles at their charges' posturing in pink leotards. Judith Warner certainly has a point that some American mothers, like their British cousins, have lost their perspective. And, I would add, I think they have lost their sense of humour.

The family of a soldier killed in Iraq is on the radio this morning and it is heartbreaking listening. They are country people who have never asked for much from life and are devastated. The family tell anecdotes of how he used to go hunting with his dad and brother. Then there is a tape recording from one Christmas when he was five.

'What did you get from Santa?' a relative asks.

'A machine gun,' says the little boy.

'Are you a good shot?' they ask.

'Yes,' the little voice replies.

The Washington Post publishes 'Faces of the Fallen', three pages of photographs of the American soldiers who have died in Iraq and the war against terror. It is February 2005, and already well over 1,000 have lost their lives.

Today I try my fifth dry cleaners in an ongoing quest to get my cream rain mac cleaned. Just like the rest, the assistant says she won't do it because of the type of material. Again, I point out that the label clearly states 'dry clean only'. 'I've had it cleaned in Britain loads of times and no one has questioned it once,' I persist. 'Honestly, I won't sue you if it goes wrong. It isn't an expensive coat just a dirty one.' But she won't budge and nor will the manager.

Three or four times more US citizens than normal are making formal plans to emigrate to Canada, lawyers estimate in the media. And numbers of passport applications have been steadily increasing over the past few years (under future rules, citizens will need them to get into Canada, Mexico and the Caribbean as well as the rest of the world). Some 30 per cent of Americans have passports. In Britain it is 80 per cent.

PBS (Public Broadcasting Service) has pulled a TV episode of *Postcards From Buster* about a cartoon bunny that goes to Vermont to experience farm life and maple sugaring. Titled 'Sugartime!', the edition, made using federal education funding for young children, features two lesbian couples (the state recognises same-sex unions). It was dropped after the education secretary said many parents would not want their children exposed to such lifestyles.

The band of former politicians and religious leaders battling with the Supreme Court over the execution of juveniles have won their fight. It has ruled that killing those who were under 18 at the time of their crime contravenes the constitutional ban on 'cruel and unusual punishments'. The lives of over 70 child offenders on death row will now be spared.

A nine-year-old boy has been shot dead while playing in front of his home in Washington DC. This time it is in an area of town close to the wealthy, white suburbs. He was playing with a group of children when he was hit by a stray bullet. No one has so far been arrested.

It's a quiet Sunday evening and all is well in suburbia. Spring is here and the flowers are starting to bloom. The dog walkers are out for the last stroll of the evening and kids on bikes pedal home to bed. But turn the radio on, and there is a more sinister world of terrorist plots and counter intelligence. *The Danger Zone* on WMAL Washington News Talk offers listeners 'an unparalleled view into the inner-workings of our national security system'. Politicians, Middle East experts, and intelligence analysts discuss terror and tell us the things we would be happier not knowing. Be afraid, be very afraid.

Glance out the window and see a police patrol car parked outside Sally's house. I haven't seen a police car in this street since the sniper. Take another peek and see the two cops are chatting and smiling: maybe nothing much then. They drive off and I get on the phone to Sally.

'Saw a police car outside your house so thought I would ring to check they hadn't come to take you away.'

'They should have!' she replies, sounding disappointed she had missed it.

Public displays of patriotism don't seem to have diminished with the Iraq war. Above the pool at the sports centre is a giant American flag with the words 'caring, respect, honesty' on it. Next to some roadside shops, a man in Stars and Stripes shirt and cap walks up and down with a sandwich board. It is for a dry cleaners and reads '$1.75 any garment'. Outside a nearby Baptist church is a huge 'God Bless America' sign.

The first Thursday in May is The National Day of Prayer and this year will be the fifty-fourth. Organisers say millions will pray for the nation, government leaders, the media (!) and schools. Surveys indicate eight out of ten Americans pray daily or weekly, the top three reasons being to seek guidance, to give thanks or to ask forgiveness.

There are several hundred congregations in Montgomery County from Roman Catholic to Jewish to Seventh-day Adventist to Mormon and Muslim. Many are self-contained communities with Sunday schools, prayer groups, potluck dinners, movie nights and help groups for the homeless. Round here, we don't get those southern style, mainly evangelical, mega churches, with more than 2,000 attending each week. Or so I thought. When you start looking, there are actually 12 in DC, 13 in Virginia and 30 in Maryland.

Driving down a main artery which leads out of DC into the Maryland suburbs I pass Catholic, Heritage, Episcopal, First Alliance, Baptist, Seventh Day Adventist, Ukrainian, Muslim, Christ Fellowship, Presbyterian, Spanish, Vietnamese, Gospel and Jehovah's Witness churches or religious centres. Nestled in between are shopping strips with drive thru banks, Safeways, Starbucks and dry cleaners.

Them and Us

In the car park of a megachurch is a spray painted van with handwritten messages on its sides – 'Jesus Bus loves you and so do I, Jesus rocks my face off'. Bumper stickers urge you to 'Support Our Troops' and assure you that you will be loved at their church. Anyone can stroll in past the white cross, past the reception area with soft furnishings like a private hospital. There is a pink wall-to-wall carpet, fabric flower arrangements and white walls, brightly lit.

Down the corridor is a huge two-tiered auditorium with plush seats, chandeliers and stage. Tonight, a video camera is trained on the warm-up pastor, a tanned man in a check shirt with gleaming teeth. He welcomes the main act. 'More people will be saved tonight!' Just for a second, he reminds me of Jack Nicholson in *The Shining*. Nine musicians strike up on guitars, keyboards, drums and vocals, with lyrics lit up on giant screens. 'Get up on your feet and *feel* Jesus!' shouts the main man. 'Last night people were delivered and saved!' Up they get, swaying and clapping hands, some already dancing wildly. A barefoot young woman, with long hair and in a flowing ankle-length skirt, moves to the music with a rapturous expression on her face. Children in shorts and T-shirts run around with coloured flags. Teenage girls in jeans link arms and skip. A cool looking young man in a team shirt with a back-to-front baseball cap is wiping his eyes. There are all ages and all shades, people of white, African American, Latino and Asian heritage.

'I can't feel any demons in this room – everyone is open to Jesus!' shouts the preacher, a guitar swinging from his neck. A man in khaki shorts, T-shirt and white trainers, a soccer dad, is spinning and jumping wildly as if he were at a thrash rock concert. Instead, he is under bright lights at a sing-a-long Jesus session, but there is no sign of self-consciousness. The East European-born preacher tells how he was 'saved' from communism. A huge cheer rises up from the crowd.

Officials in a uniform of blazers and ties stand by with benign expressions. Now the music changes and people start joining hands and dancing in circles. A smiling grey-haired blazer wearer, with silver-rimmed glasses, advances in my direction. 'Want to join hands?' he genially asks me, as well as a lone man in jeans and check shirt. It would seem churlish to refuse. As we leap around, the men shout 'hallelujah brother!' to each other. 'Other way!' instructs our leader, just as I get dizzy. Now for a slower number. The old people sit down for a rest and my new friends and I separate, nodding and smiling polite appreciation.

Two middle aged women, one black, one white, are left lying on the floor. This must be normal as no one is alarmed and they seem to know what to do. Brightly coloured blankets are gently placed over them and boxes of tissues brought. They stay there, overcome with emotion, reaching for the hankies to dab their eyes. Nearby, a noticeboard with photos pinned to it stands by the stage. It reads, 'Remember our troops in prayer'.

People are lining up to be 'saved' now, which seems to amount to a public display of emotion in front of the preacher. I'm not sure I can carry this one off, so I make my exit, past the man on the reception desk who smiles. 'You have a good night, Ma'am,' he says, like he means it.

The DC Politics Hour with Kojo Nnamdi, on WAMU American University Radio, has just finished. Press the search button on the car radio to find a different station and land on a discussion about how to 'think about singleness biblically'. A caller says she would be delighted if 'a Godly man said God told me to ask you out'. She adds that she would want to be friends before a relationship could develop.

With soft music in the background, the programme makers now ask for donations. The announcer says tomorrow's discussion is 'how you look at the world – are you doing it in a Biblical way?'. Now some ads. A company, that places God above all, needs electricians. A mortgage business guarantees customers will be guided by a representative who shares your values.

'The Believer's love for God is constantly under attack,' says a new presenter, promising tips during his upcoming show on how to recognise Satan. Some Disney-style music plays.

Now, almost roaring with righteousness, comes a fire and brimstone preacher who cannot conceal his revulsion for the 'smiling face of Buddha next to Jesus suffering on the cross'. He is getting angrier by the minute, losing all reason and control. As he reaches a crescendo, behind the American twang there is an unmistakable Scottish accent.

Press search again and get a couple of sports jocks bragging about how much junk food they will eat in front of tonight's big game. Stop at the lights on Connecticut and notice the minivan in front is advertising the 'Glory to God Residential and Commercial Cleaning Service'.

Hershey, Pennsylvania, is a favourite weekend trip for local kids. It's 'the sweetest place on earth', a town built on chocolate by philanthropic entrepreneur Milton S. Hershey. Here the street lights are shaped like Hershey's chocolate Kisses, singing trolley conductors show you round the town and animated characters based on chocolate bars jump out at you in the 3D musical movie. You see how chocolate is made and pretend to be a conveyer belt factory worker. Milton symbolises the American dream. Poor, uneducated and a failed businessman, he never gave up and, after years of struggle, became one of the wealthiest men in the US. In the spirit of charitable giving that lives on in many rich Americans, he set aside some of his fortune for others, building homes, schools, parks and a trolley system for his workers.

Today the crowds flock to Chocolate World, stuff themselves with confectionery and move to the amusement park for thrills on the water rides. At the end of the day, you can lay your weary head on a pillow printed with Hershey's chocolate Kisses.

On my first visit, too squeamish for the rides, I try my hand at throwing a ball into a milk churn. 'It went in!' everyone shouts in disbelief. Suddenly I am the new owner of a giant, fluorescent blue My Little Pony called Rainbow Dash. Carrying this, I am a celebrity for the night, making new friends at every turn.

'Wow, how'd you win that?'
'Cool, you must be a great pitcher.'
'Where did you get it?'
'Mommy, I want one! I want one now!'
And, 'I could use you in my baseball team.'

Back home, I am touched to hear that some neighbours have clubbed together to buy a present for their postman who is in hospital.

We have only a few months left before heading back to Britain and we sign up for the neighbourhood yard sale, when those in nearby streets with household junk to sell set up in their front gardens on the same day. Elaine, a veteran, advises, 'Make sure you get ready early, some customers will come by before it's due to start.'

It is 7.30am and I am putting ground sheets on the damp grass when the first car cruises by, passengers peering out of the window. Another car pulls up and the driver winds down the window. 'What you got?' Some electrical stuff, furniture, toys and bikes, I reply. He nods and drives off. Nine o'clock, and more customers who have seen the ad in the local paper appear. A couple from Virginia are looking at the sofa (they do their own upholstery), a dad is buying the portable TV and some pans for his son to take to college. A single mum who has come up on the bus with her kids is taking a bag of toys. A car pulls up with three women inside, already piled high with bargains. They rifle through items and drive off empty handed. It's getting hotter and the girls are doing good trade at their lemonade (the pink, still, American kind) and cookie stand. Local people come round now on foot. 'We're sad that you are leaving. How many more weeks have you left?'

Sally comes over and sits on a chair amid the bric-a-brac, sipping lemonade and announcing loudly to customers, '*I'm* not for sale!'

A teenage girl stops to buy a drink. 'It tastes good girls! I used to love doing lemonade stands when I was a kid.'

Weeks later our furniture is packed on the truck ready to ship back to Britain and we hand over the keys to an empty house. We are overwhelmed with offers of help from friends and neighbours – 'Come and stay with us,' 'Stop by for dinner,' 'I'll take the girls to the pool.' We say our last goodbyes – 'You keep in touch.' 'Come back and visit…we'll miss you.' 'Don't be a stranger.' It is sad to leave. We can never be American but a little bit of America will always be with us.

Here we are on the Fourth of July weekend, our last road trip, in Memphis, Tennessee, home of the blues, barbecue and Elvis. As the military band plays, the sun goes down on *Ole Man River*, the mighty Mississippi, and fireworks light up the sky from Mud Island. The island is a park with a water-filled model of the river, as it flows more than 2,000 miles to New Orleans, running through it. As night falls, the resident ducks at the legendary Peabody Hotel, a 1925 landmark, have waddled from the lobby fountain into the elevator and up to their duck palace on the roof. The music joints are jumping in Beale Street.

The next day, we are on a pilgrimage to the Lorraine Motel, where Martin Luther King was assassinated and which is now the home of the National Civil Rights Museum. Children in America learn more about him at school than God. The third Monday in January is a national holiday in his honour, and around that date pupils are taught about his life. (Schools are not allowed to teach religion and can only include it in the context of other subjects like history, literature, social studies and science.)

After learning about the civil rights movement and the police investigation into the shooting, we drive out of town on a pilgrimage to another 'King' – Elvis. It all looks so ordinary, the roadside gates leading to his outwardly modest home, Graceland, surrounded by motels, Taco Bell and Krispy Kreme Donuts. Just time to check in to Heartbreak Hotel (complete with Elvis themed décor and TV channel) and swim in the heart shaped pool before deciding between Papa Johns or Pizza Hut for dinner.

At breakfast we meet some Geordies over for a 50th birthday celebration and a Scottish couple here for their wedding anniversary. There seem to be more Brits here than any other nationality. 'You'll love Graceland, it's just fantastic,' they enthuse. 'And it is so moving to see his grave.'

The white pillared frontage could belong to one of the grander houses in suburbia. The normal-sized rooms are decorated in lavish Seventies style, all gold and purples, deep carpets and faux fur. A favourite leather jacket, snooker cue and gun are on display alongside stage costumes and gold discs, with Elvis and his daughter Lisa Marie telling stories on the audio (no mention of drug abuse). Outside in the paddock you could almost be in the rolling fields of Virginia instead of beside a busy road in Tennessee. From the Meditation Garden, where Elvis and his family are laid to rest, comes the sound of uncontrollable sobbing. Men and women, from young bikers to pensioners, crowd round in a public, tear-stained vigil, overcome by emotion.

Now we are cruising down the Natchez Trace Parkway, which runs from Nashville to Natchez, a road winding through pines and cypresses and following in the steps of Chickasaw Native Americans, soldiers and settlers. Turn off to Vicksburg, Mississippi, where residents of the Confederate town slowly starved during the siege of 1863, leading to a critical victory for the Union army. Re-enactors keep the history alive and the Greek Revival style houses still have cannonballs embedded in the walls. Sitting in a main street restaurant, the long table next to us is suddenly filled with young women who look like Paris Hilton or Britney Spears. It's a sea of blonde hair, gold jewellery, deep tans and hot pink. Expensively dressed mothers accompany them, bursting with pride. The waiter tells us they are here for the pageant. So this is what southern belles look like these days (earlier, in genteel Oxford, Mississippi, I walked into a clothes shop which had wall-size photos of Paris and Britney). Outside I meet a local drunk. 'I can tell you're not from round here. Welcome to my town, Ma'am!' He wants to talk, to tell me his theories on politics and race. He is, I soon discover, a white supremacist. When he finds out where I'm from, he suddenly turns nasty and staggers off down the street shouting 'foreign bitch!' and shaking his fist.

Driving round looking for our B&B we take a wrong turn and end up by the railway track as a freight train goes by. When it has passed, another world appears on the other side of the tracks, dilapidated wooden homes with old black men sitting out on the steps. Painted above the small store are the faces of Martin Luther King, Malcolm X and Harriet Tubman, who helped hundreds of slaves escape to freedom.

The weather stations are excitedly tracking Hurricane Cindy, which is moving up from the Caribbean. So far it hasn't affected our route, instead heading for Texas, but then we hear that New Orleans may now be hit – exactly where we are going. Ringing ahead to the next town for accommodation, many B&Bs are already booked up with hurricane evacuees. Finally one landlady says, 'You been having trouble finding a room? Don't you worry, we'll fit you in somehow – we'll make little beds for the babes on the floor. I guess that'll be for two nights 'til we see where the storm is headin'.'

Then Cindy hits southeast Louisiana and moves across to Alabama and Georgia, now graded as a tropical storm. New Orleans has got lucky again.

We drive towards Cajun country in Louisiana, through heavy rain and dark skies. Wake up on the 7th of July at a chain roadside hotel, full of business people attending corporate meetings. The lobby is bustling and few stop to watch the news on a giant TV screen. I catch sight of pictures of ambulances and bloodied people and hear the words 'London' and 'terrorist attack'. An elderly lady with orange make-up and dyed hair is transfixed. 'It looks real bad,' she says. 'You from there? I'm so sorry.' We check mobile messages and emails, make some calls – with the time difference, surely we would have heard by now if anyone we know had been hurt? How is the city going to feel after this? In a few days time we will see for ourselves.

If anyone in Cajun Country knows where we are from or has heard the news, they don't let on. We stay in a lakeside cabin near a little town which calls itself the Crawfish Capital of the World, and stop at a neon lit roadhouse to eat. The locals are descended from French settlers and the ones here tonight like to party, giant men nimbly gliding across the floor with their ladies, calling out requests to the band and ordering more beers.

Ryan is our boatman on a trip into Cajun swampland. He's a French-speaking hulk in mirror shades who grew up here with the alligators, ducks and herons. It's hot and humid but there are no mosquitoes – they are all landing on plants on the water surface and getting eaten by swarms of dragonflies. Ryan is taking us through the ancient cypress and topulo trees, draped in Spanish moss, to see an alligator nest with an egg inside, while telling tales of a poor childhood eating squirrels and raccoons. He spots a baby alligator on a log and slows the flat-bottomed boat down so we can take a look. We reach the nest and he picks out the egg to pass it around.

'Won't the mother reject it if we have handled it?' someone asks.

'Naw,' Ryan assures us, 'they're not like birds. You could swap their eggs around and they would never notice.'

A man from Florida asks about alligator attacks on people. 'Don't happen round here. Some people even swim in the lake. What gators really like is dogs. I wouldn't let no dog on this boat.'

As we head back to the lake, the boat gets stuck in 'coffee grind', churned up mud where the water is low. Just as the boat pushes through this it hits a tree trunk. We are stuck fast. Ryan is unfazed, telling us to move to different sides of the boat to tilt it to one side as he tests the motor. 'Good thing I just got a new one,' he says cheerfully. It must be 100 degrees now and we are out of the shade and out of drinking water. Ten foot long alligators live here and this would not be a good time to meet one. Fifteen minutes go by. Most of the other passengers, from America and Europe, are calm but a few are starting to look worried. Just when we're wondering whether to ring for help, we are free and purr off to deeper waters, Ryan not even breaking a sweat. On the lake we see a big one, gliding along like a floating log.

Heading for New Orleans, we stop off at Greek Revival plantation houses with avenues of moss-laden trees and fields of sugarcane. You could have stepped back in time if it wasn't for the oil refineries and chemical plants nearby. New Orleans is similar, the historic French Quarter surrounded by city sprawl. Looking over the rooftops from our attic room, we could be in Paris, almost home.

Cutting through the legendary Bourbon Street at 6.30 in the evening, and a man is hurled across the street from a nearby bar. A bucket of water swiftly follows. The beggars sing Motown and play percussion on the street rubbish for their money. Everywhere someone is striking up an instrument to earn a dollar. Our waiter is sitting on the step outside the restaurant, smoking a cigarette, the sounds of jazz coming from the next street.

'Were you worried about the hurricane?' I ask.

'Yeah, I packed up and fixed a ride in a friend's car. We thought it was really going to happen this time. In the end, there wasn't even a storm.' But he still looks worried. 'Thing is, when a hurricane comes this early, the next one is gonna be a big one. I'll be out of here when it does.'

Chapter 17:
Back Home

DRIVING OUT of Heathrow the sky is grey instead of blue. We go past industrial units and terraced houses instead of the lush woodland outside Washington's international airport. There are noticeably more 4x4s than there used to be but mostly the cars and lorries are much smaller than on the other side of the Atlantic. It's the morning rush hour, and drivers' faces are tired and miserable but they do, unlike their American cousins, more often than not signal to change lanes, flash their lights to let a car go in front and wave thanks. Today, not a tinted window in sight.

In West London, children walk to school in their uniforms, coming out of tube stations, jumping off red buses, dodging drunks, hopping over dog poo. Cars line up at school gates, the private school mums in 4x4s, talking on mobiles. A builder in dusty overalls sits on a wall having a can of lager and a cigarette for breakfast.

In our street, a council cleaner in regulation red waistcoat is scooping up the rubbish while listening to an i-pod. More litter bins have appeared and new signs are on the lampposts advising of refuse and recycling collection days. So we are getting a bit cleaner then. The couple in the corner shop greet us as if we had never left and start talking about the cricket score. The lady in the chemist asks if we have been on holiday. In the café opposite, the immigrant chefs are serving up full English breakfast (vegetarian option), croissants, cappuccinos and mint tea. The blooms are being arranged outside the flower shop and the windows of the launderette are already steamed up.

It is days since 7/7 and the mood is wary but philosophical.

'You've got to just get on with your life, haven't you?'

'When your number's up, your number's up.'

'What can you do?'

In this overcrowded, high-priced city, there's no choice but to keep using the buses and the Underground. If anyone is paranoid or panic stricken, you would never know it.

I'm now in the habit of saying, 'How are *you*?' when I meet someone but I'm not getting the American-style response of, 'Good, how are you?'. Instead I get replies like, 'Not too bad thanks luv, but I'm really tired at the moment what with the kids and work.'

Or, 'Bearing up dear, bearing up, alright apart from my knees…'

In the supermarket, an old lady in a mac with a large handbag catches my eye next to the Marmite. 'Better get the shopping home before it rains again,' she advises. 'I'm just picking up something for my son's dinner. Nice bit of fish. He's 29 and still lives at home. I even buy his pants – Y-fronts he likes.' She heads off to the frozen vegetables on special offer. 'You should get some, you won't find peas cheaper than that.' At the check-out, a middle aged woman, elegantly dressed in cashmere and tartan, is hoping that the weather will brighten up for the weekend. 'I'm going down to Cornwall,' she says. 'I've found a lovely little cottage next to the beach, just me and my dog and a pile of books – heaven!' She knows the Friday night traffic will be 'hell', but with Radio 4 and some classical music for company, she will be fine.

On the walk home I pass two beggars, one quietly swaying drunk and a wild-eyed hippy who is shouting loudly at an imaginary aggressor. I'm sure it is the same man who used to dance down our street before we left, as if at a virtual Hawkwind concert.

Away for a few years and you see your home country through new eyes. It is like walking into an episode of *Little Britain*. There goes queen chav Vicky Pollard in her hoodie and oversized hoop earrings. That's Lou the kindly carer, and I just passed Sebastian, the prime minister's gay aide, off to work with his briefcase. Here there are more varieties, more eccentrics and, particularly in this city, they all live amongst each other, council blocks next to smart, owner-occupied town houses and housing association flats. This relationship, fuelled by the economic and class divide, is sometimes uneasy but at least everyone knows of each others' existence. Tattoos and body piercing are commonplace and acceptable. So is dyeing your hair and dressing entirely in black.

Hoodie hysteria seems to have grown in our absence. When a gang of teenage boys with hoods up goes past on their bikes, I wonder if they are off on a mugging spree, but they stop off at the youth club instead. We are still camping at home while our belongings sail across the Atlantic, and I decide to take the washing to the launderette. I can barely get in the door for a gang of hoodies, squabbling over what temperature to set the machine. I am now jammed in the door with a heavy bin liner. 'Move it, help the lady will you!' the leader says and his sidekicks grin and heave my bin bag through the door, delivering it to a vacant machine. They show no interest in robbing me of my launderette change today.

Travelling around London, it feels as if there are far more people from ethnic backgrounds than where we have come from – 29 per cent of a population of over 7 million here belong to a minority ethnic group and more than 300 languages are spoken – but it's not so. Out of a population of 500,000 in Washington DC, nearly 70 per cent are black, Hispanic, Latino or Asian.

The British papers are filled with soul searching over the homegrown 7/7 bombers. 'Where did we go wrong?' And, like in America after 9/11, 'Why do they hate us?' Waiting for the 94 bus, an old boy in a donkey jacket says the young people nowadays don't have enough discipline. 'We should bring back National Service,' he concludes. 'That would sort out the bad apples.'

There is agonising in the media over why the bombers had not integrated into British society, but I can't help thinking we are still a long way from the accepted ghettoisation that is widespread across the US. As a reporter in Britain, no one has ever suggested that a certain part of town is a complete no go area during daylight hours because of my skin colour. They have in America.

Police are everywhere at the moment. There has just been a terrorist attack, after all, but I wonder if I am just noticing them more because so many are on foot. In the US, they always seem to be in cars, watching from a distance. Here, they are walking the streets stopping to talk or to search.

Lining up at the sub Post Office, which doubles as a newsagents and stationers, they are still selling 99p plastic toys and kids' dressing up clothes. The policeman's outfit used to have a traditional pointy helmet and a silver badge. The one on sale now has a flat cap and a safety vest. No gun though. A Police Federation survey found that 82 per cent of officers do not want all their colleagues to be routinely armed on duty. Fewer than 7,000 officers across England and Wales carry firearms (for a population of 53 million), around one in ten in the capital.

'Back in London, then? Got your bulletproof vest?' a professional man in his 40s jokes at a party. No one challenges him. There is a gloomy perception that, particularly on the mean city streets, we are a bullet riddled society. Has the country 'gone to the dogs' while I have been living in my American suburban bubble? The stats show that firearms were used in 73 (8.5 per cent) of the homicides in England and Wales in 2004/5, five more than the year before, so reason for concern. But in the US during 2005, 71 per cent of homicides were committed with guns, the death penalty and a fully armed police force apparently not much of a deterrent.

The British headlines illustrate our less than charming national tendency to stab, bludgeon or kick our victims to death. Good job we have among the tightest gun laws in the world – a ban on assault rifles and almost all handguns, plus strict licences for sportspeople. With that kind of uncontrolled aggression, armed with AK-47s it would be a bloodbath. And we are not yet resigned to gun crime. Here at least the shooting of a child is still unusual enough to make it to the front page of a national newspaper and to provoke public outrage. An analysis of the figures concludes that if the USA and England and Wales had the same population size, the US would have 34 times the number of shooting homicides. We don't have to follow their example.

Signing up for the local school in Britain, all I need to do is fill in a simple, one sided A4 form and provide proof of address.

'Is that it?' I ask, dumbfounded.

'That's it!' beams the secretary.

Driving out of Shepherd's Bush a few days later, and the sound of sirens increases. Let's hope it is nothing, just the police being extra vigilant after 7/7. Turn the radio on for traffic reports and hear that some tube stations are shut down – Oval and Warren Street. Then Shepherd's Bush station is mentioned and something is going on in Hackney. I get that same sick feeling in the pit of my stomach I had on 9/11. Later, there are television pictures of the area outside the station cordoned off with grim-faced police and passengers, shots of the Uxbridge Road where I had been walking a few hours before. Unexploded bomb devices were found. It is a week since arriving back in Britain and it doesn't feel so good.

A hot Friday afternoon on the same road a few weeks later, and the pavement is full of praying men, spilling out from the nearby mosque. When they are finished, they wander across the street to the Arabic market to buy vegetables and flat breads. Mothers with pushchairs steer round them, school kids on holiday walk to the cinema and suited office workers head for the pub or the gym. I sign up at the nearby dentist for free check-ups – a few details on the computer and we are set. Past the bakers with scones and iced buns, the corner shops are stuffed with processed food, sweets and fizzy drinks. But the market is still crammed with cheap fruit and vegetables and cut price clothes, an exotic blend of cultures next to the railway bridges. 'Best falafel', 'two plantains for the price of one', 'fresh okra'.

Watching the television news, I realise the smashed up New Orleans road, now going nowhere, was one we had driven down just over a month ago. A scene of devastation on the TV screen, harrowing pictures of desperate people, stranded in a city buried under flood water and sludge brought on by Hurricane Katrina. The overwhelming image is of the poor blacks, left behind to cling onto life or die. I am appalled like everyone else but, unlike my British friends, not in the least surprised. Back in our old US neighbourhood, a doctor goes to help the victims and others donate money. It is not the America they want either.

Sunday morning, and everyone is about as usual, just getting out of bed a bit later. A few people are hanging around waiting for the corner shop to open, to buy breakfast and a paper. The park is busy and the pub will soon be open. People attend church early, discreetly, or not at all. Figures based on congregations in 2005 found 6.3 per cent of people go to church in Britain. In the US more than half the adult population live in a household where they or another member belong to a place of worship. While our devout ancestors sailed off on the Mayflower, the rest stayed behind to grow cynical from endless religious conflict at home and in Europe.

Never mind, we have football to fulfil the need to belong. All ages, shapes and sizes are part of the tribe when they are in the same shirt. Across the nation on a Saturday afternoon, reserve is put aside and complete strangers stop anyone in team colours.

'Hear Man U are two up!' a taxi driver shouts out the window.

'What's the final score, mate?' a cyclist pulls over to ask.

To have no allegiance to a team in Britain is like being an atheist in America. Best to keep quiet about it. My daughters go to their first big match back in Britain and discover it is a licence to shout and drink warm tea with sugar. On the way home, one remarks, 'People swear a lot more in Britain, don't they?' while watching transfixed as a man throws up through the upstairs window of the double decker bus.

Still, not many Union Jacks about. Patrotism just goes public for a big royal event. Or, of course, sport.

The workmen are watching their waists these days. Used to be they would always drink endless mugs of tea with four sugars, but not anymore. 'Just one for me luv,' or, 'I wouldn't say no to a nice milky Nescafe,' is the answer now. But they still like a fag and a biscuit and Capital Radio. Unlike their American counterparts, the plumber and the fitter take a lunch break, leaving behind a few dusty footprints and a mood of cheerfulness in adversity. Now, those who can't kick the alcohol or narcotics while on duty simply get pushed out by the Polish.

A cruise round certain coffee shops illustrates the best and the worst of Americans abroad. One has an American member of staff who should get one of those customer care awards. He smiles and chats like he means it – 'Stay as long as you want, it's a great place to write, isn't it? Can I get you anything else? Have a great day.' Even the crazy lady and the *Big Issue* seller get some love.

At a coffee shop further down the street, which Americans also frequent, often discussing their dental care, the scene is not pretty. A big, middle aged American man dressed in L.L Bean is not getting what he wants and he is complaining very loudly. We all stop and stare. Naturally, we are used to a bit of shouting when the pub shuts, but not at 9.30 in the morning. Whatever the worried looking assistant has done, it can't be that bad. As the manager moves in the American stomps out of the door shouting 'Asshole!' at the top of his voice. We all shake our heads and look sympathetically towards the young male assistant who is trying not to cry.

Soaked again. It was brilliant sunshine half an hour ago, how can it be raining? Because I am back in Britain, of course.

The licensing laws have been relaxed now and there is always a pub open somewhere. Strange to see groups of men having a business meeting at 10am over a pint of Guinness. I am now a lightweight when it comes to drink after years in American suburbia, and it is a shock to witness the alcohol consumption on a night out in a British pub. A teetotal Muslim cab driver sympathises as the car pulls away from drink-fuelled screaming on the pavement. 'It's not pretty, is it?' he says wearily.

At school, my children learn about Ramadan and Diwali as well as Christmas and Chanukah.

'How was it today?' I ask.

'Good, we had curry and custard for school dinner.'

Back Home

At the first fundraising cake sale I brace myself for humiliation but I needn't have worried – not a wicker basket or a ribbon in sight. This is about homemade fairy cakes straight from a recycled Quality Street tin and, for those who don't have the time or the inclination to bake, biscuits unashamedly bought at Tesco.

Tony Blair was still Mr Popular in the US when we left but here he is public enemy number one. 'I feel a bit sorry for him,' a friend says. 'He hasn't done too badly at home but everyone associates him with the war and nothing else.' It is hard to find anyone who admits to still being a supporter. The graffiti on the community centre wall reads 'Bliar'.

Back in Chevy Chase the leaf collection is history and there are email news alerts about a dog seen running loose and a lost cat. Soon it will be time for neighbourhood softball games and yard sales. The buzz is about 'mansionization' – building an enormous house on a small plot of land after knocking down what was there before. It is such a hot topic that WAMU's Kojo Nnamdi is hosting a discussion on it. Shame I missed my chance to meet Kojo.

The snow hasn't come to London this year and our sledges lie untouched in the back garden.

Here, someone is watching me most of the time. CCTV symbols are everywhere, more in London alone than the whole of America, they say. If an average British citizen gets caught on camera 300 times a day, I am probably clocking up even more in the capital. Am I concerned about my civil liberties? Not particularly. This is a small price to pay for having video evidence of a terrorist or a mugger. Most people I ask agree. It is surprising what you get used to.

Road works are everywhere, crumbling Victorian water pipes being replaced to stop the leaks that are exacerbating the water shortage, along with constant resurfacing and road widening. It gives us something to talk about but really this is no place for cars. Even out of the city there is no escape from traffic jams and every layby seems to be strewn with litter. As an Italian hairdresser says, 'It is so dirty here. And it is worse when it is hot because you can smell the rubbish. I can't breathe on the bus or the train because the British, they don't wash.' Oh dear.

Cranes join tower blocks on the horizon as a new shopping centre is built. Spookily, it is exactly the same company that has the monopoly on the mall experience in the Washington area. Will it be the same? Almost certainly similar gleaming décor and musak with some of the same chain shops, but I'm pretty sure it won't feel like America.

'Come to watch the barbarians?' an American once said to me over there. I wonder if this is what it is like for them visiting here. They expect history, culture and manners but they probably don't anticipate the added extras – public swearing, drunkenness and grumpiness. I remember all the natives who stopped to offer help when I was first in Washington clutching a map, and resolve to return the favour. Heading for the corner shop one sunny morning, I strike gold – there is a man in a baseball cap, clean cut with a college sweatshirt and jeans, definitely American and, if I'm not mistaken, lost! He's probably taken a wrong turning on the way to Notting Hill.

'Excuse me, Ma'am,' he says, 'Which way is it to Notting Hill?' I direct him to the tube or the bus but he wants to walk and starts looking worried as the directions get more complicated.

'I tell you what,' I say, 'I'll walk with you to Holland Park Avenue, you can't go wrong from there. It's alright, I'm not drunk or mentally ill.'

A few days later, a young American on the station platform asks which stop he needs to get out at for Notting Hill. The first people he tries only speak Polish or Italian. The next is a teenager who removes his i-pod to say this tube line doesn't stop there and he would be better getting the 94 bus.

'But I was told you can get from Shepherd's Bush to Notting Hill,' the American says, baffled.

'You can,' I volunteer, 'but from the other Shepherd's Bush station. You could either stay here, get off at Ladbroke Grove and walk up, get the 94 or go to the other Shepherd's Bush station.'

'I would get the 94,' the teenager adds.

'Can I use this ticket?' the American asks.

'No,' I explain, 'it's a single and you've already gone through the turnstile. You need another tube ticket or a bus ticket but if you can't get it on the bus, you have to get it at the newsagents.' The train pulls out as he wanders off down the steps clutching his guide book and looking worried. Hope he makes it.

I have now missed the number 49 three times while giving directions to foreigners heading in completely the wrong direction. This is, frankly, a sacrifice as the 49 doesn't come as frequently as the 10 or the 9. Still, it's not their fault. They are just people like you and me looking for a friendly face in a strange city.

Sources and acknowledgements

ABC News, ACLU (American Civil Liberties Union), *The American Journal of Clinical Nutrition*, Amnesty International, BBC, *Bethesda: A Social History* by William M. Offutt, Big Idea, Brady Campaign to Prevent Gun Violence, Bureau of Justice Statistics (US), Canada Firearms Centre, Centers for Disease Control and Prevention (Department of Health and Human Services, US government), Centre for Crime and Justice Studies (UK), Chevy Chase West Official Directory, Christian Research (UK), Cicadamania.net, The City University of New York (The Graduate Center), CNN, Darryl Worley (country singer), Department of Natural Resources (Maryland), Education Commission of the States, Fodor's, Gazette.Net (Chevy Chase), Hartford Institute for Religion Research, Home Office (UK), Johns Hopkins Center for Gun and Policy Research, Kaiser Family Foundation, Legal Community Against Violence, Lonely Planet, Montgomery County (Maryland), Montgomery County Historical Society, MSI Soccer, Moon Handbooks, National Climatic Data Center (US), National Hurricane Center (US), National Park Service (US), National Public Radio (US), National Statistics (UK), National Weather Service (US), *The New York Times*, Police Federation (UK), Southern Poverty Law Center, Statistics Canada, Time Out Guides, *The Times*, US Census Bureau, US Consumer Product Safety Commission, US Department of Health and Human Services, US Department of Homeland Security, The Vegetarian Resource Group, Washington DC Fiscal Policy Institute, *The Washington Post*, The White House (Office of the Press Secretary), WTOP Radio.

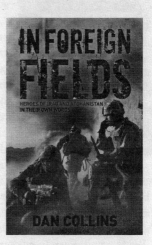

WASTING POLICE TIME...
THE CRAZY WORLD OF THE WAR ON CRIME
PC David Copperfield (£7.99)

PC DAVID COPPERFIELD is an ordinary bobby quietly waging war on crime...when he's not drowning in a sea of paperwork, government initiatives and bogus targets.

Wasting Police Time is his hilarious but shocking picture of life in a modern British town, where teenage yobs terrorise the elderly, drunken couples brawl in front of their children and drug-addicted burglars and muggers roam free.

He reveals how crime is spiralling while millions of pounds in tax is frittered away, and reveals a force which, crushed under mad bureaucracy, is left desperately fiddling the figures.

His book has attracted rave reviews for its dry wit and insight from The Sunday Times, The Guardian, The Observer, The Daily Mail, The Mail on Sunday and The Daily Telegraph;.

'Being a policeman in modern England is not like appearing in an episode of The Sweeney, Inspector Morse or even The Bill, sadly,' says Copperfield. 'No, it's like standing banging your head against a wall, carrying a couple of hundredweight of paperwork on your shoulders, while the house around you burns to the ground.'

"A huge hit... will make you laugh out loud" - **The Daily Mail**
"Very revealing" - **The Daily Telegraph**
"Damning... gallows humour" - **The Sunday Times**
"Graphic, entertaining and sobering" - **The Observer**
"A sensation" - **The Sun**
By PC David Copperfield - as seen on BBC1's *Panorama*

www.coppersblog.blogspot.com

DIARY OF AN ON-CALL GIRL
True Stories From The Front Line
WPC EE Bloggs (£7.99)

If crime is the sickness, WPC Ellie Bloggs is the cure... Well, she is when she's not inside the nick, flirting with male officers, buying doughnuts for the sergeant and hacking her way through a jungle of emails, forms and government targets.

Of course, in amongst the tea-making, gossip and boyfriend trouble, real work sometimes intrudes. Luckily, as a woman, she can multi-task... switching effortlessly between gobby drunks, angry chavs and the merely bonkers. WPC Bloggs is a real-life policewoman, who occasionally arrests some very naughty people. *Diary of an On-Call Girl* is her hilarious, despairing dispatch from the front line of modern British lunacy.

WARNING: Contains satire, irony and traces of sarcasm.

"Think Belle de Jour meets The Bill... sarky sarges, missing panda cars and wayward MOPS (members of the public)."
- The Guardian

"Modern policing is part Orwell, part Kafka ... and part Trisha." **- The Mail on Sunday**

£7.99 – and read her at **www.pcbloggs.blogspot.com**

LIFE AND DEATH IN LONDON: A PARAMEDIC'S DIARY
Stuart Gray (Paperback £7.99)

Stuart Gray is a paramedic dealing with the worst life can throw at him. *A Paramedic's Diary* is his gripping, blow-by-blow account of a year in on the streets – 12 rollercoaster months of enormous highs and tragic lows. One day he'll save a young mother's life as she gives birth, the next he might watch a young girl die on the tarmac in front of him after a hit-and-run. A gripping, entertaining and often amusing read by a talented new writer.

IT'S YOUR TIME YOU'RE WASTING
- A TEACHER'S TALES OF CLASSROOM HELL
Frank Chalk (Paperback £7.99)

The blackly humorous diary of a year in a teacher's working life. Chalk confiscates porn, booze and trainers, fends off angry parents and worries about the few conscientious pupils he comes across, recording his experiences in a dry and very readable manner.

"Does for education what PC David Copperfield did for the police"

"Addictive and ghastly" – **The Times**